RHAPSODY IN BLUE

MAINSTREAM | SPORT

RHAPSODY IN BLUE

THE CHELSEA DREAM TEAM

RICK GLANVILL

MAINSTREAM
PUBLISHING

EDINBURGH AND LONDON

Dedicated to my older brother Gary
who gave me no choice. Thanks.

First published in Great Britain in 1996 by
MAINSTREAM PUBLISHING COMPANY (EDINBURGH) LTD
7 Albany Street
Edinburgh EH1 3UG

This edition 1998

ISBN 1 84018 107 9

A catalogue record for this book is available from the British Library

Typeset in 10½ on 12½pt New Century Schoolbook
Printed and bound in Finland by WSOY

Acknowledgements

It seems trite to acknowledge players who have given millions of fans so many hours of pleasure on a football pitch for the brief moments they shared discussing their careers with me, but they were all such fine people, and it is the least I can do in return for their contributions. Cheers to the chaps in the Chelsea family.

Also to all the others who helped fill in the gaps, especially Tommy Docherty and Gwyn Williams – 'Mr Chelsea' since 1979.

My gratitude also to Paul Dutton for player statistics, Mum and Dad for attic-raiding, Roger, Mark, Barnet, Dan, Matt and all the excellent Chelsea world-wide web sites (Jax, CSR, Jer, 'The Beautiful Game' and more) for a brilliant array of anecdotes and ideas. 'Carefree!'

Neil Barnett for sharing his memories (when he can't even find his glasses) and Steev and Frannie from Chelsea's Onside team.

Mostly, though, to Yael, who played a blinder in her now familiar sweeper's role.

Rick Glanvill

Contents

A Disclaimer

We've always been a club of firsts: the first, in 1905, to gain direct access to the Football League (do not collect bruises in the amateur game), the first to produce a match-day programme (6d, 1948), the first to fly to a game (1957, to Newcastle), the first to beam back a European match (Barcelona 1966, lost 5–0), the first, post-war, to win an FA Cup final replay (1970), the first to fence in our fans (1972), the first club to sign Graham Wilkins (same year – no connection), and, perhaps most impressively, the first to have its own branded yellow dusters in the club shop (1973). Now we're one of the first in this series of 'dream teams'.

Obviously there could be 50 or so more. And, all right, so your favourite player isn't featured. So Greaves couldn't head the ball, Venables disobeyed The Doc's orders, Bonetti dropped the odd cross, Webb was fallible, McCreadie lost his head every now and then, Osgood was lazy, Wilkins brought his big brother along, Nevin couldn't tackle, Wise loses his rag, and Elliott lasted as long as an old-style English summer.

Yes, yes, yes. I know. But this isn't business. This is personal: my private collection from 35-odd years of pleasure and pain following Chelsea. And I wanted these heroes to tell the story of the Blues in each decade, not just the glory years. That's why all those equally good claimants such as Charlie Cooke (brilliant, but not as consistent as any of the selected midfielders), club record-scorer Bobby Tambling (not as exciting as Greaves or Ossie), Ron Harris (our most successful captain but not a great footballer), Holly (a near-catastrophic manager) and Alan Hudson (a catalyst for disintegration) are sadly absent.

But such periods naturally mustn't be ignored hence the eclipsing of Eddie Neddie, Kerry 'Wig' Dixon, Speedo, Stevie Clarke, Andy Townsend and others on this book's star-studded team sheet. Personal favourites of the last few years like Eddie Newton (too often sub), Dan Petrescu (too recent) and Dmitri Kharine (too windy) would also make it onto my bench. Finally, I'm too young for the Championship side. (Let's face it, who isn't?)

So is there anything we can agree on? Rudi, surely? And our all-time great goalscorer, young Jim?

The most contentious selection will, no doubt, be the manager. The rivals all had good shouts. The Doc for his bravery, faith in youth and motivation; John Neal for his adeptness in the transfer market; Eddie McCreadie, perhaps, for returning us to the top flight when the financial pressure was at its height. Most obviously, there is the great Dave Sexton, who won two trophies from three finals in three years.

They all had their faults: Neal's and McCreadie's largely being the brevity of their reigns through force of circumstance. But Docherty was self-destructive, and Sexton took it upon himself to dismantle a team The Doc, then he, had constructed; it's still hard to forgive a man who traded in Osgood, Webb and Hudson in their prime, for Kember, Garner and Garland, who never had one.

Anyway, there are more potent, oh, go on then, romantic factors to consider. In the summer of 1996, the view from the Bridge has rarely been so serene; calmer waters lie ahead, and we have the most exciting crew on board for a quarter of a century. I wanted to reflect the optimism of the times, and there was only one way to do that – by choosing Glenn Hoddle, the manager who made the club fit for the millennium in so many ways, who gave us our first, fleeting glimpses of Cup and European glory for decades, and who raised our gaze, as fans, from the basement to the heavens. Today, the King's Road swingeth once more.

God brought us Hod, Hod gave us Gullit, Gullit brought us Luca and the rest.

And you can't argue with that. Can you?

Rick Glanvill, 1996

The amendments to this new edition hardly do justice to the amazing period since I wrote *Rhapsody in Blue*. They probably require another book entirely (and preferably one not written by Harry Harris).

The significance of winning silverware for the first time in 26 years, the arrival of perhaps the most gifted Chelsea player ever – Gianfranco Zola – along with new heroes like Gus Poyet, Tore Andre Flo, Celestine Babayaro, Brian Laudrup and, well, old ones such as Frank Sinclair, the managerial madness, the stadium (or is it estate?) redevelopment, the death of Matthew Harding, the professionalisation of the football club . . .

A DISCLAIMER

It takes away the breath of any supporter who got dizzy when we signed Duncan McKenzie or finally got round to clearing the grazing sheep off that fenced bit of the Shed End. But I decided not to add Zola or any others so that this remains a record, to a large extent, of a club on the brink of a dynasty of success. That way we'll rightly recall with pride the heroes of a less glorious period.

When Mainstream originally asked me to write this book I joked that I might need to make it a five-a-side team if they insisted on 'successful' players. In two years' time I might be asking them if I can add subs – and seven, too, like in Europe.

That's how far we've come in two years. Just think what the future holds.

Thanks for buying this book.

Rick Glanvill, May 1998

1

Greavesie

On the evening of 16 October 1954, Jimmy Thompson, Chelsea's former winger, now chief scout, rang through to Ted Drake to check on the day's result. It was his habit; his diligence took him everywhere from Scotland to the south of France in pursuit of the best young footballers, and he always 'signed in'. So Ted Drake, on the way to Chelsea's first-ever Championship, answers the phone. Jimmy asks how Chelsea have fared.

'Oh,' says Ted. 'Seamus O'Connell got three on his debut, and we still went down 6–5 to Man United . . . But I tell you, you missed the game of a lifetime.'

'Maybe so,' says Jimmy, 'but I've just seen the player of a lifetime.' He'd just seen the 14-year-old James Greaves bag five.

Any story worth telling must have its heroes. And they don't come cast in any greater mould than little Jim, the demon from Dagenham Boys. And so at 14 he became one of several trawled from the East End in Chelsea's net. Resentment still simmers amongst the older generation of East-Enders at this supposed 'poaching' by the West London grandees and their local Pied Piper, Jimmy Thompson – or 'Mr Pope' as he enigmatically liked to call himself when in the locality.

The fact is, Chelsea was a better club for the kids than any other in London at the time. The Blues – the 'Pensioners' nickname had recently been dropped by the current manager in a bid to shed the old 'music hall joke' image – had an odd squad: half brittle-boned elder statesmen, half knees-knocking youngsters. And they were renowned for blooding their kids early.

Normally, the first point of contact for youngsters was Jimmy Thompson, Chelsea's eccentric roving talent-spotter. Other influential characters in the youngsters' careers were trainer Wilf Chitty and youth team manager Dickie Foss, a former Chelsea player. Jimmy Thompson's technique was to talk up the club constantly, win the kids over with his aura (and impressive bowler hat), then promise the world (and deliver rather less).

With the precision of a political circular's arrival on your coming of age, Chelsea's chief scout rolled up at the Greaves' house a month before their son was due to leave school. He left with another youngster's immediate future signed and sealed in his pocket. 'You'll never regret this, my boy,' he said, smiling his false-toothed smile. 'You have my word on that.' More cash for him, and Chelsea's production line of brilliant youths restocked. And Jimmy Greaves never did regret it.

Like others before him, the young Greavesie's first port of call was in Hendon, not SW6. There were other Dagenham Boys and other mates who started on the same day – it was another of Jimmy Thompson's selling points. Bobby Smith, Peter Brabrook and Les Allen were all in the same youth side as Greavesie.

'We had the Welsh Harp, didn't we,' he smiles, 'where I spent a lot of time, because that's where we used to play all our games. Very seldom did we play at Stamford Bridge. And that's why I played for Middlesex Youth – because Hendon is in Middlesex, our ground was in the borough. I played for Essex, London and Middlesex, and I couldn't quite work out why at the time.

'We won the Youth Cup in 1957 with Middlesex. I didn't score, but Johnny Clarkson did, another Chelsea player, and we won 1–0 against Stoke. It was a smashing club, it really was. I spent two years there as an apprentice before signing professional terms, and then four seasons as a professional. It was a lovely club to play for. I know it sounds far-fetched, but at the time I would have played for them for nothing. I just loved football.'

Greavesie was a scoring phenomenon from the word go, scoring on his debut for Chelsea's juniors. He didn't have a powerful shot, but his studious accuracy was devastating. In his second year as an apprentice, 1956–57, he established a record for the most junior goals in one season that has endured ever since: an unbelievable 114 strikes.

Ted Drake had welcomed Jimmy in typical old-school fashion: 'I expect you to become a distinguished player.' It was Dickie Foss's job to begin that process. Foss, an undistinguished wing-half for the Blues in his time, was an honest, no-nonsense disciplinarian who consistently brought the best out of his young charges. Errors were exposed and corrected; good play was rarely discussed – it was expected.

Later, first-team coach Albert Tennant worked on young Jim's flat-footed running style. He had the youngster run on the balls of his feet. It was painful, but it improved his gait and balance and enabled Jim to perfect that gliding, ghosting, swerving run that became his trademark. He favoured his left, but could dispatch superbly with both feet.

Swift elevation to the first team was inevitable in a squad that had remained largely the same as that which had lifted the Championship in 1955, lacked motivation and direction and was shipping goals. Youth had to be given its chance. He made his debut in the first game of the season after that 114-goal haul – the figure bears repeating, doesn't it – with his dad watching from the stand.

It was, coincidentally, at White Hart Lane, against the club Jimmy had supported as a child (well, he was only 17 even now) and was later to move to in his maturity. But there was no show of any affection today, 23 August 1957: 5ft 8ins, built like a jockey, ice cool in his comic baggy shorts, he regularly passed two, three players with ease, then started and completed the move which silenced the home supporters. 'I was in the right place at the right time,' he said later. We drew 1–1. More importantly, James had opened his account.

Desmond Hackett of *The Daily Express* described Jimmy's performance as the 'greatest show I have ever seen from a young player on his league debut, and I have seen the juvenile . . . Johnny Haynes and Duncan Edwards.' Tottenham's Danny Blanchflower, one of those tormented by Jimmy's winding runs, pronounced him the greatest youngster he had ever played against.

The goals kept coming: six in the first nine games. A month after his start in the First Division, Jimmy made his England Under-23 debut, scoring twice and missing a penalty in the 6–2 clubbing of Bulgaria, staged at the Bridge. (Later, at senior level, he was to star in the 9–3 decimation of Scotland.) Then suddenly he was hit by a loss of form – the uncharted territory of six games firing blanks. Wisely, he was dropped in November by Ted Drake, who clearly considered him all footballed out. A ten-day rest to remove the precocious talent from the media spotlight became six weeks as Chelsea continued scoring without him. His return was inescapable, though, and arrived on Christmas Day 1957 at the Bridge against Portsmouth. Utterly fired up, Jimmy grabbed four in a typically festive 7–4 victory. He wasn't dropped again.

By September in the following season Greavesie had an incredible return of 16 from the initial ten games. In April 1959, he slipped past Arsenal's Dave Bowen to equal George 'Gatling Gun' Hilsdon's scoring record for the Blues of 30 in one season. He went on to gather 124 goals for us in four seasons, and top-scored in the First Division for us twice: 1958–59 (32 goals) and his final campaign, 1960–61 (41).

But that curious 7–4 Pompey scoreline was unfortunately no rarity; more like the norm for Chelsea during Jimmy's time there. He'd soon learn that much. The first leg of the 1958 FA Youth Cup final (which Jim was still eligible to play in) against Wolves was won 5–1 at the Bridge. The return – a formality, surely – was at Molineux. But we went down 6–1 and lost the trophy. On another occasion we lost 6–5 (again) and Frank Blunstone preceded a carpeting of his own defenders by throwing his boots across the dressing-room floor. 'If we scored eight we could bet on you lot letting in nine!' he ranted. It was that sort of self-destructive team.

In a clash with Everton, our England keeper Reg Matthews raced to boot clear a ball approaching his goal line, hotly pursued by defender Peter Sillett. Matthews turned to hoof away, and the ball rebounded off the incoming Sillett's stomach, leaving him winded and bent double, and the ball in the back of the net.

'I remember another game,' says Jim, 'where we were playing Nottingham Forest, and it was rumoured that a guy from Forest had tapped Peter Sillett, and wanted to give us all a drink if we threw the game. And we had this meeting upstairs in the snooker room at Stamford Bridge. And we all said, "No way!" But they beat us anyway, and they finished higher than us! So that was . . . well, it was "all the best", wasn't it?'

Perhaps most memorable of all these fallible performances was one at Preston, just before Christmas 1959. 'I scored a hat-trick and we were 3–0 up,' says Jimmy, 'and I was bit of a lad then and said to the others, "I've done my bit. I've finished for the day. You lot have a go."' Midway through the second half and Preston were on level terms. Peter Sillett, Jim's big mate and drinking buddy, said, 'Come on Jim, you'll have to make a comeback.' Jimmy scored a fourth and slipped on to auto-pilot again. Preston nabbed their second equaliser. Peter Sillett called on Jim again: 'A last one will finish them off,' he said. The Greaves goal machine did the business and we ran out winners: Preston 4 Greaves 5. And Preston were League leaders at the time. The next day's paper suggested that if the groundsman hadn't turned off the lights, he'd have still been knocking them in the following morning.

There were less equivocal triumphs, of course. Early in the 1958–59 season Jimmy faced the might of League champions Wolves and their all-international defence including the saintly Billy Wright, Ron Flowers and Bill Slater. 'I've been told I was the reason Billy decided to hang up his boots at the end of the season,' Jimmy says. And with good reason: the 18-year-old cut through the champions' back four like the proverbial knife through butter, feinting and weaving to create and take chance after chance. They had no answer to his mobility. He scored five of our six goals that day and had another controversially ruled out.

Yet still the Blues bumped along the bottom. 'The side I played for at Chelsea had more potential than any I played for,' says Jim. 'But I think we lacked direction in those days. He was a nice man, Ted Drake, but I think if Bill Nicholson had had that team, it would really have got somewhere. Even if Tommy Docherty had had it later; I think when Tom took over Chelsea, he wasn't in a strong position because he hadn't had the experience anyway. But if you'd taken some of the managers of the day, like Bill Shanks, who was just up-and-coming, or people like Harry Catterick at Everton, or Harry Potts at Burnley, they probably would have done very well with that Chelsea squad.

'I mean, we had the England goalkeeper, Reg Matthews, and followed him by the other one, Peter Bonetti, Peter Sillett was an outstanding player, "Schnoz" – John Sillett – could do a good job, Peter Brabrook was as quick as anyone in the country, Les Allen, Barry Bridges, Frankie Blunstone, and we'd nearly all come through the youth scheme. Chelsea, then, had they had the guidance of somebody like a Bill Nich, could have actually been one of the top sides in the country.

'Bear in mind, they'd won the Championship under Ted Drake in 1954–55, but then it all sort of fell away; nothing was followed up. Which it could easily have been. I think we did have a much more talented side in those days even than the side they've got now. I think the only thing was we weren't committed. And that was mainly because nobody bothered to commit us. We never came close to winning anything; we came close to finishing fourth from bottom once. We were always third from bottom. I can never remember not fighting relegation at some stage of the season.'

Jimmy's prolific ability was what maintained our top-flight status (and we were instantly relegated after he left). Jimmy was a minute-man: perhaps 'idle' for 89 of the 90 in a game, but lethal and decisive in the remaining one. 'My trade was goals. I loved scoring. I would rather have played badly for 89 minutes and score the winner than play well for 90 and not hit the net.' He was an 'inside-forward', a number 8 or 10, with an instinct for threatening opposition defenders and the goal. He'd attack the ball rather than wait for it to land at his feet, immediately putting his markers off balance. He could dribble past players like they weren't there. And although he wouldn't scare Linford over 100 metres, his mental speed made him quick off the mark.

In his first few weeks in the first team, Ted Drake was so amazed with Jimmy's bursts of pace that he asked him where it had come from. 'I used to do hurdling all the time at school,' said Jim, blithely. Impressed, Ted Drake ordered up a batch of hurdles and had all the other players working their hides off to achieve Jimmy's standard. It appears to have been complete fabrication on Jimmy's part; a bit of mischief. And the rest of the players were none too pleased with this exacting training exercise. They'd been used to a more *laissez-faire* approach to exercise. It's likely that Jimmy himself was a little fazed. Like our other great goal-getter, Ossie, 'Saint James', as older fans dubbed him, never enjoyed training. In fact, Terry Venables always remembers him playing in goal to avoid some of the exertion.

'It was just a lovely club to work for,' says Jim. 'We had a manager in Ted Drake, who never really said all that much. We were the "all the best" club. All the players just used to say "All the best" to each other as they ran out on to the field. That's where that came from. To be honest I thought that was quite normal; I didn't know anything different. Ted was a nice, honest guy who I thought, probably, as far as modern management goes wouldn't qualify. Because he just used to sit in his office. I never really saw him in a track-suit apart from maybe for a session where press and photographers were there.

'Ted was a lovely man. I don't know; maybe all managers were like that in those days. I didn't know any different. Maybe Bill Nicholson, possibly Bill Shankly, one or two others, were the first of a hands-on management that has seen the game progress to what it is today. At Chelsea the team was coached, if that's the word, by Albert Tennant, and we had a trainer called Jack Oxbury, and really, you know, it was a matter of doing a few laps and having a kickabout behind the back of the goals there, that was about it. Of course, in those days there was an enormous running track, a dog track and there was plenty of room behind the goals to play. So we used to train at the back, with the dogs. The dogs used to beat us – that was the trouble!'

Peter Bonetti joined the Chelsea groundstaff when Jimmy was making his mark in the first team. 'Greavesie was a great character,' remembers The Cat. 'A man who ploughed his own furrow, just did his own thing. I can remember him on a Friday coming in to the Bridge for training, looking at the ground, walking round two laps, saying, "Well, that's me done. I've had my training session." And pissing off. Jimmy could do that. He was a law unto himself because of what he was doing on the pitch on a Saturday.

Plus, he could afford to do that because Ted Drake was a bit more lenient than most managers in those days.

'I was just a kid then, but Jimmy was lovely to meet. My first trip away, travelling with the first team, was the sixth game, the one where I broke my nose – all the others had been around London. It was at Bolton. And I was rooming with Jimmy because I was a kid on my own. And I was young, naïve and gullible and Jimmy said, "Oh, I'll take Catty with me, I'll look after him, I'll show him all the ropes." And Jimmy was only about two years older than me anyway: I was 18 and he was only 19 or 20 himself. He was this lad full of confidence. A real Cockney lad. Full of himself, and some of the goals he scored in that season '60–'61 . . .'

There was no intrigue as to why Ted Drake and others just let him get on with it – the evidence was there every week on the scoresheet. 'I think when I played for Chelsea I just had a natural ability to score goals,' says Jim, with considerable understatement. 'I feel that where it all went wrong for me in my career was when I had developed my game, I should have gone back into midfield and started playing the game from there. But that never happened, because people always want people up front who can score goals. At Chelsea I just scored goals; it was a natural thing for me to do.'

Jimmy and Chelsea loved each other; he even named his house after the club. 'I had a really great time there, you know. We were just like a bunch of kids. I'm still great pals with Schnoz, Peter Sillett I see occasionally, Peter Brabrook I saw the other week and he's looking very well.'

Cars figured strongly in Jimmy's life once the maximum wage was abolished. He was once said to have turned up for England training sessions in a different motor each day. And despite the lack of success – and win bonuses – at Chelsea, Jimmy managed to buy himself a vehicle of sorts. 'I could only afford a decent one at the end,' he recalls. 'Before that, I used to drive a 1937 Standard 8. And I'll tell you what, it would always break down. I had a ball of string in the boot, and Peter and John Sillett will tell you this, that between the accelerator pedal and the actual cable, I never had the actual cable, I used to tie it up with string. And it used to go every so often and we used to go out and change the string.

'I used to drive Peter and John, Peter Brabrook and Ronnie Tindall to training. And we all used to play cricket on Sundays for Surrey, for charity, whoever's benefit it was in these festival games round the county. And even with the car I had, I was the only one who had one. It was a real old banger. People like Ken Shellito will tell you: if I ever went over a puddle, people had to lift up their feet.

And it's true.' When he went to Milan, Jim splashed out on a left-hand drive Jaguar.

'But it was a really smashing club, there's no doubt about that,' Jim reiterates. 'The only really bad experience I ever had with Chelsea was when Ted Drake took us on a fucking ten-day tour to Bulgaria, which was behind the Iron Curtain at the time we went in 1958.' He groans at the memory. 'It was an absolute nightmare. There was nothing to do, nothing to eat. Nightmare. And I remember all the lads getting so fed up with it all we were tearing our hair out. It really wasn't the place to be!

'In those days the players had very little say in these trips. And Ted wanted to take us back there the following year! Peter Sillett talked him out of it. I don't know how he did it – well, I do, because Ted was a great golfer, and Peter said, "No, let's have five days down at Broadstairs, boss, and we can all go on the golf course." And Ted swallowed that. And I think he'd have had a revolt on his hands if he hadn't. But that was the sort of club it was, looking back. I don't know, I suppose it's much more professional nowadays – or maybe it isn't.'

That following pre-season we beat Ajax – as usual. But Ted Drake was on the way out. If the older players acted like aloof old Corinthians, their manager's mind had begun to drift. Peter Sillett recalls the moment when Ted was driving him home from training. Things were going poorly on the pitch and Ted seemed preoccupied as they pulled up at some traffic lights, staring blankly ahead. The lights changed several times without any response from Ted, and without comment from embarrassed passenger Peter. Then, eventually, a passing policeman knocked on the window: 'Are you all right, sir?' he queried. Ted Drake looked around as if waking from a trance. 'My God, Peter,' he said. 'I thought you were driving.'

So the writing was on the wall. In the 1959–60 season we scored 76 and conceded 91. The following season, though, the deficit had reduced: we recorded 98 – but conceded 100. In November that season, Greavesie had been 'tapped' by Newcastle (who offered him dosh, a job as a car salesman and, presumably, all the stotties he could eat, as enticement. Jim immediately returned the compliment with interest: four goals in a six-goal drubbing that saw the Geordies relegated).

These were tragic and unsettling times off the pitch as well. In 1960, Greaves's son, Jimmy junior, died, aged just four months. Since then Jimmy had been approached by an agent acting for AC Milan. It could be he simply needed a change of scenery. He was quoted in *The Express*: 'I want to try my luck with another club.

Chelsea have great potential, but for some reason it is not being properly fulfilled.'

The following month, as if to reinforce his point, Jimmy excelled in a 7–1 thrashing of Don Howe, Bobby Robson and West Brom. It was a momentous match for Jimmy: in amongst the five he got on the day was his 100th league goal (making him, at 20, the youngest of his profession to do so). He had now scored three or more times for Chelsea on 12 occasions. He had also notched 11 in 11 for England. 'How on earth,' queried *The People*, on behalf of Blues fans everywhere, 'can Chelsea even think of selling him?'

'The club lacked ambition,' he says now. 'There is no question about that, and them being prepared to let me go was proof of that. But I actually didn't ever put in for a transfer at Chelsea. I was not too unsettled either. But Milan had made an inquiry and obviously I felt that it would be a good career move at the time, bearing in mind that the import ban wasn't on any more in Italy and there wasn't a maximum wage there.'

The Football League had recently rejected a plea from the players for an extra £5 a week (£20 was what each club was restricted to paying its players); Milan were beckoning Jimmy with the promise of £15,000 over three years (£15 per week with immense bonuses including £300 for a win; at Chelsea the reward for victory was £4). In his entire time at Chelsea Jimmy had just one family holiday – a week at Butlins. But he'd travelled abroad enough with England and Chelsea to face the relocation with confidence.

'Of course, by the time I went to Italy in 1961, the whole thing happened in that few months, where we threatened to go on strike, Jimmy Hill won the day and the maximum wage was going to be abolished, and I was then in a situation where I could earn pretty near as much back here as over there. And I suddenly found myself having a change of heart, which was quite interesting. I'd only signed an agreement with Milan, I hadn't played for them and I wanted the registration cancelled. I went to see John Battersby, who was then the club secretary. And I learned many years afterwards what I'm going to tell you now.

'I said to him, "Look, I don't want to go." And he said, "Well, I think you've got to honour your contract." But I insisted I didn't want to go. And they got this guy from the City, R.I. Lewis, a solicitor, to get me out of the contract. As it happened, he got me a better deal. But that wasn't the point: his brief was to make sure that I went out there. Chelsea wanted the money, they wanted the 80 grand. And I was told this as little as a few years ago by John Battersby's daughter, who said, "Of course, did you ever know really what happened . . .?" And so I might have been a Chelsea player all my career. I mean, I wasn't that ambitious anyway.'

But when it came down to it, Jimmy was leaving us because of the lure of the lira. When the maximum wage ceiling was removed, he had the potential to earn just as much at Stamford Bridge and swiftly recognised that fact. 'I have to say, when you do look back, nobody fought very hard: the manager didn't, the board of directors certainly didn't, so nobody said, "Actually, Jim, we'd like you to stay."'

One man who *did* battle for Jimmy to resume his Chelsea career was Tommy Docherty. At his interview he condemned one of his rivals with customary outspokenness: 'If you appoint him, you won't get a coach, you'll get a hearse.' The Doc arrived at an ailing Stamford Bridge from Arsenal in February 1961 as player-coach to be greeted by Ted Drake with the words, 'Welcome to Chelsea, Tom, but you weren't my choice. I wanted Vic Buckingham.'

It was obvious that Tommy was the ideal replacement for the now out-of-touch and aloof Championship manager. But he was powerless in the wrangling over Jimmy's departure. 'Tom was coach after the deal with Milan had been set up,' says Jimmy. 'The deal with Milan came in about December, where they had an option to buy me at the end of the season, and it had all been agreed. But they couldn't get me over there beforehand because of the Italians' foreign import ban. Tom came in for the last few months I was there. I'd played against Tom when he was at Preston and when he was at Arsenal. He actually did say, "If I'd had my way, you wouldn't have gone."'

'I think if we'd kept Greavesie we'd have been one of the great sides of the '60s,' says Tom, who may have lacked many things, but certainly not ambition. 'He was a great kid, just a little chirpy Cockney. And the best goalscorer I've ever seen. When I eventually took over, we'd a good young side. We were scoring goals but we were losing goals as well. And I just felt when we started tightening up with the full-backs Shellito and McCreadie, who were truly great, we weren't losing goals, but we weren't scoring goals either. And if we'd had Greavesie we would have won the Championship four or five times. He'd have made that difference.'

'I knew Tom very well,' says Jimmy, 'and so if the Milan option hadn't been exercised, I could very well have stayed at Chelsea. Certainly it was no lack of effort on my behalf to stay at the club. But there was a brief to make sure I went to Milan because Chelsea needed the money. I've never been quite sure why. You look back at football in those days, and, you know, we used to play to gates of

40–45,000 . . . where did all the money go? They didn't pay the players, who were on £20 a week maximum. And I worked on the groundstaff at Chelsea for two years and I know that the stands and everything never had a lick of paint. So where did all the money go at all the clubs? Where did it all go? And why, when, come Easter, I wanted to stay with the club, did they want 80 grand? Why did they need it? Somewhere down the line there's a load of unanswered questions, which I don't think ever will be answered.'

The Doc assumed the mantle of manager in January 1962 when 'by mutual consent' Ted Drake left to spend more time with his nine iron. By then it was too late for Jimmy Greaves, who had joined Spurs the previous November. Tommy Doc had had to sit and watch as the Italian job fell through for Greavesie and Chelsea showed no interest in picking up the pieces.

'True story,' says Tom: 'When Jimmy was unsettled in Italy, and he wanted to come back, Chelsea had a clause in the contract giving first option. John Battersby was sent out to negotiate for Greavesie, but not to bring him back: "Anything Bill Nicholson bids, don't go as high." Crazy. I was only the coach then, so I couldn't do anything about it. I don't know why. I think maybe when they got the 90 grand, it was a lot of money in those days, and they didn't want to give it back.

'Spurs obviously sent Billy Nicholson over. And instead of sending me over, or the manager over, Chelsea sent the club secretary. We used to call him Snudge, as in *Bootsy and Snudge*, the TV show. There was no way he was going to get a result over there. And all I know is if we'd have got Greavesie back it would have been bingo time; I think we would have cracked it.'

Our chances of winning back Jim's hand weren't helped by the board's actions after his final flurry in a blue shirt. 'Joe Mears was a nice enough guy, but I remember when Joe was ill, old Leslie Mears and a guy called Bill Pratt – who lived up to his name – took over. I'd finished my last game against Nottingham Forest and they wanted me to go to play an exhibition game in Israel and I said no. And the Chelsea board banned me for two weeks, which meant I lost an England game, against Mexico, because of that. You look back on these things and see what players demand now, and you think, I dunno, maybe he was a prat or I was a prat, or maybe we were both prats.

'Looking back, obviously I don't regret going to Tottenham, because it was a wonderful club to play for. But what is interesting is that none of that need've happened if somebody at management level – and I take that right to the boardroom – had really wanted to have kept me during the period from Christmas to the end of the season in 1961. They could easily have done so, because I didn't want to go. I mean, *I did not want to go.* And they knew that.'

It was a costly mistake. Although Jimmy only scored four times in ten years against us and always tended to struggle against Ron Harris when he returned, first in a Spurs, then a West Ham shirt, he was there for the FA Cup final in 1967, along with another Chelsea old boy, Terry Venables. Not for the last time the old boys ended on the winning side.

But back to happier reflections for the rest of us. On that final day of the season, 29 April 1961, with Jimmy already installed as our all-time greatest marksman in a First Division campaign, we faced Nottingham Forest at the Bridge. As was his habit, Jim emerged last on to the pitch, this time as captain for the day. That in his swansong Greavesie's penalty would prove the decisive goal of seven was remarkable enough; that he scored our previous three was typical – he was Chelsea's talisman. As he was carried shoulder high from the pitch by adoring fans, the scribes were writing Chelsea's death warrant – correctly, as it happened. Kenneth Wolstenholme spoke for Blues fans everywhere: 'And one wonders, with some desperation, what Chelsea will do without him next season.'

Back to the present. At Liverpool in the 1995–96 season, Ian St John was introduced to the crowd. Needless to say, we drowned out the Kop with our chanting of Jimmy's name. Nevertheless, Chelsea fans' affection for our greatest goalscorer and his remarkable achievements with us has dimmed, and that is wrong – he is one of the greatest testaments to the enduring investment in youth at Chelsea. Tottenham may have stolen him for posterity, but we had him for four years at his peak, before the booze had taken him. And a part of him never really left.

'I don't know about being revered by Chelsea fans now,' he ponders. 'It was a long time ago. But my affection for Chelsea has never been a secret. I really do love the club. Nobody would love to see them win something more than I would – well, apart from Ken Bates. You know, and I said it a couple of weeks ago on *Sport in Question*, that people say Chelsea are a big club and a great one; they are neither. Potentially, they are. I think they've got the right chairman. Hopefully they've got the right board of directors, and maybe they've got the manager now in Ruud Gullit. I don't know, but what I'm saying is everyone says what a great club they are. They are great in that in my day it was a wonderful club to work for, a great atmosphere, and it was great all round, but they weren't a great club on the field, and they weren't a big club either.

'Chelsea: it's a name. It's probably the greatest name in the world: Chelsea. You think about it. What does it conjure up? It conjures up the best part of the biggest city in the world. Chelsea! It's magical. And they've never lived up to it, but I hope they do. I'm a great Chelsea fan, as you probably know. And I'd love to see it all happen. I openly say I think it's a fabulous club. I like Ken Bates a lot, as you know. I like Matthew Harding as well. I'd just like to see them do something to get the club really going.'

2

Venners

Of all the unsung heroes in the long history of Chelsea Football Club, surely none deserve more praise than those who scoured the playing fields of England in search of talent which, for 15 years, provided the backbone for our most sustained period of success.

Three ex-players among them – chief scout Jimmy Thompson, youth team coach Dicky Foss, and scout Wilf Chitty – were pre-eminent, unearthing and polishing a collection of gems that was the envy of every other club. The chain ran almost unbroken from Jimmy Greaves and Peter Bonetti to Ray Wilkins. Their diligence didn't just benefit their employers of course: other clubs reaped the benefits by buying our well-brought-up young men, and the England team has often looked to current or former Chelsea players for inspiration. On the last two occasions Chelsea has even supplied the national team's manager, although Glenn Hoddle was 'schooled' at Tottenham. One national hero we can lay full claim to, though, is former England boss Terry Venables. He remains the only player to have represented England at every level. And he performed a large part of the feat while on Chelsea's books and playing staff.

The lad cited by some as 'the new Duncan Edwards' arrived at Chelsea's fledgling ground, the Tudor Rose, on the same day as Allan Harris, Bobby Tambling, Bert Murray and Peter Bonetti in July 1958. He immediately made an impression. 'Venners was a character even then,' chuckles The Cat. 'He was a very confident boy. All the clubs were after him then, because he was the England schoolboy captain and had just played in the Under-15s schoolboy team with Allan and Bert. So Terry was the king-pin at Chelsea from the word go. He was very knowledgeable on the game. I can remember when we first got in to the first team together, he used to write reports on the game. You could see then he was destined for greater things, because technically he was involved in the game and coaching-wise he was very wired-in.'

So were we lucky to get this brilliant youngster? Well, in some ways. But part of it was a well-earned reputation for bringing kids through, and another was Jimmy Thompson's powers of persuasion – as was the case with another East End nugget, Jimmy Greaves. 'The good thing about Jimmy Thompson,' confides Tommy Docherty, who witnessed his ways first-hand, 'was there weren't a lot of rules about poaching kids then, and what rules there were, Jimmy paid no attention to. He looked like a spiv but he was a great judge of young players: eight, nine, ten years of age. We called him the Pied Piper – every time you saw him there were about eight budding players with him.

'He used to travel anywhere and everywhere. I mean, you'd get phone calls – would we take a reverse charge call from Inverness or the South of France? Then he used to come in and get a few hundred quid expenses and go to the dog track. Joe Mears was also chairman of the FA, so he had to be very careful. Some of the things he had to do for Jimmy you wouldn't believe, because Jimmy kept bending the rules there were. He was like Al Capone. He used a lot of aliases: Mr Pope, or the Rt Hon so-and-so. You'd get a phone call from the director of the Glasgow Presbyterian Church – that was Jimmy.

'He used to go walking with about eight of the kids down at Blackpool where he'd taken them for the weekend. Allan Harris used to say he'd say, "There's a Blackpool scout! Quick! Jump in here!" And he'd jump in behind a bus with all the lads to avoid being seen by another scout. He had a lot of trouble with Jimmy Murphy, the Man United scout. He used to call him "Lobo the wolf". He had names for everyone. And he used to sign boys, which you weren't supposed to do, and hold the registration until the boy became the legitimate age to register. All those shady tactics they all did. And the boy knew he couldn't sign for anyone else because the forms were in the safe.'

Jimmy would promise a young star and his family the earth. 'But when they'd come to get it from the chairman,' reveals Tommy, 'he'd say, "Well, Jimmy, you know we can't do that, we'd break the rules."'

The teenage Terry Venables fell under the mysterious scout's spell. 'He was just outlandish,' says Terry. 'Completely different from anyone else you'd met. He had a bowler hat, hair slicked down – a bit like Ted Drake – and he was always chewing. Big false teeth kept dropping down. You got the feeling even if he was serious he was still laughing cause his teeth were so big! But he was a great character and he just had you in fits. He did the same jokes over and over: "He can't hit the goal, he's knocked the linesman's hat off, ha! ha! ha!" You'd heard it about 30 times but it didn't matter, he was just infectious. He took about six of us once to Frinton for the day and we missed the train coming home. Oh, he was a nightmare he was.'

Terry remembers ducking behind the buses away from other scouts, all the cloak-and-dagger stuff: 'He would be telling you to meet him under the big Waterloo clock. I'd be standing under there and I would hear psst, psst, psst. I'd look round and see this little head come round the corner and beckon, and you'd follow him and he was all secretive and there was no need to be secretive. Looking back, you don't know why but you did everything he said – crazy! He drove you so mad. If some West Ham scout came he'd hide in the bathroom, so he didn't know he was there. You'd be sitting there with the scout from West Ham for an hour and a half, and then Jimmy'd come out afterwards – "Has he gone?" He was an amazing character.'

On one occasion, Jimmy massaged Terry's foot for half an hour to 'bring out the bruise' with oil 'the professionals use' so that his young charge wouldn't miss an important trial. Subsequently, Terry had the inflamed foot X-rayed – and it was found to be fractured. 'He always promised you a pair of boots or something, but he never actually came up with his promises or anything.

'But I chose Chelsea in the end because we got very close, me, Terry Moore, Bert Murray and Allan Harris, and those three signed. I didn't know whether to sign for West Ham. But in the end I thought Chelsea had a good name for bringing young kids through. Even then as a kid you're ambitious: you thought you'd get into the team at 17 or 18, and in fact I did in the end. I was a Tottenham supporter as a kid, so I thought about that. But they had Blanchflower and Mackay, you know you're blocked, all big names, and they would buy over the top of you. It was a good opportunity at Chelsea with the other three great mates already there. My mum always said, "Wherever you think you're going to be the happiest."'

Mum might not have been keen on Terry travelling two hours each way on bus or tube from his Dagenham home to the Hendon training ground. But Terry knew it was worth it, even if the pitch was on a slant. 'Dick Foss was the youth team manager,' he says. 'He was wonderful, I thought he was great. Sadly, he died recently. He was the same thing: side parting, slicked down, very smart, quite good-looking bloke, very stern, but he had a good sense of humour. I liked him a lot. They didn't really have a lot of coaching in that time, but he would give you directions, tell you what he wanted from you, and he was very successful with the kids.'

Dick, our former wing-half, masterminded the first Chelsea FA Youth Cup victory in 1960. Terry was his skipper. 'We won it two years on the trot: the first time we won at Preston, the second time at Everton, home and away. They were very exciting games both years and we drew big crowds. I think we got 15 or 16,000 people there and at the Bridge. Also they had a London Cities cup. Teams from London – Chelsea, Arsenal, Tottenham – combined teams. And they played our youth team at Stamford Bridge and we beat them as well. That's a good side we had.'

The fledgling team, packed with homegrown talent, instantly captured the imagination of the fans. 'Fantastic rapport,' says The Doc. 'They could see the great times coming back again. You know, although Chelsea won the League in 1955, the team after that wasn't exciting at all, other than Greavesie. The only players we sold were the ones like Micky Harrison, Micky Block, Mel Scott, the Silletts and people like that – the ones who I felt weren't very good. A few quid for them helped pay for the youth policy. And the youth policy was even better than Man United's. They came off that conveyor belt like shit off a shovel.'

'Terry had more influence than anyone in the team because of the type of character he was and the knowledge he had,' says The Cat. 'Dicky Foss was very much the manager and Terry respected that. But even at 17 Terry was knowledgeable and in team-talks obviously spoke a lot about tactics, players, because he was very confident and had a lot of ideas, instigating new free-kicks and coming up with ideas for set plays. He was a leader from an early age, and helped the quieter ones in the dressing-room. He geed people up and slagged them off if he felt it was needed, but not in a nasty way.'

'I just always wanted to be organised and try to gain sort of percentages against the other team,' explains Terry. 'Coaching was just beginning to start then and I'd seen enough. I knew there was something out there that was more than what we were seeing and doing. I just felt that we weren't doing enough with our training; it wasn't enough if you were going to be a professional.' Terry's presence off the field was equally powerful. 'I was cheeky – practical jokes and stuff – and I was quite easy-going,' he concedes, 'and I was always trying to organise people: a bit "busy", I suppose, a bit of a nuisance. I've always taken football seriously, but I've always taken myself not quite so seriously.'

'He was a comic, a real comedian,' says Peter Bonetti. 'Like Gazza, but Terry had a better mentality than Gazza. He was a trickster, very humorous. His party-piece was mimicking people: Jimmy

Durante, Frankie Howerd, Max Wall and Tommy Cooper were some of his favourites. He would tell funny stories, get up and tell jokes.

'He could sing, too. I can remember going with him to Tin Pan Alley [Denmark Street in Soho] one day. He used to write songs in those days, and plays, and I went with him and he was doing this recording. The record never got anywhere but I thought it was very good. He must have been only 18 or 19. Terry was a very versatile man. And when you see all the things he's been through, I can understand that, because he had all that ability when he was young.'

'All the people I used to impersonate are dead, so no one would know them,' is Terry's wry comment now. Whatever, Terry made his eagerly anticipated senior debut on the field of play under Ted Drake as a wing-half at the same time as Peter Bonetti in 1960. He was dropped after a few games in a struggling team in favour of a man just under twice his age: Tommy Docherty, newly arrived from Highbury as player-coach. In time Terry won back his place and Tommy deposed Ted. For Venners and Doc it was the beginning of an often tempestuous love-hate relationship.

'He was a good player,' offers Tommy. 'He was crafty, shrewd, but he was always king of the kids. Terry was one of the lads who, if you were doing any free-kicks, he would disagree with you – in public. After they'd finished training, he would knock on your door and say, "I'm sorry about that boss." It wasn't just exuberance; he wanted to look good to his friends.'

'I think the great thing was we were all young together,' says Terry. 'We were all competing against each other every day, so you stretched yourself every day. I always make the comparison when Rodney Marsh went to Fulham: the younger lads there weren't pushing him on so he got to the first team fairly quickly. But I felt if he was at Chelsea he may have been even better. He didn't stretch himself enough until he went to a very good Manchester City team, and realised he wasn't as good as some of the others.'

The mood at the Bridge was increasingly confident. 'It was always fun and young and vibrant,' says Venners. 'There was an older group but when The Doc got there they didn't like him so it got a bit of an atmosphere. Before that all the older players were really good with the youngsters. But they could see that The Doc was going to be wanting them out, the older players, and so I think that's where that came about. Then Dave Sexton come as coach, and it was quite an exciting time. He was the first of a breed and really he's still one of the leading guys 30 years later.'

The Doc put his faith in the kids when the battle to stay in the top flight looked lost. 'Me and Allan Harris played in the last game when we got relegated,' says Terry. 'We played Burnley, and if they'd beaten us they would have won the Championship. So, last game of the season, he put a lot of us kids in, and we drew with them. I remember them spitting on us and everything coming off, because that made Ipswich win the League.'

Initially there was no problem between the strong personalities at the club – they had the same sense of mischief. 'He was a funny lad, great company,' says Doc. 'One time we were going to a Fairs Cup match from London Airport. He and the lads were calling the flights out and people were running for them. Then they were throwing coins in the air, and the money's coming down and bouncing on the tiles, and people were running with cases, stopping, and thinking, "I've dropped some money," doubling back and picking up the coins, and I don't know whether any of them missed their planes or what, but there were people and cases going everywhere. They were kids; they were like that.'

One of those kids was Tommy's £5,000 signing from East Stirling, Eddie McCreadie. He was to become Terry's best mate at Chelsea. Terry describes the left-back in glowing terms as 'brilliant but crazy'.

'He give us another dimension,' Terry enthuses. 'It was a great buy, actually: I couldn't believe how good he was. He was so fast, great tackler, good in the air, had everything. Great to get on with too: great personality, great friend.'

'Terry was very kind when I first came to the club,' recalls Eddie with obvious affection. 'I was the only Scotsman when I arrived and I wasn't exactly welcomed with open arms, I've got to be honest. Nobody gave me a hard time, but I felt on my own after training and that. I was going home to my digs, and not with a lot of invitations to come and join in with what they were doing.

'Then Terry came up to me after training one day and said, "D'you know what you're doing?" I said, "Well, I'm just going home." And he said, "Well, come and have lunch with us." And we went down to the Broadway, the café near the ground, and he kind of took me under his wing. He became a wonderful friend.

'He was a wonderful player and a wonderful influence in many, many things; very smart, very intelligent person. Very funny too – we'd many laughs together. Terry and I used to mess around together a little bit. At London Airport we had Chelsea blazers on and Terry and I were standing in one of these booths, which was unoccupied, and people started coming up to us and asking questions. And after about two or three times we decided to take it into our heads to supply the people with directions. This went on for about half an hour; we were sending people all over the bloody place. It was rather mean, but very funny at the time.

'We used to muck around like that all over the bloody world, for goodness sake, him and I, whether it be the British Embassy in Jamaica or Harrods store, trying on wellington boots and all that. And I would pretend I was deaf, and in one of these big department stores people would ask me what I wanted. Of course, I wouldn't be able to hear them. And Terry would explain to them that I was deaf. Again, this must sound very cruel, but we didn't mean it like that. Of course, within a minute or so, we had shopkeepers shouting in my ears at the top of their voices in Harrods. I guess I was the stooge, the straight man. The guys enjoyed it; they used to hide behind counters, trying not to give it away.'

'It was all good, clean, funny stuff,' smiles Terry. 'There was no harm in it. I just can't believe what we used to do: making out we were carrying a sheet of glass through Harrods, and they'd mind out of your way. Or we wanted a pair of socks for this geezer who only had three toes. They were getting me small sizes, and I said, "They're too small." They said, "He's only got three toes". "Yes, but he's still a size seven." Ridiculous things driving people mad. It seemed funny at the time!

'There were always jokes going on. The press were terrified of travelling with us in Europe. I always remember Peter Lorenzo in one airport where they had these red sort of corded barriers on a silver stand. I took the hook off and hooked it into his pocket, and when he started going downstairs he took all the lot with him. Then Brian James, who used to get very, very embarrassed, said to me and George Graham, "Do me a favour, I know they've hidden my briefcase. Don't say anything. Mark my card – where is it?" So George said, "It's in there." So he went through the door and found he'd gone in the women's toilet. There was no briefcase, and he'd come out so red-faced, it was incredible. It was just non-stop.'

So Tommy Doc had a lot in common with the youngsters. 'He was very enthusiastic; he was a character,' says Terry. 'He was a very funny guy – I mean, he really did make you laugh. He did some hysterical things. Later on we were at this reception and he was talking to this woman who he said had bad breath, and he kept making funny gestures about it. Then he took her off dancing, kept parading her to everyone, pulling faces without her seeing. And it was a packed dance floor and we were killing ourselves with laughter, and next time he come round he had a handkerchief tied round over his face. How he did it while he was dancing with her I don't know – or what he said to her.

'For a manager really he was diabolical, but you couldn't stop laughing. Then he'd tell you a porky or let you down and you'd be fuming. I used to have nightmares about him, I used to dream about him. I used to think, "This guy is awful," and you'd say, "I'm never speaking to him, I'm not laughing any more." And the next day he'd have you in fits! You used to get so angry with yourself, but he was hysterical.'

If inconsistent. 'He was just rash. He'd make a decision and then change his mind tomorrow. You'd be out somewhere and he'd say, "I want you back at 10 o'clock tonight." Then if he was in the room and he was on form, enjoying himself, us all laughing at him, we'd all go to leave and he'd say, "Where are you going?" We'd say we had to be in bed by 10 and he'd say, "No, don't worry about that." You know?

'And the next time we're having a laugh, just cause he's in the wrong mood, he'd say, "Get home." You never knew where you stood. He'd have a meeting saying, "No more messing around." And he's the one who'd been doing all the messing around! "No more messing around – we've got to concentrate on football because we're professionals." And you'd think, "Yes he's quite right." Then as you left the room something would hit you on the back of your head. You'd go, "What happened?" And he'd go, "Ha! ha! ha! I was only joking." He used to laugh with his tongue hanging out and it was such a funny sight. You didn't know where the hell you were, it was unbelievable. Never a dull moment.'

Nevertheless, the tightly organised young team tasted early success, gaining promotion from the Second Division at the first attempt. Looking likely to stroll away with the title up to Christmas 1962, the big freeze set in and Chelsea lost all rhythm. The two last games both required the full quota of points. The first was away at Sunderland, who were virtually assured of promotion. The Roker faithful were in festive mood.

'It was a great moment,' says Terry, 'because they only had to draw and instead of the usual coloured newspaper, the "pink", they'd printed a green one, they had champagne ready, and we heard all this.' A makeshift Chelsea team employed an unusually muscular approach to put skipper Charlie Hurley and the others off their game.

'It was a very windy day,' continues Venners, 'and Charlie Hurley kept coming up for corners, and he played centre-forward for part of the game and we were under a lot of pressure. Then Tommy Harmer scored from a corner off his "hickory". It was about a foot from the line and he just went like that [Terry thrusts his midriff forward] and he knocked it in, and we won 1–0.

'Then we had to beat Portsmouth on the Monday and we won 7–0. In fact Bobby Campbell played directly against me, and I scored a penalty that night, and I'm not sure, but I might have scored another one as well. I can't remember, but I'm sure we celebrated after that.'

Within a few short years more youngsters were blooded by the manager, including Peter Osgood in 1964. 'Terry was a great player at Chelsea,' enthuses Ossie. 'I think he was one of the best. And he was a strong personality – I think that was perhaps the problem. He didn't agree with what Tommy Doc said, and I think a lot of times he did go out there and say different things, and that's what got up the boss's back, I think, a lot of times.'

His manager was aware of Terry's precocious talent, but also wary of his influence on others. 'Anything Terry said, that was it,' The Doc believes. 'There were a couple of them thought that. Allan Harris, who went to Barcelona with him, George Graham, John Hollins was a bit like that – you remember I sent them all home from Blackpool in 1965? That was all the kids.'

The Blackpool incident! What exactly happened? Well, on the Tuesday before the Saturday game, Tommy had been disappointed with a 1–0 defeat at Liverpool and punished the players by denying them a night out. Late at night, one of the hotel porters had gone round and said, 'Do you know all your lads have just gone out for a drink?' And The Doc said, 'Nah, can't be right, can't be right.' And the porter said, 'Look, I'm telling you they have.' The Doc said, 'No, there's a rugby team in the hotel. It's got to be them.'

Anyway, in the early hours he went up to check on them, went in the room, and all the lads were up there lying asleep. When he pulled back the covers, though, they were all in suits – having just got in. Terry, Eddie McCreadie, George Graham, John Hollins, Bert Murray, Barry Bridges and Joe Fascione were sent home in disgrace. As a result, a hopelessly depleted team lost 6–2 at Burnley and all realistic chances of League success – we were third with only a few games remaining – vanished.

Still, the team was young like Tommy Docherty was young. 'We were a good team,' says Tel. 'We'd been playing for a long while through the youth side and we knew each other's play and it was the style of play that went from the youth team into the first team.' Much like the regime under Glenn Hoddle, it seems . . . 'It was a good blend all round. It was a good football team from the back. West Ham perhaps started overlapping full-backs with Kirkup and Birkett, but our two were really good – Ken Shellito and Eddie McCreadie. I mean, they were brilliant. So they would attack, play it to me in midfield, and I'd put long balls through to Bridges and Tambling.

'I used to play in front of Ken and I had a good relationship with him and the two forwards. Ronnie Harris was a good defender. Marvin Hinton was a great footballer. Johnny Hollins I used to like playing with because we were great mates, and we would always train extra afterwards, the two of us. Quite a few of us, after training was finished with, we'd go and do more, sprint races and little things to challenge each other with; we tried to do as many new things as possible.'

By 1963–64 Terry was our regular penalty-taker (he never missed one in eight league opportunities) and enshrined as captain – something that The Doc would eventually use against him. 'I thought it was a great privilege for me,' says Terry, 'and then later he took the captaincy off me. He never really gave me a reason. He liked changing things you know, and he gave it to Ronnie. There were a couple who turned it down, like Johnny Hollins.' The players' solidarity with the player must have irked Tommy.

Whatever, 1965 was a magical year for Terry. He made his senior England debut as an inside-forward, and won his first trophy, the League Cup. Chelsea also finished third in the League and reached the semis in the FA Cup. The silverware arrived after a 3–2 defeat of Leicester City. Terry scored a penalty in the first game – where all the goals were scored – though he's been mistakenly telling people over the last few years that he also slotted one past Gordon Banks at Filbert Street – 'I must have dreamt it,' he laughs.

By now, with Venners the generalissimo on the pitch, Drake's Ducklings had been surpassed by Docherty's Diamonds. 'Well,' says The Doc, 'that came from when I was up in the stand against Leeds United when we won in the '66 FA Cup: "Go on my little diamonds!" It just came out, because that's what they were. I could've said, "C'mon my dynamos" or something, but that would have been an insult to them, you know. They were diamonds.'

And the pivot was the industrious, voluble number 10, even though there were increasing tensions between the two. 'He was a great creator of goals,' says Tommy. 'He played a lot of great games. When we played in Europe, I used to take him with me to watch the opposition before we played them, I had that much respect for him. And I didn't mind his keenness to discuss things with me, but he would have it out in front of the players. He would say, "We're going to do this," and, "Well, I disagree there." He would make you look a bit stupid, you know.'

Terry believes time has clouded his former manager's memory: 'Well, he does only flirt with the truth, Tom,' he says. 'If it was a funny joke you wouldn't get the truth but you'd have a good story.'

And Terry believes The Doc wilfully destroyed a side that was ready to dominate English football like Leeds or Liverpool would. 'It was a very good side,' he insists, 'but it was the beginning of something. We started at the same time as Leeds – I played against Billy Bremner in schoolboys internationals, then for Leeds and Chelsea. And when we played in the First Division against each other we both had young sides, and really we used to do well against them.

'Then we got to two FA Cup semi-finals in '65 and '66 and didn't succeed and he lost his patience and he wanted to break the team up. But Leeds kept with the same players and went on to be Leeds United as we knew them . . . it was always a bit frustrating not knowing how far we would have gone. We felt we would have actually been one of the best in the land. In saying that, Chelsea did continue to do well, in a different style. They were more like 11 individual players. The King's Road boys, and all that.'

In some ways it was against Liverpool that the yardstick of quality is most interesting. In 1966, we went up to Anfield for an FA Cup third-round match against the team that had easily beaten us in the previous year's semi at Villa Park. Home team manager at the time was the wily Bill Shankly. In his inimitable fashion, Shanks had a pre-match word with the opposition captain and manager, Venners and The Doc. 'Aye,' he said, 'you're a good team – good enough to win it next year.'

After an early Roger Hunt setback, we silenced the Kop with a stunning team display. The Man Who Would Be King, Peter Osgood, did much of the damage that night, alongside our all-time top scorer, the mighty Bobby Tambling. 'It was a corner,' remembers Terry. 'Bridges flicked it on, Osgood scored with a header. And then there was a great move that went from the goalkeeper right through our team, and Bobby Tambling scored a second goal.' The latter was quintessentially the fast-passing style of The Doc's team at its best. 'It was a magnificent achievement and I think it gave us all a lift realising that we were on the beginning of something good. We always believed that, anyway: we just had a lot of confidence.'

But the semi-final at Aston Villa's stadium again proved an insurmountable obstacle, Sheffield Wednesday cantering to a 2–0 win. We were lucky to get the 0.

Terry was one of those singled out for criticism by Tommy Doc. 'Well, I always had the hump with Tommy,' counters Terry, 'because I'd played on the Monday night before the semi-final and I pulled a hamstring and was struggling for fitness. Then they gave me an injection, and Tommy pushed me. He said just being out there would be a big boost for the team and he talked me into playing.

Then when I played and didn't play that well, he blamed me for the result. You just didn't know where you stood with him.'

The Doc could be unaccountable, privately consoling and reassuring his young players, then tearing them apart in the national press. The most notorious occasion was that Liverpool FA Cup semi-final defeat in 1965, where his dressing-room manner differed dramatically from his post-match briefing. 'He says, "You've done your best, they were brilliant,"' says Terry. 'Then he went out and slaughtered us in the papers.' Tommy told waiting journalists that the players and he were incapable of winning anything and the team would be broken up. 'We should have known,' says Terry, 'but he'd have you believing whatever he said.'

On top of the Blackpool boozing incident, the demolition of the team appeared inevitable. Still, there were some remarkable performances in Europe to enjoy, including defeats of Munich 1860, AS Roma and AC Milan, clubs that would come to have greater meaning to Terry when he became manager of Barcelona. 'At the time I just thought it was normal to beat them,' he shrugs. 'But we had some great performances. We had gone into quite a lot of stadiums as youngsters because we were playing for England youth, but it was fairly impressive to us. I mean, I think Suares was playing at that time in Milan, Maldini – father of the current one, Paolo. But I think the best was Munich 1860. They had a guy called Runnymeyers, brilliant centre-forward, and a brilliant goalkeeper, a German. They had a good side and we beat them as well. That was a very good performance because they were one of the favourites. And Milan – to knock them out was fantastic, even on the toss of a coin. We still beat them 2–1 at home.'

Roma at home, for many, was Terry's finest performance. 'Maybe,' he muses. 'I scored three goals so you'd remember it for that. One George Graham passed to me, and I hit it on the volley. Another was a very cheeky free-kick. I paced out the wall, turned to come back to the ball, and then went back again and it was played alongside me by Joe Fascione and I hit it into the net. We worked things like that out beforehand. We were non-stop talking about football, like in the café on Fulham Broadway for hours after the training. Talking about what you could do, how you could get better. We were just besotted with the game.'

Such devotion paid off in many ways. The Chelsea side of 1965 was one of the great teams of the decade. Tributes often came from unusual sources. 'We were invited to play the German national team twice,' says Tommy Docherty. 'What a compliment that was for us! It was in 1965, just before the World Cup in 1966. And I asked

Helmut Schoen, "Why did you pick us, Helmut?" He said, "Because you play like a South American team. You don't play like an English team at all: your full-backs come like wingers. We haven't seen this before in Europe."

'And he said to me, "In the World Cup next year, our centre-forward will be Uwe Seeler and he's just recovering from an Achilles tendon injury, and he'll be tightly marked. Could you ask Harris to mark him close?"

'"Oh," I says, "Helmut, you're taking a bit of chance there. That's the late Chopper Harris you're talking about."

'Helmut says, "What, is he dead?"

'I says, "No, he's just late all the time in the tackling."

'So he says, "Okay, no tackle, just mark," he says.

'Anyway, I spoke to Chopper and he was as good as gold. And I think at that time they gave us about ten thousand quid a game to play the friendlies, one in Achen, and one in Dusseldorf. It was fantastic. The stadiums were packed with about 50,000 people there. We came out with our blue shirts, blue pants and white socks, you know, and we were flying. Eddie [McCreadie] was like an outside-right. He said to me, "Have you got any ideas how to beat their right-back?" Instead of stopping wingers, he was beating their right-back. We murdered them in the first game, beat them 3–1. The second game we lost 3–2. And I'm talking about Beckenbauer, Overath, Uwe Seeler and all them. It was some team. All young, 22, 21. Bertie Vogts, the present coach, was right-back.'

That's a Scotsman's recollection; the former England manager has a different view. 'It was the 1966 World Cup,' smiles Terry incredulously, 'and we were going out there helping the Germans practise – unbelievable! I know there was a reason why we went – I found out later – but I'm not telling you that. In actual fact I think it was Franz Beckenbauer's first game for Germany. Well, it was not long after that that he came here in the World Cup. Barry Bridges scored, but we beat them, out there away from home – I mean it's not bad is it? They were trying, too, because they wanted to get into the team. But we played really well.'

It says quite a lot about the relationship between Doc and Venners that the European match most often cited as the one where the player disobeyed his manager's orders on the pitch – 0–0 away at Roma – is now hailed by The Doc as his greatest tactical triumph. Having won 3–1 at home in controversial circumstances, Terry says Tommy decided upon a flat back four for the difficult second leg. But Venners discussed it with the others and they agreed that with Mr Cool, Marvin Hinton, in the side, they'd be better deploying him as a sweeper – the role The Doc had seen him perform superbly time and again.

'Obviously the tactic was not to lose a goal,' says Tommy. 'And we just played it that every time we lost it we got behind the ball. And I played Marvin Hinton as a sweeper, and he was brilliant – different class. They talk a lot about sweepers today, but he was as good as any. I heard Glenn Hoddle talking about it: I says, "I played that at Chelsea in the '60s." No one was better than Hinton at that and with Ronnie Harris as a man-marker, the two full-backs were playing like they do today, going forward all the time.'

Yet having survived the Roma barrage, we faced Barcelona in the semi-finals of the Fairs Cup in 1966. By now, Terry knew his days were numbered.

'For a long period we got on fantastic,' he says. 'It's just those things that happen in football, players and managers they have good and bad days, it's just that he was so inconsistent. But there was no doubt about it, he was a hell of a character. They were good times, they also were very frustrating times, but that's part of growing up: he was a young manager, I was a young player. Another ten years down the line and we might have done things differently. We wanted to win something, and we kept getting so close that that was the frustration, I should think. A frustration to the manager to know that he was so close and never made it, I understand that.'

When did he sense he might be moving on? 'I think when Charlie Cooke turned up in Barcelona!' laughs Terry.

'Terry was a great player when you were winning,' reckons The Doc, 'but when things were going against you he wasn't the best. I just couldn't see us winning anything with him. Because of his attitude. So we bought Charlie Cooke. I got 80 grand off Tottenham for Venables, and paid 73 for Cookie. What a buy he was! I knew what I was doing there; I knew what I was getting rid of and I knew what I was getting. I knew the Chelsea crowd would love him, and he was God, wasn't he?

'When they went over to Barcelona I stayed behind to sign Cookie. I took Cookie there and introduced him to all the players in the dressing-room before the game. And they were all, "Hello", "Nice to meet you", "Good luck". And Terry was very nice. I must admit. But Terry being Terry tried to get the winning line in just before Cookie went out the door. He said, "Charlie!", and then threw Charlie the ball. And Charlie caught the ball on his instep, flicked it on to his neck, headed it twice in the air and stuck it on his neck again and flicked it back over to Terry.

'I thought, "Oh God, Terry, you shouldn't have done that. You picked the wrong man there." Charlie just said, "See ya lads," and walked out. What an entrance . . . and what a departure as well.'

'I think I knew then,' smiles Terry. 'I got the hint when he was juggling the ball in the corner! He turned round and he had my number 10 on the back of his shirt! I was quick, you know! Things had got to a bad stage, though. I didn't understand at the time, but if someone's got to go, it's always the player. And I suppose I was upset because I felt I'd always given everything.

'I suppose I'd always wanted to play for Chelsea, and I loved it so much, I wanted to be there all my career. I didn't want to go. I always had in my mind that I would be there for ever. I felt very bad, very bad when I went to Tottenham. In fact, I couldn't settle down there: I kept thinking that it wasn't real and I'd be going back in a couple of months. I knew it wasn't true, but it was something in me thinking this was not real. I never really played for Tottenham like I played for Chelsea.'

But then – who does?

3

The Cat

Meeting a legend in his own lunchtime. Check watch. Note day. Isn't there something rather important happening elsewhere? Oh yes – Euro 96. England v. Germany . . .

Crikey. Of all the days to meet Peter Bonetti. The 'anniversary' of Mexico 1970, the only bad match in his entire hundred-year career, the 2–0-up, 3–2-down World Cup quarter-final. You remember, of course: Banks had a dicky tummy, The Cat crept in . . . and crept out again. Well, they all blamed our poor Peter, and we took it personally. But *we* know that if Sir Alf hadn't taken off Bobby Charlton, and if the midfield hadn't played so deep, and if the bloody defence had just *done something!* . . .

'I've heard that a few times,' says the slim, silver-haired 'Catty'. 'Everyone's got their own opinions on it and they're not going to change now. It's history.'

Sorry to bring it up. 'Well, it just makes you laugh. I played six other games for England, only conceded one goal, and there I played in one game where I lost – all right, I didn't play well: I was at fault for the first goal; the other two I don't think I was. What else can you say? You can talk till you're blue in the face, but the facts are I should have saved the first one, done better on it – 99 times out of 100 I would've done. But I didn't, and it was an important game to lose. You've got to live with it. Just like Pearcey's had to live with his penalty miss and Waddle with his.

'Oh, I said to my wife the other day watching the Spain game, "That's great! I'm so pleased Pearcey's had the chance to rectify it." I never had the chance, but you don't let that affect you. The good thing from my point of view was that 46 days before the incidents in Mexico I'd helped Chelsea Football Club win the FA Cup for the first time in its history, and we sampled success again in the Cup-Winners' Cup. This game is highs and lows all the time, it really is, and that proves it. So if you're a person who's always going to worry about the lows and mistakes, then you won't survive in it. That was

41

1970. I went on to play until '79–'80, so I went on to play another ten years virtually, so it obviously didn't affect me. And it would have been wrong and stupid of me if it had.'

Right. Look, I'm sorry. Won't mention it again. Instead, let's look at how one of Chelsea's greatest-ever discoveries, a keeper recognised by all of his contemporaries – and, needless to say, his team-mates – as one of the top three in the world at his peak, came to arrive at Stamford Bridge and how The Cat got his name.

Pele rather liked him. Quote: 'The three greatest goalkeepers I have ever seen are Gordon Banks, Lev Yashin and Peter Bonetti.' We didn't exactly agree with the Brazilian's assessment. That's why the terraces resounded to 'Bonetti's twice as good as Banks, alleluiah!' or, in other instances, 'We all agree, Bonetti is better than Yashin . . . Cookie is better than Eu-se-bi-o, so Tott'nham are in for a thrashing!'

The Cat's mother was born in Switzerland and his father, also of Swiss parentage, was born in London. Bonetti senior had restaurants in London, and the family lived in Putney until Peter was seven, when they upped sticks and took over a hotel in Worthing. The Sussex town and its environs formed the unlikely support system for a football fanatic.

'I played at every level locally,' he says. 'When I had the trial with Chelsea I was playing with a local Worthing Catholic team. My dad was playing full-back in it, three of my brothers were playing in it, and two of my cousins. So we were nicknamed Bonetti United because sometimes there were seven Bonettis in the side. I used to collect all the football magazines, and in those days I was a Manchester United fanatic. I used to write up and get autographs and pictures.' Well, we'll draw a veil over that indiscretion for the time being.

Like most of his contemporaries who made it, Peter played football every minute he could from dawn to dusk. The old house in Putney was local, about three miles away from Stamford Bridge, so Chelsea was Peter's local team, in a sense. And in the '50s Dick Foss and the rest had a reputation for a good youth policy and 'giving all the youngsters a go'.

'My mother wrote to them, and I must have done all right because I went back and they asked me to sign the following season. That was the beginning of the 1958–59 season; I joined them on 28 July 1958 and I started on the same day as Terry Venables, Bobby Tambling, Bert Murray, Allan Harris – these sorts of guys, who were to make it in the game as well. I remember our first day, joining up with all of them at the Welsh Harp in Hendon, and I was a bit of a green kid, because I lived in "the sticks" as they called it. So I was in trouble straightaway. A lot of those boys were East-Enders, from Essex way, and I was a quiet lad in those days, more of an introvert – well, I still am – whereas Terry and a lot of the lads were extroverts. But I think they judged you on your ability in the end and it was nice to be accepted, to be one of the lads.'

Youth team manager Sidney 'Dick' Foss, a former Chelsea playing star, was busily assembling probably Chelsea's most potent set of youngsters ever. He was a big influence on Peter. 'He was the first big man I came into contact with in the professional world. Very good, he was. Helped me tremendously, just coaching and that. I wasn't coached as a goalkeeper, because there weren't goalkeeping coaches around in those days. So I had to do everything everyone else did. Nowadays it's different, because I do goalkeeping coaching, have done for the last 13 years, and I know how important it is. In fact, in latter years at Chelsea, I was doing the goalkeeping coaching even though I was playing.

'But then, you didn't know about it. You just did as you were told. Literally. Used to train, do all the running. But it didn't bother me because I was a bit of a fitness freak anyway. I could run all day and I used to win all the runs, being skinny and that. Nowadays, yes, I'd be regarded as too small to be a goalkeeper. I was 5ft 11ins tall, but I don't think in those days it mattered: there was Alan Hodgkinson and Ron Springett, keepers who played for England, and they were all smaller than me. But I was agile, and that made up for it in more ways than one.'

Agility alone wouldn't depose the incumbent between the posts, though: England's Reg Matthews. And it wasn't as if in those days he was going to get any tips from the older custodian. 'There was a big difference in those days between the groundstaff and professionals. It's different now: you train together and all the rest of it. And although as juniors we were there with them, we didn't actually train with them. And you respected them more; it was a "Mr" relationship. I wanted to be a professional, course I did. I wanted to get to the top. But I never thought, "I'm gonna take his job." You didn't think that way; there wasn't the hype there is now. There wasn't the money there is now. It was more of a sport. You wanted to be a professional because you loved the game.'

Such a Corinthian spirit nevertheless reaped early rewards. In 1960, the youth team became the first in Chelsea colours to win the FA Youth Cup, that confirmation of precocious talent. 'It was a brilliant team,' smiles Catty. 'And the first FA Youth Cup win was my last game with the juniors. It's funny. I made my first-team debut on 2 April 1960. The week before I'd been playing for the juniors in a league game at the Welsh Harp.

'So I then played in the first team for six of the remaining seven games that season, and I broke my nose in the sixth game, got carried off. And that meant I missed the Youth Cup final the following week as well. We played Preston at home, drew 1–1 in a game I didn't play, but I was fit to play the second one, and we won 4–1 at Preston. So my last game for the juniors was in winning the Youth Cup when I was regarded as a first-team player, though I didn't think of myself as a regular. The two Silletts were there as full-backs – they were lovely people. When I first came in they had a lot of gentlemen in the side who were what you might call . . . not unprofessional, but they weren't so dedicated to training and stuff. Ted Drake was quite lenient really.'

The Cat's arrival coincided with the end of Drake's *ancien régime*. The man who masterminded Chelsea's grinding Championship triumph in 1955 had become an aloof figure with his coterie of slicked-back older players. He was out of touch in the early '60s, and an ambitious young player-coach was brought across from Arsenal to bolster the club. It was too late to stave off relegation, but his impact was immense.

'Tommy Doc came in 1961, and we went down in 1962,' says Catty. 'I was already in the first team and here again, he was another man who was a great influence on me. Although I had my skirmishes with him, Tommy was a great influence in my life, a helluva lot. Great man. I liked him tremendously, even though we had our punch-ups, so to speak.

'Tom stood out because when he came in he got rid of all the old pros, the Silletts, Peter Brabrook, Tindall, and brought in all the players from the youth team. I can remember a team where there was Allan Harris playing, Terry Venables, Bobby Tambling, Ken Shellito, Barry Bridges, Bert Murray, and me – that's seven out of the same junior side. The six of them were juniors one year and he put them all in the first team the next. Then you had the likes of John Mortimore and Frank Blunstone who were from the senior group that stayed on, and then he went out and bought Eddie McCreadie – his first purchase, who was a fantastic full-back – and Graham Moore.

'So we didn't have the experience. And the first year we were all together, we went down. But we came straight back up the following year, because by that time we were that bit older, more experienced, more knowledgeable, better players, and we were a good side – without actually winning anything apart from the League Cup in 1965.'

In common with other young players, Catty was alternately bewitched and bewildered by The Doc, now installed as manager. And when Dave Sexton arrived as coach, two influential figures shaped his career. 'Whereas Dave Sexton was a coach – tactically, technically, Dave was very good on that side of things – Tommy was extrovert. He used to motivate more than coach. That was his greatest strength. He could gee people up. He could bellow at people. And Tommy would do what he thought was right no matter who they were. If he wanted to drop someone he would drop them. And of course us youngsters used to revere him, because of who he was and what he did. And he certainly helped all of us because he was slinging so many youngsters in. People like Ron Harris and Johnny Hollins when they came were being put in early, whereas they might not have been at other clubs. He gave them their first chance and they took it.'

Needless to say, Peter grasped his too. The nickname showed the regard his team-mates had for him. 'That came very early. Ron Tindall started it after my first few games. We all used to meet upstairs in the billiard room above the offices at Stamford Bridge, and have our team-talks in the back room next door. And I can remember before the game playing darts or billiards. I was a quiet boy, and Ron Tindall, one of the senior members at Chelsea, wasn't. He was a lovely, lovely man. Anyway, while I was playing, I can remember him starting off – to make me relaxed, I suppose – doing a commentary. He was saying, "And look, the camera's on Peter Bonetti . . . 'The Cat' is coming up . . . he's getting ready, preparing for the game . . ." And it stuck. He gave me the name probably because of my agility. I suppose it helped; I felt it gave me confidence, or helped me to relax or whatever. And it's great in a sense because, even now, the England Under-21s and the seniors whom I worked with under Graham Taylor, even they called me "The Cat". It's nice. Ossie and the rest of them call me Catty. I take that as a compliment.'

Threats on The Cat's nine lives, in the figurative sense, came early. In the promotion campaign of 1962–63, and Tommy Doc's first full season, he was near ever-present and often under pressure behind a young defence as the runaway leaders hit the skids after the 'big freeze'. The crunch came in the last two matches. Chelsea needed to win both: away at promotion favourites Sunderland, and home to Pompey a few days later. At Roker, a mix 'n' match team in which Catty was probably relieved to hold on to his number 1 shirt scored through former Spurs star Tommy Harmer, but withstood a barrage – of sorts – from the Makums.

In reality, it was the young keeper's commanding presence in the box that was decisive. 'I remember thinking all through the second half that I couldn't understand why they kept thumping the ball into our penalty box when it was getting them nowhere,' said Tommy Harmer years later. Catty's only other involvement was fielding a succession of pass-backs. Yet, in the last minute, he was called upon to pull off a full-stretch save from Mulhall that Roker skipper Charlie Hurley described as 'out of this world'.

'A lot of people remark on the save I made against Sunderland,' says Catty. 'I was under pressure for the entire 90 minutes there, but that one won us the game, because we won 1–0, and had to win to go up. That was one of my most important saves from Chelsea's point of view. If that had gone in, we wouldn't have got promoted. End of story. We wouldn't have gone back and scored because it was the end of the game. So certain saves mean more to you than others, but they're not necessarily the most eye-catching.

'I can remember making a spectacular save against Munich 1860 at Stamford Bridge in the Fairs Cup in 1965–66, when we beat them 1–0. And not many people remarked on it. Yet I know it was important because I had been thinking of going one way, and then suddenly I had to turn in mid-air. And it was behind me, and I remember hooking it out. A lot of people said, "Good save", but to me I felt it was one of my better saves because of what was going through my mind at the time.'

As Brian Glanville's book *Goalkeepers Are Different* attests, the man between the sticks has a unique perspective on the game. 'A goalkeeper will remark on a save; an outfield player or a commentator won't necessarily. I've seen a goalkeeper make a fantastic save, because it's got a deflection or whatever, and he might not have got the credit he should have done. Other times commentators amuse themselves, saying, "Oh, that was a brilliant save," when I think, "That wasn't fantastic, that was a bread-and-butter save."'

'That was a great team, great days,' muses Tommy Docherty. 'And The Cat, Bonetti, was different class. He was a great goalkeeper. One of the best ever. He was a lovely lad, smashing kid and brilliant goalkeeper. Great professional. Hated to be beaten even in training. I saw Swift and Trautmann and Bert Williams and Banks and Shilton. On crosses, there was nobody better than him. And for 5ft 11ins, he was absolutely brilliant. He got the name of being a wee bit shifty with his money. I think every time the ball went into the goalmouth he thought it was a fifty pound note, the way he clutched it. He wouldn't let it go at all.'

This was one of The Cat's great innovations. Not only was he one of the first keepers to throw the ball out when he had possession (well, did you ever see him kick it any distance?) but he claimed more crosses than any previous custodian. Remember the classic Bonetti act: a high jump amongst towering strikers, the clean claim of the ball, and the crouch. Then the frail, hunched look up and green-gloved wave to defenders. A swift motion, then a roll out or an arm's-length throw. Defence becomes attack.

'Yeah,' he grins. 'Funnily enough I was watching some of the old classics on Sky the other evening, and some of our games were on: the Cup final and the replay at Old Trafford. And I'd seen a couple of games a few months ago when we played Man City and Villa in the League. And, I must admit, I did surprise myself. I knew I came for corners, because that was my strength, but I didn't realise how many I came for and how many I caught. So it's nice even now, looking back, that people used to say that was my strength, my cross-claiming, my ability to hold balls in the air.

'Looking at Euro 96, too many goalkeepers punch the ball away, as if they're protecting themselves rather than the goal. Balls that are hit in, he's only got to catch it and it's safe, you can start a counter-attack. But they just punch it away and I think it's idiotic. I still coach people to catch.

'I don't know why I decided to do it, really. I think it's like asking why did George Best dribble so much? Why did Bobby Charlton hit balls so much? It's part of your game, your character and all the rest of it. I did it as a kid. I used to try and hold on to everything: even if a ball was going in the top corner I'd try and catch it rather than flick it away. The goalkeeper who stays on his line might have let three goals in from those crosses. I'd rather someone came out eight or nine times and dropped one, than didn't come out at all.' And, oh, how we loved sneering at inferior keepers, 'Huh, you should have caught it . . .'

A video of our January victory over holders Liverpool in the 1966 FA Cup would make scintillating viewing. The team prepared for the showpiece clash of the third round with special training at Lilleshall. Chelsea, beaten in the semi by the Scousers the year before, steeled themselves for a torrid atmosphere at a damp, sanded Anfield. Roger Hunt scored after two minutes and then attempted to hassle The Cat, who was shielded from the worst of it by the zealous John Boyle – a member of The Doc's 'slippery pitch' team. But the Chelsea keeper was in simply sublime form, swallowing Liverpool's shots with disheartening ease. 'One of the brightest displays of goalkeeping seen for years,' cooed *Soccer Star*.

In a bubbling second-half team display, Ossie, in an early phase of his extended run in the team, showed the grace and intelligence that was to mark his career, and scored the equaliser. Tambling got the winner. A famous victory that served to spread the gospel of St Peter.

Then, of course, Peter had the first branded goalkeeper's gloves – he was the trendiest keeper too. Even opposition fans quite liked him – he wasn't brash and lairy like some of our fellas. And neutrals bought his gloves. 'Same with all the rest of it,' Peter smiles. 'The jerseys, the shorts, etc. Didn't take off as big as it has nowadays because there wasn't the commercial aspect then. It was more difficult to promote things. I was born 20 years too early, without a doubt. I know that more and more. But having said that, I wouldn't have changed my time in the game for the world.'

Not even the clashes with The Doc? By 1966, this was a regular feature. 'Well, he and I certainly didn't see eye to eye after a while. I had a bust-up with him really after the World Cup in '66. I was with England all through the '66 campaign and we were away for five or six weeks. We'd travelled around and had the pre-tournament friendly games against Colombia and San Salvador. And I can remember the week before the final, Tony Green, the secretary from Chelsea, rang me and said, "Peter, at the end, if you get to the final next Sunday, we want you to report on the Monday to Germany. The first team are going out there pre-season training. Tommy says you've got to come and join up with them on the Monday. I've got tour tickets here and everything."

'I rang from the England hotel reception and said, "Tony, doesn't Tommy know I'm with the England squad? I want a break. I've been away for five or six weeks. All the lads have been off all summer." And he said, "Well, Pete, I've had a word with you. I'll go back and tell him." Back came the word: Tommy Docherty – typical Scot – "I don't care what he's been doing all summer – it's of no interest to me whether he's been with England. I want him out there."

'So I just rang back and said, "I'm sorry, you can stuff your tickets. I'm going away for a week's holiday, with the family, on Monday and I'll be back the following Monday. If he wants me to fly out there then I will be glad to do so." I hadn't seen the family for five or six weeks and they wanted me to go on this ten-day pre-season tour of Germany. But that was Tommy. That was the start of my bust-up with him. So come the following week I got back and flew out to join them and he didn't even come to meet me. Didn't speak to me for two or three days. Just had a go at me. He played me in one of the games, and I played well, as it happened.'

The Doc saw an ulterior motive behind Peter's actions. 'When he was in the 1966 World Cup party he was tapped-up by the West Ham players. So that's why I signed Alex Stepney. Peter's wife Frances, whom he's now divorced from, she used to moan and groan and say, "They're always away, Mr Docherty." I said, "You're only away in football when you're successful. If you want him to be home every night, I'll transfer him to Leyton Orient tomorrow. He'll never be away anywhere if he plays for them."

'I bought Stepney as insurance, when the chance came. Sir Matt Busby came down from Manchester United for either of them. And I said, "Oh, I'm keeping the better one." Peter was being a bit, not naughty, but a bit silly. I said to him, "No, you'll stay here." I knew Chelsea supporters would go mad if I sold Bonetti; whereas they wouldn't be too bad if I sold Stepney.'

Stepney had saved six penalties for Millwall the previous season. But The Cat he wasn't. Before his departure, Tommy Doc embarked on a typical piece of brinkmanship. 'When we got back to England,' recalls Peter, 'the board fined me a week's wages. I couldn't care less – it was money well spent. And then Tom was saying to Alex and myself, leading up to the start of the season, "I'm thinking about playing you a game each." Alex and me, by then we'd become great buddies. And we were saying to Tommy, "Aw, come on, this is ridiculous!" Even I was saying, "Alex, if you start off, fine. I'd rather you start off and you play every week. And if I win my place back, fine." And Alex was the same. But Tommy Doc was winding us up, because he was annoyed with me.

'My main contention is that he was jealous because England had won the World Cup, because he was a Scot and they hadn't done very well. Obviously I wasn't doing what he said, and he obviously thought he'd play the dictatorship card. As it happened I played the first game, and it was against West Ham, and of course they had players like Martin Peters, Geoff Hurst and Bobby Moore just after winning the World Cup. I remember I played a blinder – that was one of my best games. And we won 2–1. First game of the season, and of course he couldn't do anything else but to keep me in then.'

But Peter wanted out – to West Ham or Man United preferably. He'd already asked for a transfer. 'I can remember the moment vividly. Man United were one of my favourite teams – not now, of course. And so I was driving home from training that day – it was a Wednesday or Thursday evening – and blow me down, I nearly crashed the car, because the radio said, ". . . And Alex Stepney of Chelsea has just signed for Man United."

'I went, "You bastard!"'

'During the World Cup games, West Ham were interested in me, because I'd fallen out with Tommy again. West Ham had put a bid in of £70,000, which was a lot of money. And Tommy came back and said, "It's not enough." So Tommy was just waiting. Didn't put a price on me. Just wait and see what people said. Then said it's not enough. I don't think he wanted to sell me in the first place. But we were having these barneys, and by then, I must admit, I did want a change. I'd been at Chelsea ten years. Little did I know I'd be there for another ten! And in a sense I was my own worst enemy, because at the time I could have got away I was playing the best football of my life.' But the barneys persisted. 'Just little lies here and there along the way, and promises that weren't fulfilled,' says Catty.

Nevertheless, Doc did stand up for his keeper on occasions. One in particular sticks out. Chelsea embarked on a pre-season tour of Australia in 1965, and were winning by a two-figure margin when disgrace looked about to pay a one-off visit at the Bonetti door. 'It was only one of these friendly games. The ball had gone out for a goal kick and I've gone to get the ball and the referee's just pointed for a corner. The referee's given a corner and I said, "Fucking hell, that wasn't a corner." Just like that. And I never used to swear in those days, I must admit. The referee was a Hungarian-Australian or something, and he's heard this and thought I was swearing at him, and he's threatened to send me off. And of course Tommy comes running on from the touchline all annoyed, saying to the ref, "What are you doing?"

'"I'm sending him off – he swore at me."

'So Tommy's saying, "He's a good Catholic lad, he's never sworn in his life; he wouldn't swear." And sure enough I didn't. And I never got booked in my life, let alone sent off. If it wasn't for Tommy sticking up for me I would probably have been sent off. In the end the referee said, "Oh, all right, then." Didn't even book me, just forgot about it.'

The pre-season tours were a chance for bonding, but The Doc, although a disciplinarian, could be quite unpredictable on a night out. 'The biggest thing with Tommy was he wanted to be one of the lads, yet being a manager, you can't be one of the lads. As players who become managers at clubs nowadays know, like Glenn Hoddle and Ray Wilkins, you've got to step the other side of the line. And Tommy, whenever we went out for a do or whatever, he wanted to come with us. But you can't do it.

'Preparing for the Cup final in 1967, we'd gone down The Brain for every round. So before the final, we'd been invited out to someone's party, just someone's friend's cocktail party, and Tommy came along and was saying, "Right, okay lads, you can stay till midnight." It was still early in the week but we still had to be very good. Then all of a sudden something went wrong. He got upset – I think some guy chatted up the woman he was after, something silly – and next minute he's got all annoyed and he's gone, "Right. That's it, lads. I want you all in by 10 o'clock tonight, and that's that." And then he pissed off. That was the typical Tommy. If things were going for you, fine. If things weren't, he'd change just like that. You couldn't plan like that. He was changeable.

'Like the Cup final we got to in 1967. "Yeah, don't worry lads, I'll get you Cup final tickets!" We end up being able to buy 12. And we found out later that he was supposed to have had loads. That's the sort of thing that happened. He'd always look after himself first, and the players came second. He was a bit of rogue from that point of view. The lads used to call him Tommy the Tyke. He was a likeable rogue. Give him his due, though – he got things done.'

When Dave Sexton replaced The Doc in October 1967, he was more The Cat's type of bloke: studious, quiet, professional. 'With Dave it was first and foremost the players. I'm very close to him even now, because of him being the manager of the Under-21s and me the goalkeeping coach. I'd like to think I'm a good friend of Dave's. We don't socialise, go out with the wives and all that, because he's very private. We only socialise at football. Tremendous manager, very knowledgeable. He was an honest man, and had integrity. He was a football man through and through; talked to you all night long about football.'

Catty and Dave both lived in Sussex and travelled in together. It led to accusations from some quarters that the manager had his 'favourites'. 'There were no favours given,' says Peter. 'Dave was still a very professional man and did what he felt was right, irrespective of who the players were.'

Yet man-management was never Dave's strongest suit. 'He had problems with some of the boys in the team – 1972 or thereabouts – when things were on a bit of a decline. But I think he was the scapegoat for that, to be honest. I think he was disappointed with them, because he wasn't a shouter. He wanted loyalty returned and I think one or two let him down; I think they'd be the first to say that. And I think that's what got Dave the sack in the end. Some of the players needed a bit of discipline and Dave was trying to do that and they were doing things behind his back. It was a question of the board saying, "We back you, Dave, or we back the players." And they backed the players.'

Yet the record books show Dave Sexton to be Chelsea's most successful manager ever, redesigning the bustling team he inherited from The Doc. 'Well, he got us the success the club had not had before: FA Cup, Cup-Winners' Cup,' says Peter. 'He knew how to buy players and get them to play. Tactically he was brilliant, knew what tactics to use. And I think he knew how to get the best out of players.

'Ossie talks about the blend we had in those days – and we did have a blend. We had four skilful players in one team. We had Ossie, Cookie, Huddy, Peter Houseman – what I would call exceptional, skilful players. In one team. Then you had the likes of the assassins at the back, as Ossie called them: Ronnie Harris, Eddie McCreadie, John Dempsey, David Webb. And then you had the runners, good footballers still: Holly, who had the lungs, Tommy Baldwin, could run all day. And Hutchy the big strong guy up front as well.

'We had a tremendous blend. That doesn't just happen by accident. Someone's got to have that in mind. A manager's got to bring that out and put it together. And Dave did. He was a very meticulous person. Very much into tactics and coaching – he travels all over the world to coach even now. I think he probably lost one or two of the players when we'd be working on certain things. Even with the Under-21s, I see him out there talking and I think, "Dave, you're losing them," because they haven't got the footballing brain to see what he's saying.'

The pinnacle of the '70s team's success was the long-awaited capture of the FA Cup in 1970. The old music hall song 'When Chelsea Won the Cup' was finally rendered obsolete. We'd reached our second final in four years, and there was to be no repeat of the tragedy of losing to Spurs. Yet it was Leeds, the team of the moment, and one who'd beaten us 7–0 within recent and all-too-vivid memory, who stood at the end of the tunnel.

The build-up for Chelsea was magnificent, even though Huddy, one of the heroes of the earlier rounds, was unavailable (except for functions and soirées, of course). 'I remember going into restaurants and at the end of the night the manager saying, "Oh, don't worry about the bill, it's been a pleasure to serve you." I lived in Banstead in Surrey then, and I went into a pub-restaurant in Sutton with a group of about ten people – neighbours and friends – and at the end I went round to collect the bill and the waiter said someone else had paid. I said, "What?" And it was a fellow who supplied all the one-arm bandits, who was quite a wealthy man. I said, "But there's all of us." He said, "He wants to pay for everyone." Course all my friends were saying, "Cor, we'll come back here again." So you got perks. It's lovely.'

The final itself was spoiled by the quality of the pitch, which may well have earned a blue flag from the beach inspectors, but was unworthy of the 'hallowed turf'. The 2–2 scoreline was, perhaps, an unfair reflection of Leeds's superiority. In extra time Peter's aerial dominance was vital to a tired defence. The replay, at Old Trafford 18 days later, produced several heroes in blue: Ossie, for his diving header, Webby, for his cheeky winner, Cookie for his second-half brilliance, and, perhaps greatest of all, Peter Bonetti, injured in a mid-air assault from Leeds striker Mick Jones, who limped and dived to repel almost everything that Don Revie's men could throw at him.

'Certainly the FA Cup final, and the replay, I'd a lot of stops to make and catches to make and, yes, it was satisfying, because we won and if I hadn't played so well, we might not have done so. I watched a replay of the Old Trafford game the other night. It just looked funny me hobbling about. And it looked odd me bouncing the ball, because the rules have changed. I wouldn't say it was my best game by any means. I've played in a lot better games than that where I've been non-stop. But from the point of view of winning something and making important saves, and having a good game overall, yes, it must stand out.

'In the European Cup-Winners' Cup the following year I probably had nothing to do. One save, I think, in the last couple of minutes and that was about all. I don't remember anything else. There were lots of other games where I've played well and it hasn't been so important. I mean, I always used to play well against Nottingham Forest for some reason – away and at home. The number of times we went up there and won 2–1 and I was under non-stop pressure, making saves galore. And yet we'd win the game. It was only a league game. Well, I say "only", but it was important, obviously.'

With The Cat so consistent, the man with the worst job in football for some 20 years was Chelsea's second-string keeper. When Peter contracted pneumonia before the Cup-Winners' Cup semi-final, John 'Sticks' Phillips deputised. But for the final, Dave Sexton opted for his half-fit old trooper. 'I felt sorry for all my understudies,' he smiles. 'I know it sounds big-headed but I did: John Dunn, Johnny Phillips, Tommy Hughes. Tommy more than anyone because he came in once and let in five, then he came in again and let in six . . . I thought, poor old Tommy. It's very difficult to come in and take over from a man who's been playing for years and whom people revere. I mean, Banksy when I came in against Germany! People expected wonders. Banksy was a fantastic goalkeeper, and me coming in and making a mistake . . . and you suffer for it. I know what they went through, because in a sense they must have gone through something like that.

'When John first came in people automatically put this rivalry between us. But we were good mates. Lovely lad. Honest. Wasn't a drinker. He did come in and take over for a while. I remember one season, the year Chelsea were relegated: 1975. I went to America that summer because I thought I was going to be on a free transfer, yet again, and only played about eight First Division games that year. I played in the reserves that year and we won the Championship. And then when John broke his leg that pre-season I came back from America hoping to get my free transfer and then Eddie McCreadie called me because Steve Sherwood wasn't playing well. Next minute, come in, play a blinder, first game they've won in weeks, and I stay in for another four years or whatever!'

That season, along with all the other pros at now cash-strapped Stamford Bridge, Catty took a wage cut to ease the club's outgoings. 'It was more Eddie than us,' he says. 'We just said yeah, fair enough, it's not going to hurt us. Eddie was another Tommy Doc in a way: very extrovert, very confident man. And he just wanted to do something for the club and said to the lads, "Look, how about taking a wage cut?" So we said, "Fair enough." So we did.'

That doesn't exactly square with Ossie's view of the 'tightest bastard you'll ever meet' . . .

'I know. He thinks I'm tight.' He relates his version of their £5 bet before the Hautcharage game (one that tallies more with checkable events, it has to be said).

'He said, "Catty, I'll always take your money."

'"Ossie," I says, "I bet you a fiver you don't get six."

'"You're on."

'And of course, we beat them 13–0 and Ossie got five. So I bloody asked for the fiver! He always used to have a go at me and I'll tell you why. I wasn't a socialiser, going to the clubs and boozers. I was a quiet person, and more or less stayed in the hotels. Holly and Peter Houseman were my mates. They used to go out occasionally, but not as much as some! And, of course, Ossie and them were always saying, "Come on out." I was a bit more of the elder statesman anyway, six or seven years older than Ossie, and I'd say, "No, lads, you go out and enjoy yourself." And Ossie would say, "Oh, you old misery." And I'd say, "I don't enjoy drinking, I'm not a nightclub person." They used to think it was because I didn't want to spend my money. It was nothing to do with that. And I tell you what: I always used to stand my ground. And in the end they got fed up with it.

'But I remember Eddie McCreadie when he was manager. I always used to sit in the front of the coach going to away games and on the way home. And after one game, the year we won promotion, 1977, when Cookie and I were back together again, Eddie came up and he said, "I've got to admire you. They often give you stick about not going out and not doing this . . ." I used to get up early and go to church on a Sunday, do my own thing. "You stick to what you believe in," he said. I said, "Are you criticising?"

'"No Pete," he said. "I admire that. It's just that the lads at the back there, they're all getting together, all going to have a piss-up now, and they know you don't drink and now they've accepted you. That must be nice, feeling comfortable doing your own thing." I thought that was great. I took that as a compliment.'

Two years later, Peter finally quit Stamford Bridge with the record for goalkeeping appearances at one club. It was a glorious career: in 1969 fans had voted him Chelsea's greatest-ever player. Predictably, he was to return home – as one of the League's first specialised goalkeeping coaches a few years later. Those who saw him in his prime will never forget the extraordinary saves that he made look routine, and the sense of security he brought. In 1992, as we shuffled away from a game in which unfortunate Beasant errors had largely accounted for a 3–2 home reverse, a friend muttered, 'I always said we got rid of Bonetti too soon.' No one laughed.

Back in 1970, at the conclusion of that match between Germany and England in Léon, Catty went up to his manager. 'Sorry, Alf,' he muttered. 'Don't let it worry you, son,' responded Sir Alf.

And he never did.

4

Clarence

'It Might Be Cold Tomorrow'
I've never felt so happy
And yet sad,
I love you today,
It might be cold tomorrow.
                    Eddie McCreadie

'"Clarence", that's what we called him. Like the cross-eyed lion off
that show *Daktari*.' Well, Eddie McCreadie was fiercer than most
left-backs, and a far better player than his peers too. But it speaks
volumes for the turbulent relationship between manager and
player that Tommy Docherty's first words are teasing ones. 'If I
met Tommy today, we could sit down and have a good chat, but we
wouldn't be great friends,' says Eddie. And to think it all started
so well . . . 'He was brilliant, fantastic.' The Doc can still eulogise
about his first great purchase. And smile at the memory of how
one of Chelsea's finest-ever acquisitions came about in April 1962,
the serendipity of it all. 'There was a fellow recommended me a lad
called Gourlie of Arbroath, played left side of midfield. So I went
to see him play at East Stirling, and they gave me the team sheet,
sitting away at the back of the stand, and this left-back, I couldn't
get him out my mind at all. I thought, "Why the hell are you
playing here?" He was great in the air, he was quick, his control
was magic. I didn't know whether he was a left-back or an outside-
left. He was just a revelation. I never even knew if Gourlie was
playing that day or not. Afterwards I met Jack Steedman of East
Stirling.

'He says, "Hallo, Tom, what're you doing here?"

'I says, "I'm looking at the boy Gourlie from Arbroath, he's not a
bad player." Then I says, "I wouldnae swap him for your left-back."

'"Oh," he says. "Now you're talking!"

'And I asked him to tell me about this boy McCreadie . . .

'"Ah, he's a good lad, Eddie, I want a lot of money for him," he says.

'I says, "How much d'you want for him?"

'"£8,000."

'"Oh," I says, "behave yourself, Jack. You could buy the whole of East Stirlingshire for eight grand."

'Anyway, we bartered away and got him for five, plus a friendly at East Stirling. There wasn't even any more if he played for Scotland or anything. And they were delighted.'

Eddie remembers the evening well. 'I believe he'd gone to see the winger Joe Fascione who played there. Anyway, bottom line of it was that most people knew that Tommy Docherty was at the game. When you're in the Second Division, at East Stirling, and Tommy Docherty's 100 miles anywhere near the place, people tend to know about it. But the biggest surprise I got was when I walked off the field after the game and one of the directors of the club asked me to come into his office, saying Tommy Docherty wanted to talk to me. That was quite an exciting moment.

'A couple of years earlier I'd been offered a move to Fulham and one or two other clubs. I asked my father at the time for his advice, and he told me I wasn't strong enough. He told me that if I went down to the First Division in England at that time I'd get my ass kicked. He thought it would be more beneficial for me to play in the Scottish Second Division, which was renowned for a lot of tough tackling going on. He felt I should learn that part of my game before I went down to England. I took his advice and for two years nothing happened. I was rather disappointed perhaps in my decision, feeling that my opportunity had left. I felt that I had a certain amount of ability, but how far I could go at that time I had no idea. But I knew there were clubs interested in me. I was fairly confident in myself, although not over-confident. I felt I had certain abilities; when anything was put in front of me I kind of went at it. I always worked hard, which helped me a great deal.

'So I remember Tommy Docherty telling me, "I'd like to take you down to Chelsea, and this is what we're going to pay you. I'm flying back to London in the morning, but perhaps you would like to talk this over with your parents before you sign."

'"No," I said, "I'll sign right now." I wasn't interested in the contract and how much or anything, I just wanted the opportunity.'

The Glaswegian played two games in the stiffs during the 1962 close season. But the club had been relegated and Tommy was reconstructing the squad in preparation for promotion, and he immediately threw Eddie into the first team. 'My first game against

Rotherham away was like a cup final to me,' says Eddie. 'Just pulling on the famous blue Chelsea jersey was a thrill indeed. I remember distinctly the atmosphere in my first home games as well. It was an atmosphere I'd never experienced before. You were very conscious that you were not alone out there.

'And I remember even now from my first game – remember this was a side with Terry Venables, Barry Bridges, Bobby Tambling, all these wonderful players – and from the first ball that came to me, the first thing I thought was, "Man, this is *easy*!" D'you know why? It was amazing. When you get the ball in the left full-back position you're looking for someone to give it to, and there are a few people hiding from you that didn't want it. But in this game, every time I got the ball there were about three or four people looking for the ball. And if I wanted the ball the passes were so good I didn't have to stretch for it. The passes were coming straight to my feet. I'd never experienced that before. And I just thought, "Thank goodness. This is wonderful. This'll do me."'

Tommy Doc saw his fellow countryman's potential immediately. He told Eddie, 'You'll be playing for Scotland in another year.'

'D'you think so?'

'Aye.'

Eddie immediately forged a wing-back partnership with England right-back Ken Shellito – 'the best right-back I've ever seen', according to The Doc. But it was Terry Venables, newly elevated to the first team, who was Eddie's big mate at the club.

The first big test of the Docherty era came at the close of his – and Eddie's – first full season. The Blues were leading the Second Division at Christmas, but then the 'big chill' of winter '63 set in. Matches disappeared in blizzards, and Chelsea lost their way in traditional fashion. The last two matches would prove decisive. We needed two wins outright. On usual form you'd think we had two hopes – and Slim had just left town. Especially as the first of the crunches was up at Sunderland, who needed just one point to put themselves amongst the big boys.

Worse, we had injury worries (Shellito's cartilage), and The Doc was in the habit of playing a 'harder' (i.e. including John Boyle) or more creative side dictated by conditions. The Doc decided to draft in some of the recently bought older heads and, uncharacteristically, grind out a result. 'We'd people like Derek Kevan, Tommy Harmer and Frank Upton played centre-forward and things like this. It was a mercenary job to get what we wanted, and indeed we got it,' says Eddie.

Harmer scored the only goal off his 'hickory', as Terry Venables put it, following in from a cross. (The sole strike of his Chelsea career, as it happened.) The Cat made a staggering save in the last minute. And the first part of the impossible dream was performed. A matter of days later we took the pomp out of Pompey with a 7–0 annihilation. We were up where we belonged. Eddie felt it was his birthright. 'It was a great thrill, but I felt I deserved to be there. And I settled in very quickly with the team when they put me in the First Division, considering my experience – which was nil. And then moving in with such quality people and playing against such quality players so quickly . . . the coaching helped me a great deal. I thought Tommy Docherty and Dave Sexton were helpful to us all at that time.'

'Oh, he was a hard fucker as well as a great player,' says Tommy Doc. 'He never took into account that that player could have broken his leg. Twice he got done over the top, damaged his knee. And the next time we played the same team, West Brom I think, I said to him, "Now Eddie, watch him."'

'"I'm ready," he says.

'Anyway, 20 minutes into the second half Eddie got done again, didn't he. He was in the dressing-room. I came down, and he said, "I'll never learn, will I?"

'I says, "No, you'll not."'

Dave Sexton had arrived as coach after making it known he was looking for an outlet for his coaching skills. He swiftly graduated from youth-team to first-team coach under The Doc. 'He was good at little functions,' says Tommy, sharply. 'Not a great tactician, and would never gamble during a game – say, if he was losing 1–0, he wouldn't make a switch. He would say, "Oh, but we might lose." Whereas I'd say, "Well, we're losing anyway."'

Glory looked assured for the confident Chelsea of the mid-'60s, even though injury was increasingly punctuating the career of Ken Shellito. The League Cup, in its fifth year and increasingly regarded as a serious competition – though the final was still to find a home at Wembley – was the first of what seemed likely to be a cupboard-full of silverware.

In the first leg, the aspirations of the stripling Osgood were overlooked and our mighty left-back, Eddie Mac, was returned to a role from the dawn of his Scottish career. 'Well,' he sighs, 'I was fortunate that night and I was unfortunate, and I'll tell you why. I was fortunate to be in the position, because Barry Bridges had got injured and Tommy Docherty said to me before the game, "I'm going to play you centre-forward." The unfortunate thing about it was that I scored the winning goal, one of the best goals you've ever seen – and it wasn't even on television.

'Oh, man, it was an incredible goal. It was a really wet evening. They've got two head-hunters left at the back there: John Sjoburg and Graham Cross. These guys didn't take prisoners, you know. And of course I've come way back because we were getting pressed and the ball was in our box, so I've come away back into my own half, I guess about 25 yards.

'Peter Bonetti got the ball and I moved to the side and Peter played it to me. As the ball came to me, I could feel one of their midfield players come in and he was going to give me a little bit of a tickle – I knew that right enough. So I side-stepped him with the ball and I managed to run on it. And as I turned, I moved it forward and saw Sjoburg and Cross come towards me, both a bit square. And I was a bit quick at that time. And I hit it between the both of them on the halfway line and I just ran. I got through, and they had a few swipes at my heels, and I ran all the way down.

'This is heavy going, okay? Thick and muddy. I got to just outside the box and I'm stretching and stretching to get it and I hit it just a little ahead of me. I've seen Gordon Banks come off his line, and I threw myself at the ball, got a toe to it just as he came out, on the edge of the 18-yard box, and it went past him and kind of bobbled into the net. And I swear to God, if he'd stayed on his line he could've thrown his cap on it. I've got friends over here with all these tapes of the 100 best goals and that. I say, "Man, I scored a goal once, and it wasn't even filmed." I wasn't renowned for scoring goals. Out of all these games I scored five goals or so. I'm glad I didn't do that for a living – I'd have starved to death.' Eddie's was the third and, as it proved, decisive Chelsea goal: the return at Filbert Street ended 0–0.

In the spring of 1965 we had faced Liverpool in the semi-final of the FA Cup. The treble was a realistic proposition until the Scousers ran out easy 2–0 winners. As it was, the legendary 'Blackpool boozing incident' and subsequent disciplinary measures also put paid to our Championship ambitions. So the League Cup it was.

We reached three FA Cup semi-finals in three years from 1965 to 1967. A year after the Liverpool disappointment, we lost to Sheffield Wednesday on a pudding of a pitch. Both games were at Villa Park, the ground where Chelsea's cup campaigns come to die. 'Losing two semi-finals, man that was hard,' says Eddie, predictably. 'We felt very confident going into most games and I think we felt that we should've won these games and we didn't. In the dressing-room afterwards I never felt so bloody low. But we bounced back, because we were young, and we were very close as a team.'

By now, though, relations between the quixotic Doc and Eddie had deteriorated. Eddie didn't like the manager's manner, nor his mercurial mood changes. Before the vengeful FA Cup quarter-final defeat of Liverpool in 1966, Eddie slapped in one of many transfer requests. 'Eddie came in one day to see me, and he says, "I want a transfer",' recalls Tommy. 'I said to him, "What's the matter, d'you no' like it here?" He says, "No, I love it. But you're playing me out of position." I says, "Well, it must be because you've been capped 14 times at left-back!"

'"I'm a great centre-forward," he says. "You've been playing me out of position for three years and I didn't know what to say to you." So I said, "Okay, you can have a transfer." I went round the corner – it was handy, because Joe Mears's office was just near to mine. Joe said, "What are you going to do?" I said, "I'll frighten him."

'And next morning I sent for Eddie about half-ten. I says, "There's two clubs in for you." He asks, "Who are they?" I says, "Well, one's on the 'phone at the moment, I'll tell you in a minute." And I went out. And we had a wee hatch in John Battersby's office that looked into my office. And I looked in where Eddie's sitting twitching – he's thinking like Inter Milan, Real Madrid or Glasgow Rangers.

'So I come in and I says to him, "The only problem is, Eddie, it's no' money. It's a swap for two players, and we're interested in the two players."

'"Oh," he says, 'it doesn't matter as long as I get a move." And he says, "Who is it?" I say, "Mansfield Town." Before I could say anything else, he ran out of the office, and I never saw him about that transfer after that. Snudgy and I were killing ourselves laughing. Eddie just got a wee bit full of his own importance, you know.'

Tommy believes his left-back was easily led, especially being a pal of Venners, and that's why he would periodically ask for more money or a move. 'Terry had gone out and convinced him to ask for more money, when they'd gone out and got pissed,' suggests Tommy. 'But I had a big desk at the Bridge, and I stood up and he was sat down, and I looked maybe bigger than I was.' Invariably Eddie failed to get his way with the boss. Well, that's Tommy's version of events. He also suggests that if you went round Eddie's house in the evening he'd answer the door in satin slippers, a silk dressing-gown and dark glasses, which Eddie instantly refutes.

Whatever, winning had become a habit, as had the ritual post-match celebrations. 'We just used to go out after the games and have a few beers, whatever. I didn't drink beer for many years. After several years I was vodka and coke – I was quite renowned for that. But there were so many wonderful times and occasions to celebrate,' muses Eddie.

The flying wing-backs – Eddie and Ken Shellito – added to the flair and glamour of Docherty's Diamonds. 'The great Santos,' marvels Eddie. 'They played two full-backs, brothers, who played for Brazil, who used to get forward. Ken and I used to do the same. We were the first overlapping full-backs really. I think people would say Jimmy Armfield was the first overlapping full-back, but Jimmy never went over the halfway line, with all respect. Docherty and Dave Sexton, they worked on us. I mean, we trained at that. We had to do maybe five, six, seven overlaps a game each. That's hard work. But I enjoyed it; it was exciting and I think it gave Chelsea a completely different look from anyone else. And it became very successful because nobody could do much about it. We were hurting a lot of teams with it: finding a lot of spaces and holes in the defence.'

In 1971 Chelsea played the great Brazilians themselves. 'I remember Pele – I gave him a little tickle too in that game. Second half he gave me a little tickle back. But he absolutely impressed me as a human being. We were staying at the same hotel in Kingston and after the game several of us were having dinner, and people were coming round asking for our autographs and you're a little bit tired – "Okay, I'll sign it, but just let us eat our dinner. Wait over there." Not Pele, though. He was lifting up kids, anyone that came up to his table, you know, he would take the time to talk to them. And I've seen him do that many, many times. For someone who had so much wonderful ability to be so humble, to have such quality and class, to be able to spend time with people who wanted to talk to him. But he was very tough too. He could give you a few whacks too. Don't think he didn't.'

Back in '65, the 'samba' style in SW6 impressed the German national side enough for them to ask Chelsea to play them in preparation for the following year's World Cup and the South American teams they would meet there. Incredibly, we beat them – Vogts, Seeler, Beckenbauer *et al* – 1–0, then lost 3–2.

But that Liverpool semi-final defeat rankled with Tommy Doc, and his mind was set on further reconstruction. 'I went through the two different teams there as you well know,' says Eddie. 'I don't have a real clear idea of which was the better team. They were different in many important ways. In Terry's team, he was the general, really. The next team was severely different in terms of play and personnel. If you compare Bobby Tambling and Barry Bridges to Ian Hutchinson and Peter Osgood, people like Alan Hudson, who were creative, outstanding, world class . . . Bobby and Barry were obviously wonderful players, and proved it time and again. But there was something different, I always felt, about the Hudsons, the Venableses, the Osgoods, Charlie Cooke. These were, I felt, in a class by themselves. Ossie: I've never seen a guy of 6ft 2ins control the ball the way that he did. He was so deft.

'So there were more individual players in the '70s team, but I personally felt that the team spirit in both sides was wonderful and, when I was on the field, there was never any question in my mind that we weren't all going for the same thing. That team spirit was the most incredible thing I experienced as a player, and through winning and having good players you went into every game not thinking a lot about losing. And we didn't lose a lot of games for about ten years.'

Meanwhile, the East Stirling lad settled instantly into the London 'scene' and the swinging lifestyle of the King's Road Chelsea boys. 'Yeah, I enjoyed London,' he beams. 'Hell, it's one of the best cities in the world. If you're successful, as most of us were, it can be a lot of fun, and you've got a lot of nice restaurants and you're meeting a lot of interesting people there. The most difficult thing I found – and I'm not complaining, because God was kind and made me successful, and when people come up and want your autograph and that, it's quite a thrill and good for your ego – but after a few years that can get a bit heavy, and you maybe don't want it so much. I found that I was losing a little bit of patience with that. I came to realise that my privacy was rather important to me and there wasn't a lot of that when you're playing for a club like Chelsea.

'Lots of the players would thrive on it, I guess. I don't mean this to be unkind but I resented the fact that I was a fairly intelligent player and all everybody I ever met wanted to talk to me about was football. It's natural: why would they want to talk about submarines when I played for Chelsea. But I just felt, "Man, I can talk about other things, you know." I loved music and I liked discussing what was going on in the world. In that kind of life, you don't get the chance to see the real world really. People and situations put you on a pedestal. For soccer players, real life is something that happened before you got there. But then you get fame and you think you're a bit better than you are at times. And sometimes you're not as nice as your parents brought you up to be.'

Towards the end of the '60s, Eddie was finding celebrity a poisoned chalice. 'But from morning till night it was compliments. I'd pick up my milk in the morning and the milkman would be out there saying, "Great game on Saturday." Then into my car and drive to training and somebody would wind down their window, "Saw the game on Saturday. You were fantastic. My son loves you to death."

Your whole life is compliments, compliments. And I don't care how good you are or how intelligent, that has a weird effect on your life. I didn't have it as bad as Ossie or Alan Hudson, the adulation they got. But it was tough. I don't think I smiled too much. But after matches we'd laugh and we had a good life.

'But I became very serious. You play a game on a Saturday and the emotions are very high and before you know it you're back on Monday, getting worked up for a game on the Wednesday. You're up and down, up and down. I've got to tell you, it's not a lot of fun if you're trying to go to sleep on a Friday, and you've got to play at Old Trafford next day against Besty, you know. The elation is unbelievable, playing. But you might go there and have your ass kicked in front of 50,000 people; and that ain't a happy thought.

'I felt an enormous pressure. I was so tensed up, especially before big games. I think it probably got more after a few years, the more successful I became. Because every week, if you're not playing against Besty, you're playing against Peter Marinello, Peter Thompson or some of these incredible European players, or playing for your country. You were playing against some of the best players in the world every week. And if you've got that frame of mind, you go out tensed up like a rock. It doesn't make you a happy camper amongst your family. It's hard being in the public eye like that, and having to make a good account of yourself off the field too.'

Yet into the '70s, Eddie held his own against the best the world could throw at him. 'I don't think anyone ever gave me a good shallarking, so to speak,' he muses. 'I was kicking everybody's ass. You won't believe who gave me the worst time I ever had in my life, in probably my third year at Chelsea: Peter Brabrook. He was a wonderful player; but he lacked a little bit of consistency at times, shall we say. I play against this guy – Chelsea v. West Ham – and, man, I never saw the ball. He couldn't do anything wrong against me. He killed me. It was the most embarrassing thing.'

Often as not, Eddie's earth-moving challenges earned him that sort of enmity amongst other players. 'There were a few people after me over the years, I know that. Playing over 12 years, you make a few enemies. I remember playing a game down at The Dell, against Southampton. On the Friday evening we were sitting looking at their team, in the paper, and there were five guys in that team who'd wanted me real bad for years. All there in that team. I've gone into games when I've known there's a couple of guys wanting to take me out, like Leeds United: there was a bunch of them. Billy Bremner, Bobby Collins, Norman Hunter all wanted a piece of my ass. But in this game, there was five of them. Peter Osgood said to me the night before, "Nobody would blame you if you pulled out of this one!"

'I got myself so worked up that the game started for about two minutes and the ball had come to Terry Paine and I just whacked him. I thought, "Shit, if I'm going to go down, I'll go down fighting." The referee warned me immediately. Two minutes later, somebody else came in and I laid him out as well. The rest of the game, nobody came near me. I heard afterwards all their team were saying, "Screw that shit – that McCreadie's a nutcase!"'

Eddie's no-nonsense approach stood him in good stead, for the most part, in the European campaigns that peppered his remarkable career. 'Milan, Vienna, Munich, Roma, Barcelona . . . all the games we won were great performances. The Germans we played were so strong and so fit. They would just run and run and run. And the Italians were just wonderful passers of the ball, but they were always pulling your shirt or spitting in your face and stuff that used to get us all wound up. You'd get that abroad. I remember we were in Haiti, playing a friendly. We were in the West Indies on tour, and we played in a packed little stadium in Port-au-Prince. Police were patrolling around the field with dogs and guns. And they scored their first goal, and the police were shooting their guns in the air!'

Then there was the infamous Roma incident during our 1965–66 Inter-City Fairs Cup campaign. 'At Stamford Bridge, the 4–1, Terry scored three goals. I decked the right-winger that night. You'd never see me punching – I didn't do that. But this guy grabbed me by the throat. I went on an overlap, got my cross in, and he came across me and kicked me right in the shins. As I got up the Italian right-winger put his hand right round my throat. He'd kicked me. And I was, well, have some of that, you know. And I decked him. But otherwise, it wasn't my style. "We won't do anything about it now, I'll save it for you . . ." that was me.'

The altercation was whipped up by the local press until the Roma fans were in riotous mood for the return. Eddie was the main object of their wrath – though The Doc provided an alternative target after dropping his shorts at Italians watching his team train. 'They threw stuff at me the whole game,' recalls Eddie. 'Pieces of iron, coins, ice – from somewhere – bricks, you name it.'

We secured a creditable 0–0 to frustrate the natives even further. 'After the game, when we went through the club compound, which had a wire fence round it, and on to the bus, there were about two or three thousand people waiting outside. We all got on the bus with some of the directors and a couple of the wives. I said to everybody,

"You want to get on the floor, because when we get out of here it ain't going to be fun: these windows are going to come in." They were all going, "Yeah, right, sure!"

"'Suit yourself," I said. And I sat right at the back and put Harry Medhurst's big kit bag right up in front of me. We moved out of the compound. And I tell you what, all the windows came in like that: crash! They chased us for about 40 miles. They got suspended for three years if you remember. That was scary.'

The journey home can't have been eased by Eddie's acute fear of flying. Still, it was part of the job. The alternative was retirement. 'I just used to sit there,' he says, 'and I'd take sleeping pills and everything. I remember we were going to a tournament in Mozambique in 1969' – the cup now displays dried flowers in the Chelsea offices – 'and it must have been 25 hours on the bloody plane. The guys knew just to leave me alone. I didn't want to talk to anyone. I used to sit beside Tommy Baldwin, and Tom liked to read. And he turned round to me after a few hours and said, "How are you doing?" "I'm all right." He says, "I know you don't like flying, and I know you don't want to talk, but I just wanted to say that I think you're very courageous, for someone who's so afraid of flying to get on like you do all the time." That immediately made me feel a bit better about myself, because it's not fun. Of course, with team-mates like Hudson and Osgood, they'd be creeping up behind me and banging the back of the seat, making a ruckus and saying, "Aargh, the plane's going down!"'

The sparkle finally left Docherty's Diamonds in the depressing semi-final defeats by Sheffield Wednesday in the FA Cup and Barcelona in the Fairs Cup during a few desperate weeks in the spring of '66.

The Doc's management style looked to be reaping the whirlwind. Eddie had mixed feelings about Tommy. 'He was most helpful to me in my career, and I've got a lot of admiration for him. But there are several parts of that style of management that I do not respect. I asked for a transfer many times, but I wanted to get away from him, not the club.

'He was a very, very funny guy. One of the things I learned from him was motivation. He'd really get you to believe in yourself. There was a lot of conning to it as well. A couple of years after I joined the club, I was training one Tuesday afternoon on the pitch at Stamford Bridge just in front of the old east stand. I had my back to the tunnel and I was knocking balls to Ken Shellito 40 yards away, and Ken was hitting them back to me. A lot of them were awkward balls, and I was controlling them, and Tommy was standing behind me with someone. I could hear him saying, "Look at that . . ." I knew he knew I could hear him. "This guy is the best in the world . . . look at that quality." I'm hearing all this shit, and I believed it all. In actual fact, maybe he was right!'

But by 1967, a reconstructed Chelsea team reached the FA Cup final almost despite itself, amid the now-customary rows over bonuses and players' tickets. Spurs had the game won in 25 minutes. 'I remember the terrible feelings immediately after the game,' groans Eddie, 'what with the semi-finals the years before, but I've always tried to move on quickly and forget disappointment, look for more positive thoughts in my mind.'

Three years later, under new boss and former coach Dave Sexton, there was the chance to make amends. This time the opposition was Leeds United. Don Revie's dour, cribbage-playing Yorkshiremen squared up to Dave Sexton's gallivanting glams: tooth and nail versus vodka and Coke. There were scores to settle – professionally. 'I wouldn't go over the top of the ball unless someone had done it to me. But this Leeds United team, man, they had about seven or eight guys in that team who would break your leg at the drop of a hat. I didn't respect that. They were one of the finest club teams in the world. But I just thought, if I ever have a team, that is not the way I want it to be.'

Leeds it was who drew first blood at Wembley, a soft Charlton header plopping between Eddie and Ron Harris before softly billowing into the net. 'I've had people look at that film and say, "Well, you know, Chopper Harris could've done better." I say, "Listen, I screwed up there! I'll show you again." I was in front of Chopper. Once it'd gone past me I don't think he'd much chance. The pitch was really heavy. I anticipated a bounce as Charlton headed it down, and as we know it didn't bounce. I wanted to dig myself a hole right there and dive in.' (An easy task, given the softness of the soil.)

Eddie continued, 'That's what I'm telling you about having a bad day at the office. I didn't make many screw-ups, but that was one for sure. The biggest pleasure I got in my career was in the replay at Old Trafford. Somebody from the press asked me at Wembley after the first game what I thought. I said, "Well, I think we got our asses kicked a little to be honest." And he said, "How do you feel about the replay then?" I said, "I think we'll win." I never felt more confident about anything in my life, because at Wembley I thought they were the better team. We didn't play as well as I knew we could and I thought, "Man, we're gonna win."'

Ossie's goal equalised Mick Jones's opener, and from then on there was only one winner. Webby's goal was a fulfilment of the inevitable. 'In the last ten or 15 minutes at Old Trafford, I looked at them and I was dragging myself around the field – we all were – but I looked at them and their heads were down. I knew they'd gone, the whole lot of them. And that gave me a lot of pleasure. I thought, "Well, my God – we have whipped their asses. Ten minutes to go, but they've gone." And if you can wear a team like that down mentally, then it says a lot for the character of your team. I don't think we played any great stuff that night either, but we did what was necessary.'

By now Eddie was rooming with David Webb, but he hung out with Huddy, Ossie and Hutch. The four of them were inseparable. 'They were, shall we say, very interesting individuals, on the field and off the field,' says Eddie. Not that he was immune to interesting behaviour himself. His penchant for vodka was becoming legendary, especially on close-season tours. One famous occasion during an otherwise tedious official reception at a Caribbean governor's palace still gives Webby nightmares.

'We were leaving, getting cabs, and someone said, "Where's Eddie?" He was up on this balcony, and he'd had so much to drink that he said "I'll take a short cut", and while we was laughing about it, he hung over this balcony, about 50 or 60 feet up. Hanging by his hands, he was. I said to Ossie, "Christ! – he's going to kill himself." So Ossie and someone else ran upstairs to grab him. He'd gone larking about, but now he's hanging on by his ankles, sideways. I was underneath, and I said, "If he falls, you know who'll have to catch him." I'd have kicked him but he was so drunk he wouldn't have known.

'You read about trashing aeroplanes, cameras and the like, but when you look back at some of the weird things we did, all trying to outdo each other . . . In Barbados we went to another reception. I roomed with Eddie, so we said, "We'll have our own little party back at our hotel." So we rifled all the food out of this woman's huge fridge, whose house this party was in, and we took it in bags to the hotel. We got back and started drinking all the rum, and I said, "Right, what did you get? I've got some eggs and that." Eddie said, "I've got some steak." I asked him where and he said, "Here." I said, "You silly sod!" He hadn't nicked steak; it was one of those big slabs of toffee! This woman kept her favourite brazil nut toffee in the freezer. And he thought it was frozen steak.'

'They were all wonderful guys,' says Eddie, 'just a little bit wild: guys who were a little bit frustrated at not being able to do things most normal people did because of who they were, because of the training they had to do every day, because they weren't supposed to drink as much as others.'

Frustration of a different kind interrupted Eddie's career. In the four years from the 1970 Cup triumph, he was plagued with injury: a broken nose, troubled groin, knee and ankle ligament problems, hamstring, broken cheek. 'Ach, desperate,' Eddie shakes his head. 'They tell me I'd dished out a few knocks, but I tell you what, I got a lot of knocks too. But the worst one I had was the one that really put me out, when I did my Achilles tendon. That kept me out for 18 months, and I never truly got back. I was never the same. It was just too painful. I couldn't kick with it, and I'd lost a yard in pace because of it. I came back and I played about five games in the first team. My last game was in 1974, against Leeds United at Elland Road.'

In 1972, Dave Sexton had made his loyal lion club captain, the representative of the players. 'It helped, gave me a little bit of a lift. Dave Sexton was a wonderful man, and an absolute gentleman. He was most helpful to me. I learned a great deal from him as a coach about the technical side of the game.'

Eddie had already passed (with distinction) his FA badge – he and Terry Venables went together to Lilleshall in the '60s. And so it seemed only natural that Eddie should eventually succeed his former boss as coach – though perhaps not as early as 1974. 'Well, let's say I wasn't going to be any threat to a first-team player's job. Dave sounded me out about reserve-team coaching. I said I'd think about it. And I went to Rhode Island Buccaneers in America, who were inviting players over to guest with them in the close season.'

Eddie needed a change of scenery. Apart from the injury problems, the stress of 12 years as a player was increasingly taking its toll on his personal life. Unusually for a footballer, Eddie expressed himself in lyrical prose, writing over 300 poems. 'I wrote about myself, life, people, different personal things that I felt. It was part of my escape from football, if you like. And it was part of trying to find out who the hell I was. And that's the honest truth. You train every day, you travel everywhere from Manchester to Munich away from your family, and you meet people who want to talk about soccer every day. So your life is like a vacuum. You don't get a chance to express what you are and you tend to lose who you are. Poetry gave me an opportunity to find out what was inside me.'

After a few months in the States, Dave Sexton called Eddie back to the reserve-team coach's job. 'And I was fairly successful,' says Eddie. 'We went to the top of the league, and then – hell, it seemed like within about ten minutes – I was first-team coach, then manager of Chelsea. Dave had gone, Ron Suart took over and things weren't going as well as people would have liked. My job then meant I had nothing to do with team selection. All I did was train the players and work with them tactically. He had team selection, but that wasn't going to work for too long. But we sorted that out. And I find myself being manager of the greatest club in the world as far as I'm concerned – but at the most desperate time. What a time in its history to take over the club!

'I think taking them back to the First Division was the hardest thing I've had to do in my life. But I'm glad I was there, because I loved the club and I still love it. It was the most wonderful 16 years of my life. I had the energy and the will to put it back where it belonged. I prayed to God I had the ability to do it. There were so many people depending on me to put it back. But it was a great deal of pressure.'

Hampered by a lack of money for players, Eddie knew youth was his only option. 'They all had a part to do: Ray Wilkins, Ian Britton, Garry Stanley, Tommy Langley, Jock Finnieston, Kenny Swain, Stevie Wicks. I think within seven months I had seven or eight teenagers in the side. In my playing days the Osgoods, the Hudsons, were exceptional. And if you look at most of the players that I put in my team, you'd say Ray Wilkins, and before we go any further, you have to say that there were some wonderful players but not a lot of exceptional ones. And it made it harder, because I realised I had no money to buy players, and I realised looking at my colleagues, guys I'd played with for ten years, people like John Hollins, Marvin Hinton, Peter Houseman, I realised that these fine, wonderful players – and my friends – were not going to put the club back where it wanted to go.

'Fortunately I had a great belief in my ability to judge young players. I felt, "Well, if we're going to do anything here, we have to start from the bottom, and build the club from the kids." I had to sit down with John Hollins, Stevie Kember, Marvin Hinton and Peter Houseman and say, "Look, I'm going with the kids." That was one of the most difficult things in my life. I think they knew, the majority of them. Nobody gave me a hard time. It must have been terribly hurtful for them but I think they knew it was their club too. Perhaps they didn't agree with it, and perhaps they thought I was a nutcase anyway, because the first team I ever picked had four teenagers in it and Ray Wilkins as captain. Obviously people thought I was a nutcase to start with. Anyway, I got a little bit of kick back into the club really quickly. I knew I had to stimulate the fans and stimulate the club, and there was no better way of doing it than with such fine young players.'

In his second year in charge Eddie secured promotion from the Second Division. 'I've had many compliments for what I may have achieved at that time, but I would push it aside,' says Eddie now. 'Because the credit goes to the players. These young men were under tremendous pressure. None more so than Ray Wilkins. And they all responded magnificently for the club. And history should be very proud of them. It's a shame it broke up, but that team, all these kids, did brilliantly. My job was easy compared to what they had to do.'

But in the summer of 1977 – the year of punk – chaos reigned at cash-strapped Chelsea. In the course of a few months in the close season, Blues fans watched as our most attractive team for years lost its inspirational manager through sheer intransigence: 'I wanted a contract. This is something I don't think people understood. What they were telling me was they couldn't give me one because the club was almost bankrupt. I knew that.' Eddie, remember, had organised a voluntary pay cut from all the players. 'But all my players were on contracts; I'd done the contracts for them myself. I felt hurt. My God, after what I'd done for them? They can't give me a contract?'

At the time a car was reported to be the sticking-point. 'That was just part of it. It wasn't the money, it wasn't a car, it was the contract. It maybe sounds silly to people now. I said, "I understand the club's going through hell, I read about it, I've been living with it for two years. But I feel I deserve a contract." It hurt me real bad. I'd been there for 16 years, I loved my club and still do, and going through in the two years what I went through, knowing what I had to do for my club . . . When we finally took them up against Wolves, I thought, "Thank God! I've got the club back!" And then walked into a situation where the directors of the club are telling me they can't give me a contract.'

Eddie resigned, and retired from English football. 'People have asked me if I regret my decision to resign from Chelsea, and I say, "No." At the end of the day, I thought about it long and hard, thought of getting myself back there, and I was thinking of the club, and I was thinking of the kids, the players, and that was the thing that would more than anything have taken me back there. But they'd taken the heart, the guts, out of me, really, with their attitude. They were all good people, but I just thought, "Surely this is not the way I should be treated."'

Peter Bonetti led a players' deposition to have Eddie reinstated: 'Eddie had rung me up and said, "Pete, it looks like the board have accepted my resignation. That means I got fired. Can you have a word with the lads?" So I went to see Brian Mears. I said, "Look, the players are behind Eddie, we're sorry to see him go. He's a great manager, got us up to the First Division . . ." And Brian Mears said, "Peter, thanks very much. We respect what you're doing, but you can't interfere. We've made our decision, and we'd look silly if we changed our minds."

'I felt, "I've got to get out of here, I've got to get away from this,"' says Eddie. 'I've been here all my life, and for it to end like this, I thought, there's something so wrong. I started blaming myself: "Maybe it's been my fault; maybe I shouldn't have asked for a contract, just gone along with it and things would have worked themselves out down the line." As far as the fans are concerned, I know there are a lot of different opinions about what went on, but it's very simple, and it's very bad. But the judgement is theirs.

'The hardest thing was my players. I didn't get the chance to talk to them or take them into the First Division. I'm just curious, and people have asked me many, many times over the last ten years, "How do you think that team would have done in the First Division?" My answer to that is that I think I would have had to add two or three players and if I'd been able to do that then I think they'd have been very successful over the years. And I've no doubts about my own ability as a manager either. I feel regretful that I had to leave so abruptly. I feel very bad about having to leave my players and not reach the potential they had with them. The last thing I would want to do, being there so long, was to leave with an impression that I was trying to hold the club up to ransom or anything.'

It was a terrible, wasteful end to a glittering career. Eddie moved to the States. Within two seasons we were playing the seaside towns again – but at least, thank God, that shower of a board was on its way out.

5

Ossie

He was, as Tommy Docherty put it, one of those players every manager prays will come along. Peter Osgood, the six-foot-two-inches son of a builder from Windsor was to become one of Chelsea's all-time heroes in the striker's role. On the terraces, we sang of his birthright as the Blues' new messiah. He would also come to personify the '60s as interpreted by the swingers on the King's Road, in the extended neighbourhood of Stamford Bridge.

At 16, Ossie was a bit of a hick – the farmer's boy, as team-mates dubbed him – but his lithe, deceptive frame supported staggering agility, and he was quite obviously gifted to an inordinate degree. 'It's just bred in you and that's it,' he shrugs. 'I always had good balance for a big lad, and I was a good weight as a schoolboy. I was very thin, and pretty quick and good at it really.'

Peter captained his school team at seven, then skippered the Windsor Boys, and Berkshire. He honed his skills against a wall his dad had built outside their house: 'Lovely big wall. There were angles on it and I used to knock the ball in left foot, right foot, and I used to keep doing the angles and let it run past me, different things you do when you're on your own.'

Professional football was only one option; his father was keen for Ossie to work alongside him in the trade, and Peter's footballing ambitions vied with hod-carrying on the sites. 'I played for Spital Old Boys in Windsor: a nice little club. When you were a schoolboy in Windsor the only team you want to play for is Spital Old Boys. I didn't know Chelsea were even after me. I had a trial for Reading when I was a young lad, about 15, and nothing materialised from that. I was captain of Windsor, captain of Berkshire, and I thought, well, that's where all the scouts come and watch, and they don't fancy me. So I went and played in local football, and you normally signed apprentice professional at 15 then.

'But I was 16 and my uncle Bob wrote off for a trial without telling me. I got the forms back saying report to Hendon on a Saturday morning, about 11.30. So I got there, my brother took me and the secretary of Spital Old Boys, and I said to the Juniors manager, Dick Foss, "Mr Foss, I'm Osgood down from Windsor, is there any chance I can play in the first half-hour of the trial game, because I've got to play a cup game for Spital in the afternoon." He said, "Certainly." And after half an hour I came off, and it was, "Can you sign here?" And I'd actually signed for Chelsea, and it was as simple as that. He'd seen more in half an hour than these people had seen in 15 years.'

Chelsea manager Tommy Docherty was present at the revelation: 'Aw! He was just fantastic. I said, "Dick, why are you not going to play him in the second half?"

'"Oh," he says, "I'm going to sign him." I never said to Dick sign him or don't sign him, that was his job. And he wouldn't let him go out for the second half because he wanted to sign him and there were a lot of scouts there that day. And I said to Dick about a month later, "I'm thinking about bringing him into the first team, what d'you think?" He says, "It might be a bit early, boss. It might be, but I couldn't swear on it. He's just a natural." Then he said, "Yeah, I'd throw him in if I were you – I mean you could always pull him out again, couldn't you?" I says, "Yeah. Why not?" And, of course, he just never looked back, did he?'

While Tommy may be overstating the haste with which he blooded the youngster, there was no doubting his faith in Os: 'He'd fetch £20 million today. I would say he was a better player than Alan Shearer. He was great in the air, he was big, he was elegant, he could move, he could tackle, he could score goals. He had everything. He actually had everything. And he was so full of confidence it wasn't true.'

For Ossie, though, the first barrier was to break into a star-studded youth team before signing full-time pro forms. 'Let's be fair,' he says, 'they had a good youth side anyway; they were always first or second in the league. We were blessed here at Chelsea at the time, because we had people like Greaves, Tambling, Bridges, all these players, the Venableses, the Harrises, the Bonettis, they'd all come through before me to the first team. And Dick Foss was responsible for that, so he obviously had a good eye for kids. I was quite a leggy lad, so he thought the strength was there, and it would come and mature, which it did. When I came and played in the youth team, Johnny Boyle was there, Jimmy McCalliog, Peter Houseman, Johnny Hollins. So that was the sort of side you were playing with – it wasn't too hard.

'Once you got here and you were accepted and you played in the team, they were a good bunch of lads. We all got on well. The nice thing about Chelsea Football Club, and I had 12 years here, was there was never a row amongst the lads, not ever, it was terrific. Great bunch of lads, great dressing-room, from the kids, to reserves, up to the first team.

'Johnny Boyle was my first room-mate. "Trampus", I call him. And then sometimes when John wasn't in the side I might go with Ronnie Harris or someone like that, which was a bloody nuisance. It was a waste of time: he'd be up at seven o'clock waiting for the *Sporting Life* to come, you know, Saturday before a game. He was a pain in the arse. He'd be up shaving at 7.15, whistling. "For God's sake, Ron!" Off the field he was a nuisance, on the field he was a great skipper. He was a great leader.'

The farmer's boy's qualities swiftly adapted to whatever level he played at, and the youth policy, sown by long-gone manager Billy Birrell and nurtured by former inside-forward Sidney 'Dick' Foss with his coterie of scouts and coaches, was now bearing golden fruits. 'In my first game in the youth team I scored three goals against Portsmouth. I think I've always scored on my debuts for Chelsea. I've always scored in every cup debut I played for Chelsea as well. I played in the Junior Floodlit Cup against West Ham. They had Harry Redknapp, Sissons, Marty Britt. Johnny Hollins was our captain then. It was 2–2 in the first match; I didn't play. I was on the building sites still – I hadn't signed full-time. Dick Foss put me in for the replay and we won 3–1 up at West Ham. I scored two goals, and we won 5–3 on aggregate. I always remember Johnny Hollins coming up with the match ball and saying, "There, son, you deserved that." The next day, I was on the building sites again!'

Ossie's ability wouldn't restrict itself to junior levels, though. Even though The Doc had found successors to Jimmy Greaves in Bobby Tambling, George Graham and Barry Bridges, all hard-working creatives, none had the finesse or the impudent genius of the young Wizard of Os. Tommy Docherty had been in charge three years by the time he was able to deploy this precocious lad. The bombastic Glaswegian made a strong impression on his young striker: 'He was a lunatic,' grins Ossie. 'I loved him. I know a lot of people don't like him, but I've got a lot of respect for him and I still call him Boss now. He was fun to be with, he was a fun manager, you knew how far to go with him. If he didn't like you, you were out, you were gone. That's what happened to Terry Venables and George Graham. There was a big clash there and he said, "Hey, I'm the Gaffer, and off you go."'

The other half of this mutual appreciation society returns the compliment. Tommy Docherty describes Ossie as 'different class, the best. Wonderful. Never caused me a minute's trouble. I got on great with him. We used to have a drink together, go out for a gin and tonic with him. He was great. You could rely on him in any game, even the five-a-sides or a friendly match. But the bigger the game, the better he liked it. I mean, the goal he scored against Roma, when we beat them 4–1 at the Bridge; well, it was out of this world.

'The best goal I've ever seen scored by anyone to this day, including little Jimmy [Greaves], and Besty's against Sheffield United, was Ossie's against Burnley. Peter Bonetti pulled down a cross, and Ossie was on the edge of the box, and Bonetti gave it to Ossie and it was a bit muddy. He beat a couple of players, played a couple of one-twos, went past about six, Adam Blacklaw came out, and Ossie buried it in the back of the net. Even Bob Lord was standing up cheering it. It's the best goal I've ever seen. A Burnley player never touched the ball from the time Bonetti got it. And Burnley had a bloody good side then. They were a top side.'

Not as good – on the day – as the youthful crew Tommy Doc had assembled by the mid-'60s, evidently. In 1964 Ossie broke into the first team at the age of 17 and joined a side realistically chasing a unique League, FA and League Cup treble. He made his debut watched by just 7,936 against tough-nut Workington on a foggy December night in the League Cup – in fact the only one of the three trophies Docherty's Diamonds were to win that year – and he scored the only two goals of the game. It was shortly before Christmas. And, appropriately, born was the king of Stamford Bridge.

The Doc rested his teenage phenomenon for another ten months, so Os missed the two-leg final, despite petitioning the Boss. 'Tommy played Eddie McCreadie at centre-forward here at The Bridge. They beat Leicester 3–2. Gordon Banks was in goal and Eddie scored. And they went away and drew 0–0, didn't they? So the Doc was right and I was wrong. Cheers, Boss!'

Sensations of a different sort made the headlines as the season closed, though. The Blackpool Incident, as it's popularly known amongst its veterans, put paid to the Diamonds' showcase, and ultimately destroyed the team (or at least the eight involved) and its manager. And it might have swept Ossie up with it. 'I was lucky,' chuckles Os. 'I was in the England Youth team, away representing my country. But I joined the Chelsea team and went off to tour Australia next season and, oh, it was a terrible atmosphere by then, it really was. And I always remember getting to Bombay and he said, "Young man, come here." I said, "What's that, Boss?" He said, "If you'd been there it would have been nine." Thanks very much!

'But that trip was when he put me in the side. He pushed Barry Bridges out to right-wing and played me centre-forward with George Graham. That's obviously when I made my impact. I scored about 26 goals in 13 games or something over there. It was a great side, a terrific side. It was fun to play with. George was great. For a big man, a lovely touch. Brilliant in the air, great timing of the header and he scored some great goals from corners and free-kicks. His touch and passing were superb. He was a strong lad, too; could take a knock. I was disappointed that George went, but that's just one of those things – he, again, fell out with the Boss. And that was that.'

Burnley were second in the table when Ossie, still paired in the middle with 'The Stroller' at the expense of Bridges, went up to Turf Moor in January 1966. The striker, a few weeks shy of his 19th birthday, grabbed both in a 2–1 victory. The Doc's appreciation of his second, sensational goal was echoed by *The Guardian*:

> Osgood obtained possession well inside his own half and embarked on a serpentine course towards the Burnley goal. He left Merrington, Talbut and Angus strewn in his wake and as Blacklaw came out drove it into the net with his left foot.

Brian Glanville (no relation, I promise), reached for the hyperbole about this young prospect:

> He swerves and glides past centre-halves as though they were concrete pillars, lays off the reverse pass with the confidence of a veteran and takes on three or four defenders in turn as centre-forwards used to before they became mere battering rams or walls to somebody else's pass.

Ossie was simply instinctive. 'The whole thing just drew me,' he claimed, somewhat metaphysically, at the time, 'I could feel it building up but couldn't stop.' He still gets letters from Lancashire about it: 'I'm a Burnley supporter. I was there when you scored the most fantastic goal ever at Turf Moor and we still talk about it today . . .'

Well, things had steadily built up for the ex-hod carrier. Ossie's next first-team game after Workington had been the 4–0 Inter-City Fairs (now UEFA) Cup home drubbing of AS Roma. That same season, 1965–66, Ossie stormed the First Division, making over 30 league appearances, scoring seven league goals (his first against high-flying Sheffield United), making his first FA Cup semi-final appearance after scoring three times on the way, and starring in all but one of the 11 European matches of a quite staggering campaign taking in, Roma aside, Wiener of Austria, the mighty AC Milan, Munich 1860, and finally, and mortally, Barcelona.

The Fairs Cup campaign enjoyed an inordinate number of classic moments, many of them goals supplied by Ossie. AC Milan, for example: 'Well, we went over there, lost 2–0, came back here, won 2–0. And we went over there again and we drew. Terrific. I hit a volley, a terrific volley, in the home leg. George got a header too and we went over there and we played brilliant. It was a shame to win it on the toss of a coin, but we were happy to go through on that. I'm not sure whether Buller [Ron Harris] was lucky or not, it was the first time it'd been settled like that. I just couldn't believe it: toss of a coin after all that effort, three games and you go out. Felt sorry for them because they were a great side as well. They had a lot of respect for us, which was nice, and we respected them. I think the guy that marked me was Maldini, father of Paolo Maldini, who's currently one of the world's top players. Maldini was a helluva player. Schnellinger marked me down here, the blond German. Came in scything, he did. But I liked it because he kept diving in all the time; I like them to dive in.'

The fourth-round meeting with Munich 1860 is remembered for less Corinthian reasons. 'Me and Boylers were probably two of the worst pranksters at the club. When we were out playing in Munich that game, we saw Laurie Pignon, a great old writer, and we pinned a Durex to the back of his jacket. As he was walking around, it was getting longer and longer. It was so funny, I tell you.' This was the big time for the Windsor lad. Married at 17, father at 18, he had earned £10 a week working with his dad, but could now afford to squander the odd condom. 'Oh! You don't realise how big it is at the time. If you play for Spital Old Boys and you go and play in a cup game, it's a big thing; if you go on and play for Chelsea in Europe it's a big thing. But it's your job and you go and do it. And then you look forward to it, you know, it's what you want to do: you want to taste the European side of it, and you want to play against the best, you want to beat the best. And it was a tremendous time, it really was.'

All this over a backdrop of increasing enmity between the turbulent manager and several of his finest players. 'The thing that brought matters to a head,' says Os, 'was that we lost two semi-finals in a month. We lost against Barcelona 5–0 in the replay game – that was Charlie Cooke's first game. And we lost to Sheffield Wednesday in the FA Cup. It was a diabolical pitch, which didn't suit our passing game. They had Vic Mobley, Gerry Young, all these big guys so it suited them, and they beat us 2–0. That was the breaking up of the team, I think. It was a great side, probably better than the '70s side, to be honest. Young players, you see. You had your Harris brothers, big John Mortimore, a strong lad at the back. There was Venables, Holly coming through.

'You had George Graham, Bobby Tambling, Bert Murray, Barry Bridges, Peter Bonetti, a great keeper. Ken Shellito was an England full-back at the time; he was very unlucky in his career. He would have been England captain. I don't think that George Cohen would have had a look in if Kenny had been around. Incredible side, incredible talent. I just don't think the Boss gave them time. They'd just come up from the Second Division to the First and they were still learning their trade, really. The average age was about 21 or 22. If he'd given them another couple of years it was frightening what they could have achieved.'

Naturally, given the burgeoning Docherty reputation for unpredictability, none of that was likely. Some of the Diamonds were sold off in the summer of '66 – Graham, Bridges, Venables – and the team finished ninth, the lowest ebb since the return to the top flight in 1963. That said, they reached the FA Cup final the following spring, and might even have won the double but for a desperate incident the previous October. 'I was obviously the golden boy,' recalls Os, 'what with George Best growing up. We'd just played Manchester City at Maine Road, beat them 4–1, and had gone top of the league after ten games in the 1966–67 season. I'd been in the World Cup squad. I was at the top of my form and I was flying, I really was.'

Man City fans in the Kippax End decided to chant 'Os-good, no good' to the tune of a famous clock chime. We'd often holler 'Os-good is good', you see, as Kenneth Wolstenholme enjoyed pointing out in his commentaries. Intemperately, Ossie gave the Sky Blues faithful a soldier's farewell and his obscene gestures were reported to the FA. It was stupid; he was later to discover that 'old farts' have long memories. And there, perhaps, was the first sign that he was letting things get to him. Still, it showed that opponents regarded the teenage sensation as Chelsea's danger man.

'Again, I was in a good side. We had a good balance. After that Saturday game at City we went on the Monday to play against Blackpool, and during the game Emlyn Hughes came across and sorted me out once, made a bee-line for me. Anyway, it was a 50:50 tackle, I went in, we clashed shins and crack, I heard it go – it went right round the ground. I thought, "Bollocks!" That was it. The funny thing about it was Norman Medhurst, whose dad was the physio, Harry. It was Norman's first game as physio, and when he came on, I said, "Norm . . ." "What's wrong? Your knee? What's wrong?"

'I said, "Norman, I've broken my leg." They needed two stretchers: one to take me off and one to take him. Unbelievable.'

It took Os a year to fully recover from the broken leg. He missed the '67 Cup final against Spurs, put on two or three stone in weight and, it was said, lost his pace. 'Well, I don't know,' rues Ossie. 'But at the time I could go past people as if they weren't there. And then later on you have a little bit more guile and more about you. But I played for England in 1969 and got in the Mexico World Cup squad in 1970. And won cups for Chelsea, which was good.'

Manager Doc believes the experience changed Ossie as a player too. 'It set him back a couple of years, I'd say. But I still feel he recovered from it. He doesn't; I do. You know when they recover from a broken leg or a broken ankle? It makes them a bit nastier. He began to look after himself a bit better after that. He began to sort out the fellas who were going to do him. He used that against certain players. He would go in hard for the ball, but against other players he had to be a bit more wary.'

It was the only miserable spell in Ossie's 12 years at the Bridge. But during recuperation another shock was in store. In a pre-season tour match in Barbados, Tommy Docherty, not for the first or last time, cloaked himself in controversy. 'Well, there was this little coloured referee,' he relates, and the story sort of goes downhill even from there. Docherty then made an unrepeatable remark to the local official, who reported the Chelsea manager to the FA. 'And I got suspended for a month,' says Tommy. That might not have been a problem had not Joe Mears, Doc's chairman and champion, died earlier the same year. 'Joe Mears was brilliant,' recalls Doc. 'He believed in letting the manager manage. And we had this wonderful relationship; I said to my wife, "If ever anything happens to that man, I'll leave Chelsea."'

Charles 'Bill' Pratt was Joe's successor. 'Pratt by name, prat by nature,' says the Doc. 'He was an antiques dealer. I knew then it was just a matter of time before I left. There was just the usual board meeting one day and he asked me one or two things about the situation of being suspended after the West Indies, how when your coach gets suspended you're not allowed to come to the club, and how can we run the club if you're not here.

'I said, "Well, you've got my assistant here, Dave Sexton. He can run things till I come back. I can be on the phone; I can run the club but not be there." Anyway, it was all sealed up before I came in, I think. He said, "Well, under the circumstances, don't you think it would be better if we amicably come to the end?' And I says, "Well, if that's the way you feel, to be quite honest, I've been thinking about it." Brian Mears was sitting there, Joe's son, and I says, "Since the chairman passed away, actually. I couldn't work with you Mr Pratt" – I wasn't cheeky or anything – "because you've been 25 years vice-chairman and you know nothing about football." And Brian was sniggering, as if to say, "You're right, actually.'"

'It was just a clash of personalities,' says Os. 'Joe Mears died and Joe was a big influence on Tommy. Joe was a big, strong man: "Hey, Tommy, come here," and he'd put his arm round him. "Slow down, son, let's just think about things." Whereas the other people couldn't handle him. He was too strong for them.' So Dave Sexton was swiftly installed. It was October 1967. Chalk replaced cheese. 'Absolutely,' agrees Ossie. 'Tom was flamboyant and outgoing; Dave was very reserved and quiet. Very methodical. He was there quite a while before, of course, under Tom. And we were quite pleased he took over, because in the early days as coach Dave was one of the lads. Oh yeah, he was as good as gold. He'd socialise with you, have a beer with you. I was just coming into it of course, and the lads thought the world of him. They were so pleased he got the job, to be honest.

'His coaching ability was fantastic. He was brilliant. But man-management was a problem. I mean, I saw him the other week at Brighton and I gave him a cuddle and all that and said, you know, "It's all forgotten." And he said, "I know, it was forgotten a long time ago, it's lovely to see you." And it's nice, it's nice to see him now. I said to him, "If we had that time again I'd have done things differently," and I think he would have as well.'

Not the glory, of course. Not the cups, the European adventures, the camaraderie. But perhaps the intransigence. And maybe even the training. 'I think probably not putting enough into training, the stamina side of it, was one of my biggest mistakes,' says Peter. 'The ball work was lovely, I loved it; I could have stayed out there for six hours on ball work. The physical side, on the other hand: I couldn't do the running – just didn't fancy the cross-country runs, or "doggies". See, I liken myself to a foreign player where they don't do all those sorts of things, they just work with the ball. And I would've been better off working with the ball for three hours, and the others working for an hour doing cross-countrys. I'd have got my stamina up that way.

'But you couldn't, so of course I just used to stroll round. Me and Marvin Hinton used to stay at the back. When it was foggy we used to cut corners and everything. Epsom Downs was a funny thing. We used to have Sunday and Monday off after a game sometimes, and we'd go in Tuesday, straight to Epsom Downs racecourse for a five-mile cross-country run. Epsom's up and down and Ron Suart used to stand at the top of this hill. Lots of times it was misty up there and we used to go down the hill and just sit there about 15 yards away from him – we could see him, but he couldn't see us. Then we'd wait for the rest of the lads to go down the bottom and come back up, then we used to jump in behind them, puffing, like. The only thing was we always came back with Dave Sexton – he always had to wait for us – because the bus had gone by the time we got there. Me and Marvin, Looby-Lou.'

Ah yes, the nicknames of the '70s squad: 'Great bunch of lads. Peter Bonetti was Catty. Johnny Hollins was Ena – Ena Sharples: always talking, never stopped rabbiting. Eddie Mac was called Clarence, the old cross-eyed lion. Every time he combed his hair we stood behind him crossing our eyes. Dave Webb was just DJ, his initials. Chopper we called Buller, for bullshitter; he'd come in, say to Demps, "Oi, Ossie's just told me you put lacquer on your hair." I haven't said a word, of course. And then Demps would fly up: "Yeah, and what about your bald spot, Os?" So Buller was right. He didn't get the Chopper name for the same reason as Linford Christie. It was for the other type of tackle, I promise you.

'Hutch was Hutch. Tommy Baldwin was Sponge, not so much for soaking the pressure as for drinking, really. Charlie Cooke was Cookie; although we called him Diddies one time when he had the little tits. Peter Houseman was Nobby, but I don't know why. Then Alan Hudson was just Huddy and I was just Ossie. Huddy's a Chelsea boy, a trendy boy and, let's be fair, he dressed in all the gear: the big kipper ties and all that. I was never that way inclined, but Huddy used to come in with outrageous gear. It looked good on him. He's always been very smart, with the long hair – it was like the Beatles' style.'

There was an incredible camaraderie that found expression in all sorts of ways, not of all of them liquid. 'Demps always got a lot of stick because of his hair. But it was spread about really. We all had fun. They were fun to be with.

'One of the funniest stories ever involved the groundsman, George Anstiss, whose son John has now taken over. George was out there on the pitch with these four or five old boys he had – it was unbelievable. They used to go out and fork the pitch and sweep up. They had this bloody great big Alsatian; he was a brute and they couldn't let him out on the ground except at night with the nightwatchman; nobody else but him could get near that dog. He was a vicious bastard. And, anyway, Webby had this Alsatian, similar sort of size. So Webby brought him down to the ground one day and they were all out there on the pitch, George Anstiss and these old boys, forking away. And then Webby said, "Come here. Sit down. Hold him, Os." So I held this dog by the side of the pitch, and Webby started running out on the pitch, and said, "When I get out there, Os, let him go, cos he'll run to me." So Webby ran out on the pitch and shouted, "The dog's out! Watch out!" And of course, I let Webby's dog go, and spades and forks and brooms went everywhere, and these poor old boys are trying to run to safety . . . I tell you, me and Webby pissed ourselves.'

Fun it may have been, but Dave Sexton, in his monastic, methodical way, was intent on bringing the club the serious success it craved. His style wasn't always in harmony with that of the players, even if his coaching was universally approved. In many ways, he was the antithesis of the image Chelsea – Hudson, Osgood, Cooke, McCreadie, Baldwin and Webb – were carving out for themselves as playboy footballers. 'Everybody says I was a clubbing man, but I wasn't,' says Os. 'We used to go down the King's Road, I'd have a few beers and go back to Windsor and that was me. Huddy, Tommy and Cookie were the main ones. They used to go to Tramps. I mean, I've been there loads of times, but basically I lived in Windsor and I had a family. I was lucky in that respect. Huddy didn't, he was a bachelor boy. Tom was the same.

'Footballers now drink just as much as we did, don't worry about that. No disrespect to them, but we never got up to the antics they get up to; we never got pulled in the papers as much as they do now. And it's not just drink, it's drugs as well. I have never even smoked in my life – hate the stuff, bloody stink. And I mean, we'd have a drink, have a laugh, but today they've got too much time on their hands, too much money and they just can't handle it. They're on unbelievable wages: good luck to them, don't get me wrong. It wasn't hard to pull the birds in our day, though. They were around, of course they were. You were in the public eye. Well, the King's Road was buzzing, the Stones and the Beatles were flying high, and we used to go down to the King's Road and I used to walk in and there'd be Princess Anne sitting in a restaurant. Tennis players, all those sort of people, down in Alexandre's restaurant. Michael Crawford used to be down the Bridge.'

November 1973 was typical. 'I walked into the dressing-room one day. We beat Everton 3–1, I scored my 100th league goal, did a lap of honour, came in, and Richard Attenborough had brought Steve

McQueen into the dressing-room. Things like that happened in your life. Michael Caine, people like that, you'd meet all the time through Chelsea. And Raquel Welch! I got a big bollocking off Dave Sexton for that as well. I didn't arrange her coming to the ground, it was done through the club. She was over promoting a film, and she wanted to come and watch Chelsea play because she'd heard about the King's Road. She was a special lady, a lovely lady, a very beautiful lady, and she was nice to talk to, and she said she was looking forward to the game and it was a pleasure to meet her. It got a bit embarrassing when she was shouting, "Bye Os! Bye Peter!" and the game was still going on. She probably thought, "He's not doing much, I'll just give him a shout."'

The successor in the Chelsea chair to Charles Pratt, who had died in 1968, was the latest offering in the Mears dynasty, Brian. It was his board that embarked on the ill-considered redevelopment of Stamford Bridge in 1971. 'We called him The Saint, because when we went on tour, he had this white suit and all he wanted was a halo. You've got to say he wasn't the best chairman in the world, but as a person he was terrific, he was one of the boys. He wasn't as strong as his father, but we respected him; we really liked him.' Not so much as to avoid taking advantage of his *bonhomie* on occasion . . . 'We used to sign his name on the bills now and again. Huddy was good at that. He used to get a few bills and he knew who it was but he used to pay them; there was no problem. He was as good as gold.'

Brian was the most successful of the Mears clan in football, and oversaw the club's most glorious days. The greatest, for its unlocking of the trophy room, was the FA Cup victory in 1970. And the focal point of the club, the main man, the king of Stamford Bridge, was Os-good, Os-good, O-o-osgood, Os-good . . . 'You'd feel fantastic when you heard them singing that,' smiles Ossie. 'Denis Law was king of Old Trafford, in front of Besty and Charlton. Come down here and you've had Greavesie and all them, and all of a sudden they pick on you as the king and that's unbelievable. I see Matthew Harding now and he says, "The old king's here!" Yes, it's an honour. It's lovely to be remembered.'

And to be remembered for such gallant moments, as the scorer of goals, winner of matches, saviour in darkest hours. 'Over the years we had so many great games, we had ding-dong battles and things. I loved playing at Palace: Mel Blyth, and John Jackson in goal. I always scored against him for some reason. I got four past him once. We won 5–1. It was like a frosted pitch, solid with ice, and Charlie Cooke was like a ballerina, slipping past them. Of course, Charlie wasn't a goalscorer, so nine times out of ten I was just tapping them in. Thank you very much, Charlie! Then you look at the Cup final replay and when you score a goal like that, a diving header, and it helps us win the FA Cup, I think that sticks in your mind.'

He remains the last man to score in every round of the FA Cup. And, probably, after them. Following the FA Cup final replay victory, Ossie found himself in the company of a stunningly beautiful woman. Touring the finest joints in Manchester with his belle, Ossie lavished money on food, cocktails, the works. In the early hours, the wooing paid off. 'You've given me the most fantastic night,' the woman said, promisingly. 'Now I'm going to give you something in return.'

Well, Ossie's feet barely touched the floor as he raced her back to his hotel room. Opening the door in eager anticipation, he was confronted by the most passion-killing sight known to man – a bunch of mates and vague acquaintances crashed out all over your bedroom.

'It was the team's families,' explains Dave Webb. 'No one had anywhere to sleep. My brother was up there with one of my mates, Ronnie Harris had all his family and they were supposed to have gone back on the train. So they all stayed over and came back on the train that we went home on in the morning. So in all the rooms, there were players as pissed as farts, and bodies everywhere.'

But back to more successful scoring attempts. 'I played against QPR and scored three goals in the 4–2 win in the quarter-final, I played against Watford in the semis and scored goals. But I'd say my greatest moment was winning the FA Cup; it was so special, it meant that we'd won something after so long.' There were many heroes of the 1970 FA Cup squad, some more loudly acclaimed than others. Ossie rates Peter Houseman as the greatest provider he worked with. But Alan Hudson, who missed the final through injury, was the most gifted. 'Huddy was a great passer of the ball, with tremendous vision. He couldn't score goals but he had a great shot on him, and he had a great engine, which people overlook. He scored one of the greatest goals I've ever seen at Coventry. An unbelievable goal! He must have beaten four or five players and he went through and slotted it like a Brazilian. It was absolutely unbelievable, and he still reminds me of it today.'

Then there was Champagne Charlie . . . 'The lovely thing about Charlie was if you were winning 1–0 with ten minutes to go, you'd give it to him, he'd take it away for five minutes and they couldn't get it off him. The bad thing was if we were losing 1–0 we couldn't get it off him either: "Charlie! We're losing this one!" But he was a great dribbler, great runner, terrific player and a great character.'

This was a vastly different side from the one constructed by The

Doc. The Diamonds were like a hot jazz combo: a tight ensemble, not unduly blessed with flamboyant soloists. Dave Sexton's outfit was more like a collection of bebop players, taking turns to express themselves individually, capable of sublime virtuosity or off-key exasperation.

Ossie, with that arrogant swagger, was a big-occasion performer, if not to the extent of the tricky Scots winger Cooke. And the greatest stages were to be found on the Continent, as he recalled from the '60s excursions. So when Chelsea's Cup triumph earned entry to the 1970–71 European Cup-Winners' Cup, there was no happier traveller. 'Oh yeah, we knew if we were right on the day, we could beat anybody, and we proved that with Leeds and Real Madrid – all right, they weren't at their best, but they were still a top club, and a big scalp to take. And we beat some good sides along the way.

'If you think about CSKA Sofia, it was unbelievable. We beat them over there and it was the first time they'd lost in about 20 years. Tommy Baldwin scored a goal in front of 40,000 Bulgarians and they were just stunned. They couldn't believe it. But they were a very, very good side: they were the top side of the time. We also played against the Greek side, Aris Salonika. Horrible, they were: spitting at you, touching you up. Horrible. I'd never had anything like it. Crowd kept laughing. I thought, "What's happening? Hang on" – he kept touching me up all the time. We drew 1–1 over there. I missed a penalty, funnily enough, but I laid one on for Hutch and he scored. Made it one each, which I was pleased about. We came back here, and the fella sorted me out in the first 20 minutes and I had to go off – he gave me a good dig. But we beat them 5–1. Again, a great performance.

'And then we played Bruges. I didn't play in the Bruges game away, where we lost 2–0. But I was up for the second leg. In January I went up before the FA and got banned for six weeks after three bookings – unbelievable. They were clamping down on discipline and said they were going to make an example of the next one to go up. Sexton said we'd appeal, Brian Mears said, "We're going to fight this. My father was well respected." So I went back and got eight weeks! An extra two!

'My ban finished on the Monday and we were playing Bruges on the Tuesday, having lost 2–0 away from home. And Dave Sexton said to me, "I don't know whether I'm going to play you or not." I said, "You must be joking: I've been doing cross-countrys with Ron Suart every morning." I used to have to meet him at nine o'clock, do the cross-country, then go training with the rest of the lads. Anyway he played me and I scored in the last two minutes, making it 2–0,

2–2 on aggregate. Tommy scored and I scored again to make it 4–0 and we were on our way. I jumped the dog track when I scored the second goal against Bruges, ran across to the far side, and went behind the goal. I saluted the fans, because they had paid to see that and it was a privilege to say, "There you are – you're here and I produced for you." That's what it was all about. I just loved scoring; the fans were expecting me to score.'

With cup-holders Manchester City despatched in the semi-final 2–0 on aggregate (both games missed by Os with a knee injury), it was off to Athens to face once-awesome Real Madrid in the 1971 Cup-Winners' Cup final. 'Sometimes you think your name's on the cup,' says Ossie. 'But we'd been playing for nearly 90 minutes, 1–0 up, Osgood goal as usual. And ten seconds to go they're going to bring the cup out. I've gone off with a knee injury because I'd had a painkilling injection in my knee and it wore off. Anyway, they score. Soft goal as well. After another half an hour and no goal I said to the lads, "You know, sometimes your name's on it and sometimes it isn't." And they said, "What are you doing tomorrow?" I said, "Well, what do we normally do on a day off? We'll go and have a drink."

'So me, Charlie and Tommy Baldwin went down the Hilton and we're sitting in our swimming trunks and all that, having cocktails and stuff, and Huddy comes along and says, "What are you doing?" I said, "Having a drink – that's what I normally do." He said, "Aw, but you've got a big game tomorrow!" I said, "Huddy, you go and look after yourself, son, we'll be all right." And, of course, Charlie turned it on, Tommy Baldwin was superb and I scored another goal. But that's what you did. You relaxed and did your own thing.' For the second time in a year, the streets around the town hall thronged with long-suffering supporters; the relief of Mafeking was nothing compared to the relief of Chelsea fans. The open-topped bus may have been the novelty it was in May 1970, but it further laid to rest the ghost of underachievement in SW6.

And so the holders returned to the playing fields of Europe the following season. The first round paired the Chelsea aristos with the yeomen of Jeunesse Hautcharage of Luxembourg. 'Oh, that was funny,' grins Os. 'Like playing the butcher, the baker, the candlestick-maker. That's all they were. They were smashing lads. But it was embarrassing, really. There was a one-armed lad, went to take a throw-in, picked it up, and, of course . . . it was ridiculous. We were killing ourselves laughing. But we went out to enjoy ourselves and do it right, and we beat them 8–0 over there. And when they came over here, I said to Peter Bonetti, "I'll have a bet with you. I bet I score six goals at home."

'We had the bet. He said, "Right, you've got a fiver on." And he's the tightest bastard you ever met, Catty, I tell you. And on the night, I'd scored five and we had a penalty. And I was just going to take the penalty and there was a tap on my shoulder. It was Catty and he says, "Nah, Ossie, you don't take the penalties. Johnny Hollins does." So I said, "Hang on a minute, Catty . . ." He said, "You're unprofessional, you are." I said, "Catty, we're winning 20–0, and there's two minutes to go . . ." He said, "I don't care, Holly takes the penalties." And he took the fiver off me soon as I got in the dressing-room.' Well, it may be true that Catty prevented Os from taking the spot-kick (which Holly converted), but the incident came far earlier than Ossie remembers – it was the fifth goal. Poetic licence, apparently.

Still, the boys could afford to be generous at the time. Despite crucial injuries to Ian Hutchinson and Eddie McCreadie amongst others, and setting aside the débâcle at Wembley against Stoke in the 1972 League Cup final, the team was still there or thereabouts. A desperate FA Cup fifth-round defeat at Orient, where their big centre-back Harris stifled Os after we'd gone two up, however, showed that the team needed renovation. (At one stage, as Orient's three responses rattled in, a Blues fan shouted, 'What's the matter, Ossie – he's not going to eat you!' to which the big defender nodded his head and said, 'I will!')

But in perhaps the greatest testament to extravagant ambition Chelsea embarked on a stadium redevelopment that was ultimately to set the club back some 20 years. Brian Mears announced the plans in 1972 with the fateful proclamation, 'Chelsea will never be the same again.' Dave Sexton, perhaps eyeing his diminished transfer budget, pronounced the plans 'startling'.

'The thing is,' says Os, 'when the stand was built, what we should've done was strengthen the side. We had three finals in three years and we should have built on that, gone on and won the league. We didn't. And Dave Sexton says, "Right, we've got the best midfield in the country: Charlie Cooke, Alan Hudson and John Hollins." And then goes and buys Stevie Kember. And he changed the system to 4-3-3, put Huddy on the wing, me in midfield, and it was absolute madness. All right, you go through a lean spell, and they try to change things; they panic. You shouldn't do that. All right, drop us for a couple of games, fine. Stick us in the reserves, let us get our confidence back – well, I never needed confidence, nor did Huddy. But it was just one of those things, you had a little bad period.'

Garland, Garner and Weller were not of the same quality as Ossie, Tommy B and Hutch, and by 1973–74, relations between ebullient players and taciturn manager had deteriorated dramatically. In the first week of the 1971–72 season, Dave Sexton had slammed Ossie for an unsatisfactory approach after a 3–2 defeat at home to Man United. A petition and demonstrations demanded that he be taken off the transfer list. And he was. But matters came to a head one day in 1973, as the new east stand accelerated over budget and past deadlines like a runaway express, and the team struggled for form.

'Well,' explains Ossie, 'Dave called me in and said, "How d'you feel about being captain?" So I said, "What d'you mean, Dave? Ronnie's okay."

'"No," he said, "you're the leader. They all look to you. I think it might do you good."

'"Well, if you think so," I said, "I'll think about it."

'We played Liverpool on the Saturday. We got beaten 1–0, and he calls me in and he says, "I'm going to make some changes." I thought, "Here we go, he's going to make me captain." And he said, "I'm leaving you out; I'm dropping you." So from being captain the week before I was out of the team altogether. But that was Dave; that was him. We'd just got beaten 1–0, and I might have had a poor game, but they were a great side, hard to play against. So then he dropped me against Sheffield United and Chelsea beat them 2–1. We were playing next week in the Cup, and I went in on the Monday and we trained with the reserves. He asked me if I wanted to go up and I said I'd rather train with the reserves, which we did, Huddy and myself, with Dario Gradi.

'Dave called us across and said, "Come on, you've got to train." We said, "Well, we're not in your plans, you've won Saturday, you're not going to change a winning side, why don't we stick with the reserves, stay out of your way?"

'"Well, if you feel like that," he said, "you might as well go home." And again, that was him.

'"Fine. I'll go home then, I don't want to train; that suits me." And then Huddy says, "Same goes for me, I feel the same way. Is there any chance I can have a move?" And Dave says I asked for a move and I never bloody did, so I never got my five per cent when I left here. But I think the thing that hurt me most was when I went to Dave and said, "Look, this is silly, let's forget it all. I'm due a new contract, let's negotiate, and I'll put my arms up and say, let's forget it." And he said, "Fine." Three weeks later I saw the chairman, Brian Mears. "Mr Chairman, what about this new contract?" He said, "Don't know anything about it." So Dave hadn't bothered. And that's what hurt me more than anything. So I went to Southampton.'

Dave Webb points to other incidents that signalled Ossie's departure. 'Ossie was writing a book with Nigel Clarke [the *Daily Mirror* sports writer]. They'd all gone round for lunch to Barbarella's and a couple of them were injured. Dave Sexton sent someone round, then he sent someone else round. Charlie and them had come back badly drunk, they'd drunk 30 bottles of Mateus Rose or something – and it all went off between them and Dave. They were doing the same thing when they suspended Ossie and Huddy that time – we had to play QPR without them and I played centre-forward. And I said, "Can't you un-suspend them?" And Dave said no. He was really dogmatic on that. That was where there was a problem. If he'd been a bit more flexible that time, it wouldn't have happened, but it got too deep.

'And I always remember getting Ossie – it might have been at Peter Houseman's testimonial – to come and apologise, to go outside the Café Royal. I went to Dave Sexton and said, "I've got Ossie outside." And Dave wouldn't go. He said, "He knows what happens. I'll be in the office at 10 o'clock tomorrow morning." And he slagged me off, Ossie, saying, "You've mugged me off." And I was upset and that, and that was one of the points I knew Ossie had to go then, because I knew there was too strong a character at both ends.'

Ossie turned from sinner to saint in a few short weeks. 'I walked away and thought, "What have I done?" I was going through a divorce at the time as well which didn't help – your mind's not your own. But I would never have walked away from this club. Never in a million years. It was childish, really. And the annoying thing about it was they backed Tommy Docherty in the old days and sold Venables, Graham, Murray, Bridges, terrific players, and then they sacked him after a few months, and they did exactly the same with Dave Sexton. They let him sell me, John Hollins, Webby, Huddy, and then he was gone.'

Ossie returned to Stamford Bridge on a couple of occasions. The benefit match for Peter Houseman's children was one, and perhaps the only time he was actually barracked by Blues fans. Someone shouted, 'Are you playing here Osgood?' And Ossie said, 'No, I'm counting the crowd.' And he was – it wasn't like the old days. Then, after a period of four years away, the king, now slower and less motivated, returned to his realm. It was 1978–79.

'It was stupid,' he says. 'I should never have come back. But I wanted to. But I was equally silly walking out in 1980. I should have stayed in the reserves and brought them through and got a job there. I loved working with the kids. I was still scoring good goals, and they were doing all my running for me. They just loved my presence, which was a compliment to me.

'We had a great little reserve side, brought some great youngsters in. Then I think we had three managers in one day didn't we? Ken Shellito got the sack, Frank Upton took over. That was funny. We were at Molesey, in the dressing-room. And Frank's walked in and said, "Right, from now on, you call me Boss, you don't call me Frank."' Ossie shakes his head at the memory.

'Anyway, overnight, who's put in charge, but Danny Blanchflower. And next morning, of course, we've got a meeting again at Molesey. He walks in. I said, "Morning, Frank!" He was one of them, he was. And he looked at me, saw the lads piss themselves. "Morning, Frank!" He never lasted even 24 hours. Then Geoff Hurst came in and I fell out with him – we're great mates now – but he sat there for three months, watching Danny go wrong. Oh, it was pathetic. It was Brian Mears's fault again, basically. He wanted the best for the club, but he didn't have any idea. He should never have got Danny in. It was a disgrace. He tried to get us to play the way Spurs did, but we never had the players. It was mad.'

Ossie has no doubt who his ideal manager would have been: 'If I could have had Dave Sexton, Tommy Docherty and Lawrie McMenemy all rolled into one, I'd have had the perfect manager: a fantastic coach, a guy who was flamboyant and outrageous and great fun, and a guy who was very astute and a calming influence – Lawrie.'

His own Chelsea career still shines in his memory. 'The cups, the good times. A lot of goals you remember too. I got a great left-foot volley down here against the Arsenal in the Cup semi-final, April 1973, and that's always on the box. The AC Milan goal was a terrific volley; keeper never moved. Real Madrid – you know, I bent it round the keeper into the corner. But I would say, basically, that the FA Cup replay diving header and the Burnley goal were my best.' He might also add the classic at home to Derby in 1972, when he dummied two defenders and fired a left-footer in off the post from the edge of the box. And another great thing about Ossie: he scored most of his goals against Everton – eight of his first century were against the dratted Scousers.

For the last three seasons, Ossie has been the sponsor's match-day host, occasionally emerging from the east stand to accept the adulation of a new generation of fans. The irony of working inside the structure that destroyed his team isn't lost on him. 'I say to everybody on match days, "Just think of that: when you're sitting out there, you're sitting on my lap, because they sold me to build that thing."'

6

DJ

'Unfortunately.'

Such is David Webb's jocular response to his citation as The Man Who Won the Cup for Chelsea. For a quarter of a century he has borne that exquisite burden. 'It's just unfortunate,' he says, 'because it's the only one.'

Webby – Desperate Dan in his '70s heyday – was one of the most influential and crowd-pleasing players of Dave Sexton's star-studded team. He even returned successfully in 1993, after 19 years' absence, in a capacity he is fond of calling 'Red Adair manager'. But it is as the quintessential swinger, the seemingly carefree cockney, and one of the gutsiest and most cultured defender-cum-strikers of his day, that he is best remembered.

The most striking images in the gallery of Chelsea folklore are his: Webby, praying, in his temporary goalkeeper's jersey one Boxing Day; Webby foraging forward with the score at 0–1 and five minutes to go; Webby sprawling, snapping back, bewildered but unbowed by Eddie Gray's footwork; Webby rising above the Leeds defence to glance the winning goal off his cheek, and running round the pitch in ecstatic relief at the final whistle; Webby leaning down from the open-topped bus, handing the FA Cup to a gaggle of scarlet-tunicked Chelsea Pensioners; Webby, the first player to wave to a chant of his name, cupping his ear to the crowd like he couldn't hear us, and holding up crossed fingers before the last hurrah at Wembley, 1972.

No player before or since has given out to the crowd to the same extent as David 'DJ' Webb, though Dennis Wise has come close. By the end of 1971 he even had his own official fan club. He loved it: walking through the crowds in his latest flash suit before games, signing autographs, posing for photos. 'In them days I was a bit extrovert anyway,' he says. 'But you got that feeling from people at Chelsea, it was very showbizzy. And if you kind of played up to it . . .

'When I first went there I hadn't had that kind of warmth with the crowd. My first game for Chelsea was away at Manchester United. We hadn't won there for years and we beat them 2–1 or 3–1. I had an outstanding first game and the next home game I could play was Leicester. They had a big fella named Frank Large up front – always a bit tough. The first ball that came along I hit the tackle and the ball's gone through and there was a hush from the ground as if the crowd thought, "Well, he'll do me." I took off from there. You kind of capture them and you have to make sure you keep them. I became very popular because I did the things that most of them wanted to do. I defended as well as I could and when I had the chance to be a bit flamboyant I would be. It wasn't all just jokes and fun, it was a bit of flamboyance tied in with seriousness.'

It is for the flair, though, that Dave Sexton's men are fondly remembered – the team that launched an army of fans worldwide. 'We were one of the few teams who people recognised,' says Dave, 'whereas today everyone is. It's the winning profile. You can have all the other stuff, but the most important thing is what you do on that pitch.'

Webby arrived in February 1968, a time when Chelsea, post-Doc, was undergoing team surgery. Dave Sexton had tracked him since throwing him in as a youngster at Leyton Orient, Dave's first full management post on quitting Chelsea a few years earlier. The manager had moved on, via Arsenal, to Stamford Bridge; the player was at Southampton.

'I wasn't mad keen to go to Arsenal,' mutters Dave, understandably. 'Next thing, he got the manager's job at Chelsea. So at the end of the following year he came in for me. There was all this talk about me going there and Barry Briggs, a British speedway rider who was one of my best mates, said, "Let's see them play." So we went up to the game against Liverpool. Dave Sexton was supposed to have left me tickets, but when we got there there weren't any. So we actually bought two tickets off Stan Flashman. Mind you, they were good tickets: they were probably the tickets which was left for me in the first place!'

One incident in the game sold Chelsea to Webby: 'Charlie Cooke hit the ball round one side of Ron Yeats, and ran off the pitch, round the track, round the other side of the corner flag, and got the ball. And I thought, "Bloomin' hell! Wouldn't it be lovely to come and play with this mob!" They were just different class. I was so excited about going to Chelsea from then on.'

With Joe Kirkup heading south, Chelsea paid the Saints £30,000. 'The wonderful thing no one knows, and I tell players this now,' confides Dave, 'was I was on £85 a week at Southampton and I dropped to £65 a week at Chelsea – you imagine that today! But I knew my career was going to be that much better playing for Chelsea, and I just wanted to go there. So I never went there for money; I just went there for the football.'

Dave Sexton knew what he was buying: much more than a centre-half. In fact, Webby wore every shirt number except 11 in his Chelsea career. The only position he had a real problem with was right-back. 'I was never happy there,' he says. 'I always wanted to be where the main trouble was.' That versatility was a vital element in our most successful period ever.

'I would have enjoyed the way Ruud Gullit played as a sweeper for Chelsea. I always used to love watching the Dutch team and the Brazilians. They were just as comfortable in the other team's box as their own. We had people like Johnny Dempsey and Ronnie Harris – terrific defenders, but once you got Ron near that penalty box . . . I was a frustrated centre-forward a lot of the time. Dave says to this day that I could have actually been a centre-forward. And in games when we were struggling, I was the one they always threw up to centre-forward – and it worked. In training I always played centre-forward. I started forward some games. I played on the wing and got the two goals against Sheffield United in 1972. I used to enjoy the glamour and all the clamour of getting goals – and some important goals I got.'

Once the drought had broken, that is. His first goal didn't come until a 3–1 win at Ipswich on Boxing Day 1968. Typically, Webby didn't do things by half. 'Dave Sexton, when I first went there, introduced me to people saying, "He'll get goals, this fella." It was a bit of a laugh cause I'd been there for almost a year and everyone said, "Well, he ain't scored a goal yet!" Harry Medhurst, God bless him, always had a little chip with me and I scored the first goal and I went, like, "One." When I got the other, "That's two." And when I got the third one we were all laughing about it. I said I was saving them all up to get them in one day.'

Poor loves – Webby always seemed to be Ipswich's bogeyman. After he bagged the brace against Sheffield, he equalled the feat in the following match against the East Anglians. But that was nothing . . . 'It was one of them clubs,' he grins. 'I did my knee against Ipswich, I scored the hat-trick against Ipswich, went in goal against Ipswich . . . The directors used to say I was the bane of their lives – they used to look on the team sheet and hope I wasn't playing. Something weird always happened whenever I played against them.'

Surely none so bizarre as on another Boxing Day, 1971, when

Dave made his first-team goalkeeping debut against Bobby Robson's side. 'Dave Sexton had taken a gamble and allowed Steve Sherwood to go home for Christmas,' explains Dave. 'Peter Bonetti was out injured and John Phillips had come into the side. But over Christmas he stayed at Johnny Hollins's and he woke up on Christmas morning and his back went, so he couldn't play. So Steve Sherwood was recalled and came down from up north, and supposedly he missed the pick-up point where they had a police escort!

'So we had an agreement with the referee that if he turned up before the teams went out on the pitch then they would let him change. I was still in the goalie's shirt, just going on the pitch, and Steve turned up. So they went to the referee and checked, and he said, "No" – said he was a few minutes late. And we thought – Bobby Robson! I thought, I've got to go on the pitch and win the crowd over or they'll think it's a Christmas joke, so I knelt in the goalmouth and made out I was saying a prayer. The tension just went and everyone looked at it as a fun day. And there was no way that I was going to let anyone score.' Chelsea ran out 2–0 winners.

On another occasion, we were beating Arsenal 2–1 [1969] with five minutes to go on a mudbath of a pitch. The Cat was fending off all sorts of missiles, and we needed to hold on to gain a merit place in the Inter-City Fairs Cup. It was a nail-biting time. Trust Webby to diffuse things. There was a scramble in the goalmouth, a tackle flew in and sent Dave skidding along in the mud. Instead of jumping to his feet, though, he stretched out and started doing the breaststroke. A magical moment.

Webby was just like that. He was a joker, a character, and a bit of a spiv too. He used to buy and sell cars, then flats. Later, he traded in bankrupt goods (which some might say applies equally to some players he's sold as a manager). It was even said by John Dempsey that when the train arrived at Euston after the FA Cup final, an admittedly inebriated Webby suggested he would buy a block of surrounding flats.

Demps was permitted to join Webby in one venture: Kleen-a-Kit, which collected London soccer clubs' soiled togs and returned them washed. Unfortunately, a few kits went a bit dodgy, Webby didn't have a business plan . . . and his partner joined forces with Bobby Moore's cleaning firm instead. His finest entrepreneurial moment, though, must surely be his copyrighting and performance – for posterity – of the raucous old soldiers' anthem, *Allouette*.

'When I was younger,' he reveals, 'there used to be a couple of poofs round the East End, Gay and Billy, and they used to run a pub and do a drag act – they were very good, nice fellas. Knew everybody, all the players. And in their pub there was a geezer there, and he's done *Allouette*, and I picked it up from him. As I got into football I used to sing it as a bit of a party-piece. When we done the *Blue is the Colour* album they asked me to sing that on it. I've got the joint copyright with Peter Lee Stirling, who wrote *Blue is the Colour* with Daniel Boone.' Ossie, you may recall, contributed lead vocal on a version of *Chirpy Chirpy Cheep Cheep*.

Despite such distractions, this Chelsea side was a serious outfit. And especially so with Webby et al at the back. Under Dave Sexton they used two main systems: zonal marking or man-for-man. 'If the opposition looked we had Ron Harris, David Webb, John Dempsey, Eddie McCreadie; they knew there was no way that they were going to have an easy time. Everyone helped each other out if they were under a bit of a burden. Most of the time you could leave that four and it would take a hell of a lot to get past them. Few teams ever got more than one or two, maximum, goals past us. What it was, was gelling the right players together. If you've got a half-decent football upbringing, you know how to defend. In the old days, there was much more of an art in defending than what there is today. I had a sliding tackle: I used to get the ball off people before they got it; hook my leg round people. Now you can't do it.'

Webby's ability on the ball is often overlooked – another legacy of the all-important Cup final – which is a shame. Unlike Ron Harris, Webby could play, and was a fine passer, capable of bringing the ball out of defence with consummate ease. Yet it's his all-action, physical approach which people now recall. He had his personal battles, of course. 'There was no one I went out with that frightened me, that was the nice thing,' he says. 'Besty, Denis Law and me, we used to bash each other, throwing ourselves in, but at the end of the day there was respect. You never did anything nasty to them, but they knew they were going to be in a game. But nearly everyone had run-ins with Alan Clarke.'

Leeds, one of the top sides of the times, were also the most disliked among Chelsea players. 'One time I played at Leeds and a fella tackled me, hit me up in the air; it was the most diabolical penalty,' says Dave. 'I came down and busted my shoulder, had to come off. Another Leeds game someone went over the top to me. I was on the floor, tackled the ball and at least three of their players just kicked me on the ground. I just got up and stood for it. Another time Dave Sexton actually jumped out of the box: Alan Clarke laid the ball off, I tackled it, slid it back, and he turned and stamped all over me.

'There were one or two Leeds players who did some naughty things. But like a lot of bullies and thugs in life, they don't like it when it's up them. We didn't go out to put it up them, we just kept trying to play our game. But one thing Dave Sexton taught all of us was resilience – there weren't many cowards, and that's the affinity the crowd had with the team. If someone was putting it about against us or someone had hurt one of us, the whole team was like, "We'll sort that one out." We were playing in Spain in a pre-season game in 1973 and someone had done a diabolical tackle on Eddie McCreadie. I got booked for having a go at this fella, and Ronnie Harris said, "It's my turn now, DJ." The geezer's near the corner flag, and Ronnie got him and all I heard was a crack. I thought the bloke's leg had broken, but Buller's broken the corner flag. Next thing the bloke's on a stretcher, and Ron is sent off. It was a bit of a joke game. It got decided on penalties, and I think I scored the winning penalty with a run-up from the halfway line, socks around my ankles; miskicked it and it toppled into the net.'

The team spirit was incredible from 1968–71 and was perhaps the overriding factor in our success in that period. Everyone pulled in the same direction – all right, maybe not for 90 minutes, but there was always a 20-minute spell . . . 'Correct,' says Webby. 'And it didn't matter when that 20 minutes fell, you knew no matter who you were playing against, they couldn't live with you. It might have been me, Osgood, Hudson, Charlie Cooke, John Hollins, not so much individually, three or four of those blokes would suddenly click and it would start to happen. There was a magnetism about that side.'

Who could forget that enigmatic little window at the top of the old east stand, the one that would wind open every now and then. The crowd recognised it was a very Sextonesque means of communication. As the fans chanted his name, the manager would indicate his tactical changes on the field of play. With Webby in the team, we learned to expect them to work. The window opened during a replayed FA Cup clash against Preston in February 1969. 'I thought, "Well, okay, we're 1–0 down, here we go." Everyone was going home. I said, "I'm going up. Holly, you go in there." And bang! – I got the equaliser with a minute to go. And everyone started to come back in the ground – it was one of the funniest sights ever. All of a sudden they've kicked off and Alan Birch charged in, tackled a bloke, chased after it, the goalie's come running off his line, he crossed it and Charlie hits into an empty net. A pal of mine said it was like watching the tide: all going out, we equalise, and all come back. And we won it in the last three minutes.'

On the back of such spirited displays, the following year was

Chelsea's most momentous for 15 years. The FA Cup final was the culmination of a fine season but a stuttering league campaign. The season had begun oddly for Dave: 'We went to Barbados on an end-of-season tour after the FA Cup and I grew a beard. I saw George Lazenby with a beard getting all these birds and I thought some of it might rub off on me. He was publicising his James Bond film and there were all these bathing beauties about the place. Wonderful hotel. Paradise. Steel band playing, all these geezers zooming around on one water-ski. So I started growing a beard and I quite liked it. I played in the pre-season match at Everton, but Dave Sexton left me out after that. A lot of people said it was because of the beard, him trying to discipline me. I don't know if it was or not, but in the end I knuckled down, shaved the beard off and got back on with the football, which is what I needed to do anyway.' Webby, less hirsute, enjoyed a phenomenal season.

By the FA Cup semi-final stage Leeds, who'd enjoyed some easy victories against us in the preceding few years, came looming out of the fixtures list like the iceberg that sank the *Titanic*. Manchester United stood between Don Revie's parchment-dry side and the twin towers. 'The best final would have been Chelsea v. Man United,' says Webby. 'About three replays they had. I went to one of them. Leeds kicked lumps out of Besty and the others, they were diabolical. I think that's why everybody disliked Leeds. They always seemed to be whingeing, moaning round the referees. We were never that way. It wasn't that Chelsea was the team that everyone liked; it was more the fact that we were like the last-chance saloon. We were the last group of blokes to give everyone some sort of boost in the season.'

The sacred Wembley turf was in a pitiful state – it had been desecrated by the staging of an equestrian show shortly before and was covered in sand. Its heaviness wasn't conducive to Chelsea's fluent passing style and, more worryingly, our back four – the foundation of the side – was performing poorly (to put it mildly in Dave Webb's case). 'It was one of the cock-ups of my career,' confesses Webby. 'I had never been to Wembley, and I went there and I'd enjoyed the occasion up to the stadium, going to Wembley. But I didn't go there focused. Every other game I had played for Chelsea, I had focused on what I was going to do on that pitch, but there I got caught up in the occasion. I was like a fan; I was too relaxed.'

The most memorable aspect of a game ruined by the pitch – the two goals apiece aside – was the tormenting of David Webb by Leeds's winger. 'The thing with Eddie Gray was he kept trying to take me on, took it as a personal vendetta. And in a way it worked. Because if you looked at all the dangerous stuff, that came from Lorimer and people who were seeing the ball so much.'

True enough – the final ball was never a killer. Gray was like a matador, teasing and pricking, but the *coup de grâce* never arrived. That didn't lighten Webby's day at the time. 'He turned me over,' he admits. 'My decisions on the day were all wrong. I dived in when I shouldn't have done, I stood up when I should have dived in. Everything I did was wrong. I had never felt so knackered in all my life. I looked round and there was no help. Ronnie Harris shouldn't have played; he wasn't fit. He had a fitness test on the Thursday, done ten knees-up to his chest – and he played centre-half. So I was right-back.' Ron had had a cortizone injection to play and lacked the mobility to face a tricky winger. Still, honours even.

'Michael Crawford came up to me that evening for the first time and shook my hand. I said, "Pah – shake my hand after that?"'

'He said, "I've never seen anyone show so much balls in all my life."'

Webby (now presumably wearing shorts that exposed less of his manhood to Michael Crawford) wasn't frightened going into the replay at Old Trafford 18 days later. He was back in the centre of defence, for a start. 'The second game was different,' he says. 'I was saying, "I've got my bovver boots on." I made up my mind, there was no fucking way anyone was going to do anything there, and I went out and I did what was necessary, and I didn't give a monkey's . . .' Nevertheless, Webby's commitment nearly led to him deflecting into his own net from a Johnny Giles cross: 'I volleyed it to stop it, and it's gone over the bar. And I thought, if ever there's a God up there he looked on me then.'

Leeds forced the issue in the first half, but the second was different. 'Catty was different class,' says Dave. 'We knew what we were doing. We had a kind of a feeling there. And when the chips were down, you could hear the teeth grinding.' The rest is history, or synchronicity. Once Ossie's diving header had squared things up, Hutch, the equalising hero of Wembley, was warming those whirlwind arms up. Webby found himself in the box from one of his monstrous throws, Jackie Charlton inadvertently helped it on, and DJ – mug of the first game – slapped the winner in off his cheek.

Naturally, he swapped shirts with Eddie Gray immediately afterwards. 'I didn't get my medal because of that. There was a little stairway up, and this bloke put his arm out and said, "No – not Leeds." I said, "Oh, fuck off." They came down with the cup and I didn't bother to pick the medal up, just ran off, grabbed Alan

Hudson, because he couldn't play, and took him round the pitch with us. It was fantastic, the feeling there.' Eventually, it was Brian Clough who fetched Webby's medal for him with a 'Well done, son.'

Even by Chelsea's legendary standards the celebrations were extensive, resuming after a heavy night at breakfast before the journey back to London. 'The most fantastic thing was getting off at Euston. I nearly missed the open-topped bus, because the bus started to move away and everyone was grabbing me, and I got caught up in the throng. I was drunk as I sat down and we'd been drinking on the train home, started drinking in the morning. Dave Sexton, bless him, sat downstairs on the double-decker bus for most of the time. It was me that handed down the cup . . . you know, that famous picture with the Chelsea Pensioners. That was outside Harrods. The bus was stopped and there were all these crowds, and I leant down and nearly fell off the bus head first, I was that drunk. A big fella, the chief scout there, Eddie Heath, grabbed me by the trousers.'

Such scenes were nothing compared to the high jinks the lads were capable of on tour. 'It was a hell of a good laugh when I played,' says Webby. 'Charlie Cooke drank a lot, Tommy Baldwin drank a lot. Harry Medhurst drank a lot. We used to do this Colonel Puffer, a drinking game. Poor old Harry. On these tours we'd be sitting around doing this game, drinking and banging the table, and as soon as it got to Harry Medhurst we'd all pretend he'd got it wrong: "Oh, Harry! You'll have to drink up!" And he'd go "Ow!" By the end he was paralytic, and we'd have to put him to bed. There were a couple of people like that who couldn't take it, and everyone used to gang up on them – we were terrible.

'Ossie was a pub man. I never have been. I was a lunch-time drinker. Every day for many years I went to a restaurant in Chelsea – Alexandre's – and I used to have spaghetti and red wine. I drink whisky more now; whereas in them days they all liked lager and I liked beer – Double Diamond. Everyone would have a drink but the old monkey would go in and it would get eaten up unless you're careful, especially when Marvin Hinton was looking after it.

'We always had a laugh,' Webby continues. 'Once we were in Tehran. It was just after the end of the '71–'72 season, in May. The Shah was still there. The worst place I've ever played in my life. Big bucks they paid the club, but we hated it there. No one wanted to play the Iranian national side – didn't give a monkey's. It was a packed house and I was sitting on the line with a big cigar with me kit on. I'd had an operation on my knee and wasn't supposed to play. Dave Sexton took Tommy Baldwin off and put someone [Bill

Garner] on and they were just as bad as Sponge, so he took them off. And he come up to me and said, "Go on, liven them up." I said, "What? No way." But I gave someone the cigar butt, and I was running along like a lunatic. Soon after that I couldn't breathe – I was in the toilet hoiking this cigar up. None of your players today would do it. Ronnie Harris chased this geezer, who'd kicked him up the backside, all around the pitch. Ossie ended up grabbing him. I thought there was a war going to go off.'

Room-mates Johnny Boyle and Ossie's favourites were the old 'apple pie bed' or unpacking all your cases and flinging them round your room – the kind of pranks Kerry Dixon was fond of perpetrating in a later era. Even the bit-part players in the '70s Chelsea were characters. 'Paddy Mulligan was all right. Quiet fella, old Biggus Dickus – he had the biggest John Thomas I've seen in my life.'

Marvin 'Lou' Hinton was renowned for his laid-back approach. He came on as sub against Hautcharage in the Cup-Winners' first leg. 'We kept laughing at him. He said, "What's the matter?" We said, "Have a look!" He had his bloody watch on! I said, "He wants to know, doesn't he? You're in the Cup and you're winning it and he's looking at his watch."

'Alan Birchenal had more front than Marks and Spencer's. We'd go away, faraway countries, British high commissions, and we used to wind him up to go and sing. We'd start singing and mingle with the people, who'd be thinking, "Who's this geezer singing at the back?" But Birch used to get carried away, grab someone's guitar – couldn't play it! – and give it "like a Rhinestone Cowboy . . ."'

The FA Cup triumph was followed by the Cup-Winners' Cup, and Webby played in both victories. On the way there were some odd moments for Webby to recall. October 1970, for example, saw one of the all-time great Chelsea fightbacks at Blackpool. 'At half-time we were 3–0 down, but we come out in the second half, after a rollicking from Dave, with about seven positions changed round, including me going up front. And we ended up winning it 4–3 with the last kick of the game.' Dave scored one of the goals, but that last kick left half the Lancashire side with their heads in their hands – it was an own goal by Dave Hatton. Marvellous.

'That was one of the most amazing games, anyway,' says Dave. 'We were laughing all the way home. Firstly, we were staying at a hotel in Manchester, and we came out of the hotel and the coach didn't show up, so we had to go to the game and back to the hotel in taxis. And we'd played in the middle of the week in Bulgaria and beat CSKA Sofia, so we were a bit leg-weary and didn't play too well, as if we were half asleep. John Phillips was playing, one of his early games. They had three shots fly in the net. But we always had resilience. We came back out and Keith Weller got two of the goals.'

Ah yes, Keith Weller – the pacy, forgotten European Cup-Winners' campaign hero. He slipped away from Stamford Bridge in September 1971, straight after we'd beaten Jeunesse Hautcharage 13–0 in the first-round defence of our title. 'I thought that was the turning-point of Chelsea going downhill,' says Dave. 'The club was so short of money, and I think the only person they could get cash for was him. I went in the next day, and was looking for Keith, and Jimmy Bloomfield came up to me and said, "Looking for Keith Weller?" And I said, "Why?" And he said, "I'm going to buy him." And I said, "No you can't, we won't let him go." So I went to see Dave Sexton and I was almost in tears. And I knew. Something in my heart knew that he'd allow the team to be broken up.' Weeks later we played Atvidaberg in the Cup-Winners' Cup, missed a penalty and went out on the away goals rule.

'They were under pressure to sell people by doing all the ground improvements. They had to get some cash and it was wrong.' It was the beginning of the end for Webby. 'I thoroughly respected Dave Sexton; still speak to him today,' he says. 'I only left Chelsea because he'd allowed the team to be broken up. And the players coming in weren't the Chelsea players I thought they should be. They were as good as gold: Stevie Kember, Chrissie Garland, smashing fellas. But you know, soon Osgood had gone, Hudson had gone, Weller had gone, Charlie had gone – probably for the right reasons, because he'd gone right off the boil. And the fellas that were coming in, people like Bill Garner, I just thought they didn't fill the boots of those that had left.'

In May 1974, with ructions between players and manager proving insurmountable, Dave Webb's contract elapsed. He didn't wish to renegotiate with Chelsea. 'Ossie's departure – I just thought it was the beginning of the end,' he shrugs. 'It was disappointing, but I couldn't see us winning anything with that group of players. Dave Sexton thought we'd have more chance of winning the Championship with Chris Garland and Steve Kember and that type of player. I don't think the club should ever have looked to do that – if it happened, it happened. Even though we never won it, we were always up there – third, fourth, fifth . . . Everyone had a good run for their money, and people would still be there at the end of the season buying tickets for next year because they knew they were going to be entertained. We're talking 40, 50,000 people – we ain't talking like 25,000 people.'

'People used to say Chelsea were the Manchester United of the south; I think Manchester United are the Chelsea of the north! The amazing thing I always say about Chelsea: nine times out of ten it was where people actually made their reputation. They never came with one. Yet ever since they've tried to bring in players with reputations. That wasn't traditionally what Chelsea was about: they brought young players through right up to the Wilkins era, and then it started to tail off, and they didn't have the players coming through after that period.

'You take the team that won the Cup: Peter Bonetti came through the youth team; Ron Harris came through the youth team; Eddie McCreadie was a £5,000 buy from Scotland; I was a £60,000 buy from Southampton; John Dempsey cost £50,000 from Fulham, Johnny Hollins came through the youth team; Charlie Cooke was £30,000; Alan Hudson, he'd come through the youth team; Peter Houseman, Ossie too; Hutchy come for £25,000 from Cambridge; Tommy Baldwin was a swap for George Graham . . . The team cost peanuts even in that generation. Everyone made their reputation, became known, at Chelsea.'

Well, kind of. In actual fact, between 1961 and 1971, Chelsea were the country's biggest-spending club, forking out £1.25m – £50,000 more than glamour boys Spurs. Nevertheless, it was such a perspective that David Webb brought to Stamford Bridge again when he returned for what turned out to be a brief tenure in January 1993.

'I always say that I was like Red Adair: go in, put the fire out, and fuck off. That was all I was asked to do,' he says, without a trace of bitterness. 'I looked and I said to Ken Bates, "You do realise that traditionally this club is built from within . . .?" And I remember having a bit of a row, because I didn't think they should let people like Bobby Stuart go, David Hopkin, Darren Barnard, Shipperley; they had something about them. I thought they had the nucleus of a future Chelsea – and yet they've all gone.'

The one remaining member of Webby's favourites emerged as a great player two years later under Glenn Hoddle. 'Eddie Newton is the most outstanding midfield player I've seen for years, but his potential has never been fulfilled. He's the one that, had I stayed, I'd have built a team round.' Flattering for Eddie, but not necessarily what the fans would have wanted to hear. Eddie was a stylish young player who has benefited most from the presence of senior players like Ruud Gullit. He may have buckled under the pressure that would have been placed on him.

Nevertheless, there were aspects of Webby's diagnosis that few would have quibbled with: his motivation of the players, for one, and also his belief in a citadel. 'I thought Stamford Bridge should be the hardest place to win a game. I was very disappointed that we only drew against Tottenham, because it would have been my sixth home game, and we'd have won all of them. And, to be fair, Ken uses the little parallels, and he said that I never won an away game. I understand that, I won five, drew four and lost four. I couldn't do any more than that.'

At the end of the 1992–93 season, David Webb conducted his final press conference as manager of Chelsea FC. 'Well,' he said, affably. 'I'd like to say this is probably the last time I'll see you here. Thank you all very much. I've had a lovely time. Hope you have too.' The gentlemen of the press laughed spontaneously. They had. He's a nice fella, DJ, and in many ways it was sad to see him go. But Glenn Hoddle waited in the wings.

'I get on all right with Ken,' says Dave now. 'Two national newspapers courted me for two weeks after and offered me absolute fortunes to do an exposé on Ken Bates. I'll never do that. I don't think football needs half the stuff that gets in. I also turned down a fortune to have a go at Dave Sexton when I left Chelsea in the first place. I've still got all the letters, and the amount of mail from Michael Attenborough and Richard Attenborough, and other people who were supporters and had stopped going to Chelsea, that said, "We're going to make the effort to come back . . ."'

But perhaps his last contribution to the future of Chelsea was the most creditable. It was he who initially recognised the potential of Michael Duberry and put him on the subs bench. So how would Webby write his own end-of-season report for his time as manager? He thinks for a few seconds. 'Paid him to do his best, stood his ground, done the test, then told to piss off like the rest.'

Unfortunately.

7

Butch

'Funnily enough I did a show the other night, one of these "There's Only One Brian Moore" jobs, and it was about Chelsea and the team that got us up in 1976–77. And it was very interesting: of the side that played against Hull in the last game of the season and won 4–0, there was only Charlie Cooke who wasn't homegrown.'

Ray 'Butch' Wilkins sits in his office at Loftus Road overlooking the pitch on which their relegation struggle – lost – was played out in the 1995–96 season. Twenty years on, did Eddie McCreadie's approach have any bearing on the way he conducted himself in his first season as a manager? 'No, it didn't,' he smiles. 'Except in that Eddie gave us a chance and my belief is that sooner or later you have to give lads a chance, otherwise you're not going to see if they're good enough. And you'll end up keeping them on your books for years, no games, and they'll end up costing you lots of money. The one good thing that has come out of our season is that I now know we have several youngsters who can come in and do a more-than-tasty job. It was just unfortunate that the time they had to come in was a time of immense pressure. Pressure when you're winning is nil. But pressure when you're losing is immense.'

The strain on the Chelsea squads of that turbulent period was equally potent, perhaps more so because of the club's well-publicised financial plight. As the fans rolled into Stamford Bridge for the first match of the 1972–73 season, they were confronted with an unsightly hole where the old east stand once was. It was as if the dentist had pulled a tooth. Still, there was encouragement on the pitch: Chris Garland, cissy haircut and all, scored twice as we did some demolition of our own on old favourites Leeds. And, in the programme, more optimism: new apprentices this year were announced as 'Lewington, Ray, 15, midfield, London; Sparrow, John, 15, defender, Bethnal Green; Wicks, Steve, 15, forward (*sic*), Reading; Wilkins, Raymond, 15, midfield, Hillingdon.' Brian Bason and Graham Wilkins were a year ahead of the new kids; Steve

Sherwood, Gary Locke, Ian 'Brillo' Britton, Garry 'Hardest/Least Accurate Shot in Football' Stanley and Steve 'Jock' Finnieston had signed pro the year before. The youth crop was looking healthy.

'I think we were a bunch of mates playing together,' says Ray. 'It was like being back at school. Gary Locke, who was a couple of years older than me, my brother Graham, who was a bit older, Garry Stanley . . . and Catty was considerably older. But we were just buddies, so when we got into the first team, that was it. We all grew up together and the bonding was immense.

'Ray is my big buddy from those days. They didn't have schools of excellence then. I started training with Chelsea at about 10½ or 11. There was an apprentice at Chelsea at the time called Tommy Jones, and Tommy had come from Townfield School, which was the school I went to. And he just said one day to Eddie Heath, who ran the Chelsea juniors, "Eddie, we've got a guy down at our place, got a brother as well, that are half-decent. Shall we get them along?" And Eddie said, "Well, let's have a look." So we came along – I was 10½, Graham was just over 11 – and just had a great time. Frankie Blunstone was coaching us. Great, skilful player was Frank. Terrific bloke.

'So we went along and it just festered (sic) from there, really. Every holiday we were invited up to train and play games, and that's where, at 11, I first met Ray Lew. We started playing games together as early as that, and that's where the partnership started. We got together because we came from similar backgrounds, Ray and I, and it was just like chemistry: we just gelled immediately. I don't think it was because we were both Londoners, because the majority of the lads were from London, but something just clicked. There were lots of lads there had wealthy parents. We didn't. We played together with London Boys, and it was just a chemistry that built up from that stage. And obviously it came to fruition when we were 18. We'd gone from youth team, reserves – wallop! Straight into the first team.'

Ray made his senior debut in October 1973, a month after his 17th birthday. We stuffed Leicester 3–0. Ray vied with Garry Stanley for the sub's position from then on. 'The squad at that time was one of immense talent. Dave Sexton had that side, and you walked into the dressing-room, and you looked around at the faces and you thought, "I don't think I should be in here." You did. Because there was just so much talent it was embarrassing. At that time, apprentice professionals – the YTS as they're now called – held these guys in great esteem. I probably cleaned all of their boots at some stage. We always looked up to the first-team players, and to get on to the same field as them, you thought, "God, this is wonderful."'

By then, of course, Charlie Cooke had taken a sabbatical from football (or temporarily joined Crystal Palace), Ossie and Alan Hudson were semi-detached from manager and club, not even appearing in programmes after January 1974. Whispers about the potential of their heir, the Hillingdon youngster, were rife. 'I wasn't aware of them at all,' says Ray, modestly. 'Because I couldn't actually see myself breaking into that set-up. I don't think anyone could. When you think I initially had to compete with John Hollins, Alan Hudson, Charlie Cooke, Peter Houseman . . . And I thought, "Good grief, I don't know whether I've made the right decision here." But you get opportunities in life and it's how you take them. I was very fortunate that there were certain people at Chelsea at the time, Dave included, who felt it fit that I should get a game. Every manager was like that, though I suppose Dave had a bit more licence to try it.'

Ray retains enormous respect for the manager who gave him his first chance. 'He had moulded a wonderful team, no doubt about that, and they won things, which is important. And people say he's a dour character, but it's an absolute fallacy: the man is just hilarious if you get him one on one. He's just a very, very funny guy. And even now, when he coaches, he's got more enthusiasm than the players, and he's 65. To watch him work is an education, it really is.'

But Sexton's days were numbered, and in 1974 he was off to Man United – a journey his young midfield protégé was later to make. The team had festered and morale was low – almost as low as our league position. Relegation, unthinkable a season or two earlier, was a real prospect. 'Ronnie Suart took over from Dave and Ronnie's first job was to drop me at Stoke. It was a League Cup game – we got beaten – 6–2, I think. He said he wanted a bit more experience in alongside Ian Britton, and also to get after Alan Hudson, because Huddy was playing for Stoke at the time. But Ronnie let me down very nicely, and I've got the utmost respect for him. He's a great guy, and I still see him around because he's at Wimbledon now.'

Tactically, things needed enhancing. Creditors were breathing down the necks of the board. Violence associated with Chelsea fans was turning away supporters. Investors and a figurehead were needed. Eddie McCreadie, Ron Suart's coach, assumed control as the season concluded dismally with a 2–0 defeat at White Hart Lane that retained Spurs's top-flight status and ended ours. Ray was made captain the night before that match – our youngest ever, Hollins apart. 'I have to say I learned at a very early age how to handle downers,' smiles Ray. 'Make no mistake, there was tension there, because we were down the wrong end of the table, and actually got relegated, but that's why there was tension.'

Still, Eddie Mac was a breath of fresh air at the club, an inspiration, a motivator. If anyone could revive the club it was him. 'Eddie's Eddie,' says Ray. 'Eddie's like, let's all have a party, let's all have a giggle. And that was the way it went. I think his first action was to throw me in as captain. I said, "Are you sure?" because John [Hollins] was still at the club, Ron Harris was there, Catty was still there. But the response I got off those guys was just out of this world. Instead of saying, "Oh, this young upstart, we'll show him a thing or two!" all they did was rally round: "If we can help you out in any way, Ray, give us a shout." And that is just top drawer.'

For the large younger contingent in the first team it was like they'd never left the playground. Now there was a new regime investing in youth. The old guard accepted it mostly with good grace. 'The only tension between the two generations was on a Friday, old against young, and we used to kick lumps out of each other. And you just kept away from Ronnie Harris on a Friday. But that was it: there was more importance placed on that Friday than there was on a Saturday!'

The average age of the side targeting promotion in May 1976 was 21. 'Well, it was if Peter Bonetti didn't play,' chuckles Ray. 'It was a young side. And Eddie, to his credit, gave us our heads. He wanted us to play in a manner that had something of him in it. Because when Eddie played he was a flamboyant character – superb full-back. And we just went out and enjoyed ourselves, really.'

How easy it was to enjoy yourself knowing that there was no money to strengthen the side if you failed is a moot point. Ray rejects the idea that the financial troubles damaged morale. Off the field, supporters humiliatingly raised 'Cash for Chelsea', encouraged by the marketing manager, spooky-looking Frank Milford. 'It was all poor publicity, desperate stuff. But I think players, if I'm perfectly honest, they play football. If the club's taken over, they're still employed, and they love playing so they play football. And Eddie was in the same boat. I think Eddie realised, as a former player himself, that although it's the club he's managing, it had nothing to do with him. He hadn't sold the team, hadn't built the stand, so it had nothing to do with Eddie. "Let's get on and play the game" – that's the attitude he took.'

'I realised quickly that I'd better know what I'm doing here, my idea of the game, what I'd learned over the years,' says Eddie McCreadie. 'I had to blend these kids together. Make sure there was someone like Ray Lewington there – Ray Wilkins was not the most aggressive person at winning balls, though he would win some. So I had to have someone there who could win balls. And Ray Lewington, who was wonderful but perhaps wasn't one of our most outstanding young players, could win balls. Ian Britton's tireless enthusiasm, his speed and his little legs going all the time helped us tremendously. Ron Harris came in many times and was subbed many times, but he worked very well for the club and never gave me any problems. Davy Hay was wonderful in that promotion season. Micky Droy, who was kind of a rebel at the club in many ways – I'd put Stevie Wicks in in front of him and explained to him, and he wasn't terribly happy, but I made Micky club captain. And he was a wonderful help.'

Ray and the other youngsters were the best news we had. In the summer of 1975 English youngsters had won the 'Little World Cup' or UEFA Under-18 tournament with four Chelsea players in the squad. 'Yeah, Johnny Sparrow, Stevie Wicks, Tommy Langley and myself. It was a fantastic experience. We beat Finland 1–0 in the final, and it was out of this world for us Chelsea boys. You went away at the end of the year to Switzerland, stayed on Lake Lucerne and it was 75 degrees and snow-capped mountains. And you thought you'd arrived. We trained and we played and it was just a marvellous experience.

'One minute you think, "Well, I'm going to give it my best shot, do everything properly, eat right, sleep right, don't go out," and then you look round and think, "How the hell am I going to take his place by the way?" Naturally, once you've had a bit of success you want a little bit more. I got a little bit of Under-23 recognition, – although it was only one game against Portugal at Selhurst Park – and that was great. Again, you're stepping into another sphere: Trevor Francis was in there, Peter Taylor, Brian Greenhoff. And again, I was thinking, "Christ, what am I doing here?"'

Another season was spent in the lower division; Ray didn't miss a game, and top-scored with 12. But the 1976–77 campaign was promising from the outset. 'After the first year,' says Eddie, 'I talked about how I'd like the players to be a bit more aggressive. They weren't brought up at a Fourth Division team to kick the ball half the field. All these kids were brought up to play the game, to pass the ball – the most important thing in the game – and to do it with quality. And in the Second Division they came up against a little bit of the hard, physical side of the game. And it hurt. So we talked about it and I told them, "You're going to have to kick a bit of ass here. This is part of the game, we're going to have to stand up to it.

And give a little bit back." I didn't make a big fuss about it, but by the time we got to the second season, they were such wonderful professionals, these kids, that they'd picked it up themselves, and nobody was going to push them around.'

In Eddie's new system, young skipper Ray was tried out in a role that Dennis Wise, Matt Le Tissier and others have fulfilled more recently: in 'the hole' just behind the forwards. It was something like Ossie's occasional position in his later years. 'I put Butch in a position that nobody really knew before. I tucked him in behind a 4-3-1-2. And it worked wonderfully well.'

'Funny one that,' says Ray. 'It worked for the first half of the season, but when you came to play them a second time, they'd sussed it out, and then I had the old man-to-man marking, and it didn't really turn out the way I'd have liked it. But the first half of the season I was just swanning it. People saying, "Well, where's he playing then?" I was just playing free really.' Eddie points out that when teams placed a man-marker on Ray it created gaps elsewhere. 'We found it to be very successful with him. I didn't want him to be running around marking people anyway, except when it mattered, but I've always felt that to get the best out of footballers, you play to their strengths. Use their strengths and then build up their weaknesses. And with Butch, I gave him a free hand. He didn't have to be picking up Billy Bremner for 90 minutes, you know what I'm saying?'

'It was great,' enthuses Ray. 'I was scoring a few goals, creating a few goals. But when the second half of the season came around I was thinking, "Christ, this is a different world, this." You start thinking a lot more where to be, where to go, how to lose this fellow. I was perfectly happy there. Dave always saw me more as a holder, to hit passes, bring people into the game. Eddie saw me as a scorer and a creator. So I wasn't really bothered; so long as the team won, I didn't give a monkey's where I played.'

'I've always believed in motivation,' says Eddie, 'and telling the guys that I really appreciate their efforts. And the kids responded that way. I didn't shout and scream at them. I may have lost my temper a couple of times, but not very often. I think more than anything I was kind to them.' The team responded to Eddie's enthusiasm and his young skipper's obvious talent. Ray was ever-present again that season, and notched nine goals. He had also made his England debut, against Italy in 1975, and closed the season as London Footballer of the Year and Chelsea Player of the Year. The 'Butch' bandwagon was rolling.

'We were wiping the floor with teams,' says Ray. 'There was a gradual build-up of confidence, and there was this feeling, "No one's going to touch us now, we're going to do it." I think we had that about us, and I think that's what comes through youth.' Ray was making and scoring: there was the audacious back-heel that laid on Jock Finnieston's second against Oldham; there was the Boxing Day victory over Fulham, watched by 55,000; and there were wonderful victories and sensational performances.

We demolished lowly Hereford in a way we have rarely dealt with minnows before or since. January 1, pissing down, and the skipper capped a virtuoso show (dressed in very 'Butch' black gloves) with a wondrous chip. 'I can see it now. It was from quite a way out – 30 yards or so – and we beat them 5–1. I've forgotten what it's like to win 5–1.' But the first real impact occurred just over a month earlier. The rampant Blues stormed into an experienced Southampton side and ran out 3–1 winners, watched by 42,654. Ray was ecstatic: 'For the first time the atmosphere at the Bridge was like it used to be in the days when I was on the terraces cheering Peter Osgood, Alan Hudson and Charlie Cooke. For the first time as a player the crowd made me go cold. It was the most inspiring thing I've ever known.'

Ray created both man-of-the-match Finnieston's goals, and grabbed one himself, drawing the keeper and slotting it past him. Grumpy Mike Langley wrote: 'Butch Wilkins did everything for Chelsea except sell programmes and pump up the match ball.'

'God,' Ray laughs, 'getting that from Mike must have been something. That must be the only good thing he's ever written. Someone mentioned this game to me the other day; they said it was the best game of football they'd seen for years. We didn't play well in the first half, but in the second half we absolutely thrashed them.' Bob Wilson cited the match as the best 90-minute performance he'd seen that season – Chelsea reminded him of Man United when they came up and stormed the First Division a few years earlier. Did Chelsea feel the same way? 'I think we all felt we could go a long way, yeah.'

Ray was making most of the advances, though: an England regular at 20, Player of the Year again. 'To be an England player in the Second Division just showed what stature Chelsea had,' says Ray, modestly. 'Lots of other players have been England quality in the Second Division, but haven't been selected. And I think it's purely and simply because of the club they play for. I played for a big club in Chelsea, and I think you get the recognition.'

Ray had assumed the role vacated by Alan Hudson with relish. The classic midfield general, old head on young shoulders, he would point to his team-mates where to go, direct them, in a way we did not see again until Ruud Gullit arrived. 'I think that's the way I always played, through schoolboy football, through all levels. It's just natural. I think once you're on a football field you're a totally different person. When I'm out there, I'm a completely different person: arrogant, 'orrible sod. I shout all the time; don't stop. At QPR, we were all trying to help Les Ferdinand score goals, and if he missed one it would be, "Oh, unlucky Les." And I'd say, "Unlucky? Get the effing ball in the net." And he'd look at me and scowl as if he was thinking, you old sod. And then we'd have a grin. I'm at home out there on the field: you know your capabilities, you know what you can do. And that's where you're at your most confident.'

There were moments in that 1976–77 season when that assurance was tested. Luton and Charlton both beat us 4–0. And then there was the replay against Southampton – sheeting rain again – in the Cup . . .

'On a bloody mud patch,' says Ray. 'I remember it. We lost 3–0. We should have murdered them; we should have beaten them on the Saturday four days earlier. Played them at The Dell and had loads of chances to finish them off; 1–1. There was about a foot of mud. I remember the feeling after the bloody game too! It was the fifth round, and it was there for us. Southampton were the holders, and I remember seeing Arsenal, who beat Southampton, beat Orient at Stamford Bridge. That should have been us. They had Channon, Ossie, Ted McDougall, a lot of experience. We blew up towards the end. Couldn't handle it. The game probably got to us a little bit, and we blew it.

'In the dressing-room afterwards was probably one of the worst moments, because we felt we had something, and we felt we should have already won at theirs. Eddie was naturally deflated, but did his best to pick us back up again. You have to keep on cracking away, unfortunately – it was nice to pack up and bugger off, but that wasn't the case. There are times when you have self-doubt, obviously, but that's inevitable in any walk of life. I think Eddie might have hit it on the head: perhaps we weren't quite ready to make that step, which is sad.'

After the disappointment of Southampton, Eddie was crestfallen: 'We lacked the maturity to slow things down,' he said. Privately, he began to doubt then that the team was strong enough to challenge the best, but publicly he was optimistic. 'It doesn't make sense to blame your players,' he says – perhaps another lesson learned from The Doc's mistakes. 'You have to be honest sometimes and say coaches don't win games, really, players win games, no matter how good you are. Coaches don't get promotion, players get promotion. Coaches don't win cups, players win cups.'

There was also the matter of Chelsea's style. The fast passing and bustling running was unsuited to poor pitches – and some canny opponents. But you have to say it was exhilarating to watch. 'Pass, move,' says Ray. 'There was lots of good football played. Always, when you're playing football as we played it then, you're having so many touches of the ball and you're winning; never get fatigue when you're winning. All you want to do is play with the ball. And we never gave it to the opposition, so we didn't have to work to get it back. All the work we did was with the ball, so it was an absolute pleasure.

'But I've got to be perfectly honest. When I played in there with Ray Lew, I never had to make a tackle. People often said to me, "It's a Bremner-Giles." Lew was doing all the destroying; I was getting all the headlines. I felt immensely sorry for Lew, because there were games he played where he was just brilliant for the team and you'd think, "How did he make that tackle?" And all of a sudden the ball's landed at my feet, I've got no one round me and someone's made a run, and we score. And it's all down to me. But they seem to forget that Lewie did all the donkey-work. I owe a lot of my success at that time to Ray Lew.'

Gary Locke was a fine performer in the promotion season. And Jock Finnieston scored hatfuls. 'He didn't get spectacular goals,' says Ray, 'but bloody hell. I said to him the other night, "I don't think you ever hit the bloody net did you?" It was either the stanchion and it came out or it bobbled in there and never hit the net. But it's imperative you have someone who can stick the ball in the net.'

Of the seniors, David Hay was enjoying the sort of form Chelsea paid record money for in 1974. And old-stagers Bonetti and Harris were contributing their bit. 'Peter was always a great influence on the lads, a super professional. Very confident guy, nothing fazes him. To have Catty about . . . A football club is determined by its senior pros, as far as I'm concerned. If you've got good senior pros at a club, whether they're playing or not, you've got a chance, because they'll bring on good habits in the younger blokes.'

Success brought the best spirit in the camp for years: 'If anything happened on the field, everyone was in – not fighting, but you look after your own. It didn't matter who got it: Ronnie Harris, or Kenny Swain up the front. You tried to protect him. That's what team spirit is all about. Ron always looked after the lads, and if anyone took liberties with them he was the first in there. I can remember he tried to sort me out in one of them things. He was like a dad to us on the field. And we always used to have a real laugh coming back. Obviously we were doing quite well, so it was always very boisterous on the coach. It was at a time when you could have a can of beer on the coach as well. But we used to come back from an away game, and everyone would be across at the Rising Sun: girlfriends, friends as well. All buddies together, just having a bit of fun. And then you'd just disperse, go for something to eat and away you go. It was just turning up and training, there was never any effort. It was always a pleasure to be there.'

By September we were top, and even a worrying slide-off couldn't derail the Chelsea express. Eddie McCreadie's press conference after the brilliant 1–1 draw at Molineux that clinched promotion with Ray pre-eminent was typically upbeat: 'We're going to shock a few people next season. We're not going up to the First Division to survive. We're going to attack. Chelsea will help make football tick again.'

'When you think about that last game against Hull,' recalls Ray, 'the end of our promotion season, there were 44,000 at Stamford Bridge, and it was stopped about eight times through punters running on to the field. I was frightened someone was going to get another goal, because if we scored again the game might never have got to the end! Chelsea was always a monster club. And when you think 44,000 for a Second Division team . . . I think outside of London, where would you get that – Manchester? Liverpool? It was just phenomenal. The fans, the players . . . we were desperate to get back in there.'

That season, in fact, Chelsea merchandising was the third best-selling in the country after Liverpool and Man United. Everything set fair for calm, sunny waters. Then, typically, disaster was clutched from the jaws of victory. Eddie McCreadie couldn't find agreement with the club over a contract in the summer and the man who took us up was shamefully let go. 'I'd been there a long time,' says Eddie McCreadie. 'I'd given good service to the club, and after what I'd been through there, they're telling me, "Well, we can't give you a contract." And, at the same time, every day for two weeks after that season finished, I've got players in my office. They said, "You'll never get Ray Wilkins bound to a contract." And I said to Ray, "I've got to discuss a contract with you." And he said to me, "You put in there what you think. I'll sign it."'

'We were all very sad,' remembers Ray. 'Supporters, players, everyone alike. Because Eddie was such a likeable guy, and it was like taking someone away who was a father-figure. And of course it comes out later what the reasons were, or what the so-called reasons were, and then you start to think, good grief, what's it all about? But they'd obviously set out a policy at Chelsea and it was one that couldn't meet Eddie's requirements, which was a little unfortunate. He'll still be remembered fondly at Chelsea.'

The return to the First Division in 1977 saw our one-time England right-back Ken Shellito in charge. In October 1976 Chelsea had fielded a side of ten former juniors and one amateur, Kenny Swain – a team that cost nothing. Ken had the responsibility of bringing many of them through. 'One to one, technical work, he was just different class,' says Ray. But, perhaps mindful of the fraying edge of the McCreadie system in the promotion campaign, Ken reassessed. 'Well, we had a winning formula,' says Ray, 'and we didn't really take it on from there . . . I think when we went up, we obviously had to think, "Well, hang on a minute, we're now playing against the business." So Ken thought we'd have to adjust to the situation.'

The manager reversed the two Rays' roles, pushing Lewie forward and pegging the skipper back. 'We were playing against a better category of player, so you obviously have to be wary of what they're going to do to you as well as what you're going to do to them. When we were playing in '76, you felt we would always outscore teams. And that's where we would win the game.'

With no money available again, the suit was cut according to available cloth. Twenty-nine of the 36 playing staff lined up in 1977–78 were former juniors. With Finnieston injured, a forward line of Trevor Aylott and Tommy Langley wasn't likely to frighten defenders for long. Beating Wolves 3–1 away flattered to deceive. By Christmas, Trevor's not-so-clever tally was two; gangling Langers had notched three. That made Ray, now playing in a holding midfield role, equal top scorer. 'Really? Good grief!,' he frowns. 'That says it all. You're naturally going to struggle, aren't you? It was very, very sad.'

Bill Garner's single goal at Old Trafford was a rare (and, in retrospect, predictable) ray of light in a torrid two years. At least there was some continuity in Petar Borota replacing The Cat – he gave everyone kittens. 'He was a case, Petar,' laughs Ray. 'I remember a game up at Nottingham Forest; we were about 6–1 down, and when the sixth went in I looked up at the scoreboard and the clock said 70 minutes. I thought, "Good grief, this could be horrendous." He was an eccentric; may have been one of the first keepers to come up for corners. Ever such a good bloke; trained like a sack, honestly. Worked his socks off. Used to wear studs about two inches long – I'm sure they were to bump his height up a bit: "How tall are you?" "Six foot three." Great physique, very agile. But for our football perhaps a bit eccentric, especially when you've had Catty in goal and John Phillips.'

The abuse of Ray's brother Graham became intolerable. A talented, accident-prone player, he'd popped his cork early on by scoring two own goals at Burnden Park to gift promotion rivals Bolton a 2–1 win. Dickie Davies announced the result on *World of Sport* and could hardly contain his mirth. Chelsea fans don't forget moments like that. Especially in adversity. 'Sometimes they gave him a little bit of abuse that was totally out of order,' says Ray. 'He was very skilful; had two great feet. Lacked confidence – and he was the older brother, which was very sad. I remember I went along for a trial one night to play for Hayes Boys team a year above my age group, and Graham came along to watch. Then some guy hadn't turned up. So it was, "Graham, have you got your boots?"'

"'Yeah, I've got me boots here."

"'Have a game."

'He got in the bloody team and I didn't! But it was tough with two of us, because if he was having a hard time I'd worry about him, and if I was playing poorly he'd worry about me. You've just got to try and keep your pecker up.

'It was like it was when I was going through a torrid time at Chelsea. It was 1978. And I was on valium, the lot, because I couldn't handle it. I had the injuries, a groin strain . . . some bad times. And it was Graham who kept talking me round, helped me through it. I think I missed a penalty against Bolton, and coming off down that tunnel . . . my goodness, it was just horrendous. So from one great season where everyone was so elated, the next season was pretty desperate stuff. I think we all took a little bit of abuse that year if the truth be known. And the only thing you can say when people give you abuse is that they care. They don't go there just to give you abuse because they don't like you. If you muck up, their club has lost.'

The squad wasn't up to the challenge even with the sporadic Clive Walker breaking through. Ken Shellito resigned at Christmas 1978. Danny Blanchflower took over – one of the Chelsea board's increasingly bizarre decisions. Two years in the top flight was drawing to a close and Ray was suffering. 'Danny pulled me about a month beforehand and said that he thought it was best for everyone concerned – God bless him – and he just put it to the board that they should let me go. Obviously at the time I didn't fancy that at all. Because I was with my mates. We'd gone down, and I wanted to help come straight back up again, like we had before. Then once Man U came in for me, there was not much of a decision to make.

'A lot of people put two and two together, with Dave being there, that it might be Manchester United. But it was after the Cup final, Man U–Arsenal, that Dave came in. I was very sad to leave. I didn't really want to leave. I love London, and I'd only just got married and we were very, very happy. And although we'd just gone down, we felt that we could get back up. Looking back, I'm pleased I didn't ask for a move, because I go back now and there's a pleasant reception. When I meet fans they ask me if I wanted to go, which is natural – typical Chelsea support. But Danny made it clear he didn't want me around, and he got lots of money at the time: £825,000 was a few bob.'

Blanchflower appeared to believe the squad needed rebuilding – without our talismanic England star. He bought misfits and mavericks. By September 1979 we were languishing in our worst-ever League position, 18th in the Second Division. His replacement by Geoff Hurst and Bobby Gould left little cause for optimism. They avoided the drop to the Third (uncharted territory for the club), but the euphoria of 1977 seemed a long way off as storm clouds gathered at the close of the decade. Someone had left the cake out in the rain. Again.

Ray still enjoys himself on returns to his second home. Just a shame that QPR saw fit to dispense with his services. The warm reception afforded him shows the affection in which he is still held, and perhaps a sense that he was let down as much as we were. 'The place is dying for a little bit of success,' he notes. 'I was talking to Matthew Harding the other day, and he was saying that up at Aston Villa in the semi-final against Man U the support was just unbelievable, like a home game. I just hope they can be patient. You know they've had to be patient for a long time, and I just hope they can keep it up a little longer.'

8

Patsy

In the early '80s, as the nightmare end of the Mears empire was played out before our incredulous eyes – as Chelsea looked to have been sold off for flats and houses, mirrored by mostly desperate, meaningless activity on the pitch– we wondered whether we'd ever be a proper football club again. The dash and vigour of Docherty's Diamonds, the virtuosity and glamour of the Sexton years . . . and now this: Geoff Hurst and Bobby Gould's hapless hoofers. I give you Alan Mayes, Dennis Rofe, John Sitton . . .

Thankfully, an odd sort of saviour appeared for the most pressing problem in April 1982. He was bumptious, wilful, aggressive, but a football man and a proven businessman; a man for that decade. Make no mistake – Ken Bates, for all his perceived faults, saved Chelsea Football Club. And in charge of the footballing front from 1981, we finally had, if not a football genius, then the closest thing for almost a decade: John Neal. The pensive, unassuming north-easterner, and his vital assistant Ian McNeill, set about restoring pride in the great old name of Chelsea. There were omens: in 1982 we tonked Champions of Europe Liverpool 2–0 in the FA Cup. Ha!

Then, at the close of the following season, while Leslie Mears was flogging the family silverware (or selling his shares) to a property developer, John Neal began assembling a fantastically cheap and able squad. Speedie, Spackman, Dixon, Niedzwiecki, McLaughlin, latterly Mickey Thomas . . . and one other who was worth the £500,000 total expenditure on his own: the wee wizard, Pat Nevin.

On the surface, the Glaswegian was an unlikely footballer, too cerebral for the laddish, anti-intellectual atmosphere of the great game. And he recognises the fact. 'My whole career,' he marvels, 'is one succession of flukes after another. I can think of odd decisions which, if I hadn't made, would have meant I would never have got into football. I stopped playing football when I was 16 because Celtic didn't want me as a pro. And then this boys' club asked me to go along and one of my mates said, "Ach, go and play a couple of games." So one game we're playing and my mate, just as a sideline, just said, "Right, bet you a fiver you can't score."

"Fiver? No problem."

"Yeah, but you need to beat four men."

"All right. Fiver it is." Took the bet, got the ball. Four men. Goal. And I was centre-midfield at that time – I never played on the wing before Chelsea. And as I walked off the pitch this guy grabbed me. "You. Come 'ere."

"What?"

'He says, "What was all that about?"

'I just told him about the bet and said it was just four guys, nothing special. It turned out that was Craig Brown. And the other team I was playing was Clyde. I didn't know who Craig Brown was. I didn't know it was Clyde. When he told me I thought it was the Under-18s or something. And he said, "That was our first team you just took the piss out of. You'll sign for us then."

"I'm not interested; I don't like playing football."

'And he goes, "What are you doing then?"

"I'm going to college, doing a degree."

"Well, while you're doing that we'll pay you X amount a week."

"All right."

'And that happy accident of somebody winding me up, me being in a fucking mood, and doing it, led to me playing for Clyde and then signing for Chelsea. Craig Brown gave me ten, 15 caps when he became the Scotland manager.

'It was flukes with Chelsea as well. I'd been saying no to Chelsea for nearly a year. Ian McNeill contacted me a couple of times. But I was having the time of my life in Glasgow, and I wasn't interested. And he just kept on badgering and badgering. And in the end I just took it as a two-year sabbatical from my college course. And it's never stopped since that two years.

'I went down to Chelsea and I arrived at Euston Station to be met by Gwyn Williams. I was really quite strong-willed, and I'd been promised something and I was told I wouldn't get it. And I said, "Right, when's the next train home . . .?" Gwyn Williams was like, "No, no, no . . ." He'd never come across anybody with this attitude. He tried to make it up with me: "Calm down, calm down. You'll lose your chance to play professional football."

"So what?" I think Gwyn was, like: "Fucking hell – this boy doesn't give a shite, he's got the wrong attitude."

'I was asked by Ian MacNeill to go and pick him up,' recalls Gwyn, 'and I said, "What will he look like?" Ian said, "He'll be a smart, immaculate, well-dressed young man." And after looking round

Euston Station for half an hour and not finding him, I eventually said to the scruffiest geezer sitting in the station with his legs crossed, "Scuse me, you wouldn't happen to be Pat Nevin by any chance, would you?" And he went. "That's me."

'He was a great character. I'd see him doing the tricks in the dressing-room, sitting down, juggling the ball, going in and out of the cones with the ball as quick as anybody could have a straight run. He was dedicated, worked hard. Wanted to go back in the afternoon and do more. When the kids were training he'd often ask to go and train with them, and he was a great example because he worked hard. He didn't take liberties, didn't have a carefree attitude. He was excellent, and deserved everything he got out of the game. And I have great respect for how his family and his father supported him. His father was a railway worker and he'd get that overnight train down, irrespective of the weather, week-in, week-out, and come to watch Pat, home or away. He'd be there every Saturday. And after the game, he'd go back to the station, back to Glasgow.' Nevin senior bought him his first proper kit aged eight. It was blue and white. 'That's Rangers!' kids would chide Celtic-supporting Pat. 'No,' he'd insist, 'it's Chelsea!' And it was Chelsea for the major part of his career.

'When Pat first came here,' says Gwyn, 'Craig Brown, who is now the Scottish team manager, was manager of Clyde. He was livid because we'd pinched him for thirty grand or fifty-five grand or something and he was livid. And he was on twenty-five pounds a week as a part-timer at Clyde and Craig had offered him five pounds a week more, and thought that entitled him to two hundred and fifty grand.'

Chelsea recognised that Pat was a little different, and so, through Kate Hooey, now an MP, arranged a further education course. With all the other distractions of London, the course was the first casualty as soon as he made the first team after a few weeks. People soon drew comparisons with that other gifted Scot, Charlie Cooke, but Pat was more consistent than the mercurial, mustachioed St Monancian. The only other thing they had in common was that they both lived in the Stamford Bridge Café on the Fulham Road. Cookie would pop in on his way back from clubbing, just before training. Pat was there all the time. 'If the fans ever wanted to see me I was in there,' says Pat. 'Day and night.'

Not even fry-ups could bulk up the Glaswegian's slight frame, but his balance and technique more than compensated. 'People often say, "God, he's gifted." No gift, all work. All pure work. My father was a pretty good coach. Read quite a lot about football and about techniques. And the other thing was this Jimmy Johnstone book, because he showed you a couple of tips about dribbling with cones, which I took to the extreme. Eventually you know where the ball is. You're looking everywhere, but you know that that ball is gonna stick at your feet. If I don't do that with the ball and the dribbling, it gets ragged. But I adapted it myself, put one cone there and another there, like a slalom – the hard way, the outside. You end up dragging the ball, which is where that "teasing" comes from: you leave the ball there, and as they come in there's a long drag, one long touch. I'd seen this method and I'd adapted it for myself.

'At my first training session down at Aberystwyth, I was playing centre-forward, so they played the ball up to me, and Micky Droy came up behind. And there's a certain turn where you're leaning your body that way and dragging the ball that way and as soon as you feel the person move that way – turn, low centre of gravity, zip round. And I left Micky and I'm way over there. And you could just hear Micky say, "Fuckin' 'ell, I'm too old for this game." And it was a real moment of joy. And you could see them all going, "what?"

'I was very organised. I taped most of the games – although sadly for the first two or three years that wasn't many, because Batesy wouldn't let the cameras in. But I taped most of the games. Primarily for mistakes, where I'm going wrong, but also to see what things worked and why they worked. And there are certain things that I thought, "Hey, wait a minute, I've not done that for a while," and I went back to practise them. I tried to copy a move Roy Wegerle used and I nearly broke my ankle: it was too brilliant. Now and again there's the odd thing I have totally copied, like the Beardsley shimmy. I never used to do that; it's totally learned from him. Later Andy Roxburgh gave me a video by the Dutchman Coerver. And it was all the techniques I'd been doing plus about 100 more. And I went, why was this not available to me five years ago? I could have lived in this video. If I was a kid now, I would be watching that video, going out practising.' (Coincidentally, Charlie Cooke is a representative of Coerver Coaching in the States.)

Meanwhile, John McNeill was perhaps most relieved that Pat so immediately impressed. 'He put his job on the line over me,' says Pat. 'Batesy said, "We're going to spend that on him? Is he going to make it?" Ian said yes. "Are you sure? Would you stake your job on it?" "Yes." Thank goodness for Ian.'

Pat joined a Second Division side virtually hand-sculpted by John Neal. 'He had a talent that not many managers had. Anyone can spot Vialli, to be honest. But not everybody can go to the Scottish Second Division and spot somebody for 95 grand as he did. He put that team together for a cost that was just hilarious. He picked them and grouped them together well. It's this team dynamic thing; I think he understood that. He was a brilliant man-manager, as far as I could see. He knew how to man-manage all these different people. He knew how to deal with David Speedie, and he also knew how to deal with me. He was totally different to me than he was to anyone else in the team. And how he knew to do that I'll never know – no other manager has done that before or since.

'I've never told anyone this: the first training session, John Neal organised a competition. Put these cones out. "Right lads, we'll have a race. See the cones: dribble there, dribble back, dribble there, and dribble back again. First to finish." So I beat them by about a lap. And I caught John Neal's eye and he was sitting there sniggering, and you could see he's thinking, "That'll show these buggers that the boy can play a bit."

'After three or four games in the Chelsea first team, when I was a young man trying to come through, he gave a team-talk and went through his tactics. And I was sitting, not even watching him, and he said, "Go on there and give the ball to Pat and we'll win." I was sort of taken aback. The rest of them looked at me. How did he know I wouldn't crumble under the pressure? How did he know that I would respond to that? It was a lovely feeling of total belief in me. I've never had that anywhere else. He left me alone most of the time and he would never tell me what to do, ever. And he never said why he didn't tell me. And it's so stupid to think since then how many managers and people have tried to coach me. He never once tried to do any coaching with me. Years later I caught up with him and he said, "I had a lot, but I didn't have many like you."

'"What d'you mean? Fannied about a bit?"

'"No, no. You're intelligent. And you had sense."

'I said, "Ach, be serious." But he said, "Football things. You read things in the games, you read people within the games and you knew when you were needed. I could see that from the start with you."

'Everyone who was watching Chelsea at the time just thought I was a mazy dribbler. That's not how John saw me. He could see the other things, the other ways that I looked at it. And he'd spotted that in the early years I had Johnny Hollins playing behind me, and I spent huge amounts of time helping him out during the games, tackling back, covering. Very few people ever mentioned it. John Neal never told me to do it. Holly neither. I just knew that was the thing to do.

'Then on top of that, the backing that the fans gave me was terrific. I was just totally confident. Off the field, you would see no confidence at all. You just had to ask me, if you met me, to talk about football, and I was "no good" there, I was "shite" there . . . I can remember half a dozen games out of maybe 700 that I like. I can remember walking away or driving away, feeling good, smiling to myself.'

An early milestone was the drubbing of fellow promotion hopefuls Newcastle United, 4–0. 'A lot of people talk to me about that game,' he smiles, 'and apparently it was a kind of a breakthrough game; things kind of turned for me with the fans. They sang my name. I tended to thinking of my footballing self in the third person. I couldn't really take it in, although there were a lot of nice things being written in the papers. I don't know what sort of a buzz other people get from it, but it had no effect on me.

'But the 4–0 game had two effects. Kevin Keegan was really nice about me after the game; he said a lot of good things about me. And that had a wee impact: "I can't believe it, he rates me." More importantly than playing well that day and fans liking me, I learned a huge lesson that has stayed with me my whole career. We hammered Newcastle, everyone played well, and I remember saying to Bummers – we were 2–0 up – "If we get a goal in the second half, I am just going to take the mick, I am just going to enjoy myself."

'And from saying that, the first time we had them in trouble Kerry scored and I said, "Right, let's have fun now." And I did. And it's very well known that since then I've been able to "showboat" like that. And it wasn't to take the mickey out of other people, it was to enjoy myself, express myself and let people enjoy being entertained. At the end Keegan came over and he said, "I'm really impressed with you. I'm really impressed with what you did." And I'm thinking, "Not half as impressed as I am with you, mate." Because there he was, 34, 35 years old, playing for Newcastle in the Second Division, and he worked harder than anyone else that day. Four–nil and he gave nothing. Brilliant. And his attitude, it just underlined how never, whatever I do in this game, will I change this attitude. Fans, they're not conned, they watch week-in, week-out, and when they see someone like that they accept him. I will never stroll about, do a Stoichkov or a Hagi. I will do what Keegan did then, because I admire that.'

The fans were affectionate. One woman – who shall remain nameless – sent Pat a recipe a day. 'She helped me a lot. She doesn't know how much. A lot of fans of that intelligence did.' But it wasn't all plain sailing. From the outset Pat realised that professional football was a rum old game. 'The first game of that 1983–84 season was against Derby County. And I played for the reserves at Luton

Town. I'd just sat my final-year exams and said to Chelsea that I couldn't play. So I came down on the Friday overnight train and I got no sleep. Tony McAndrew and myself were playing and we won 2–0. And news floated through that the first team had won 5–0. And I went, "Yes!" And Tony McAndrew went, "Yes!" And the rest of them went, "Fuck."

'And it was at that moment I realised that some have a different attitude to the game. Honest to God, I've never – even when I've felt I've been cheated and should have been playing, which has happened a lot – I've never wanted my team to be beaten. It's not the way I learned, about life, about football. When the team spirit is good you can see it on the park; you can just see it. It's visible: the way people work with each other, the way people do things to each other, cover each other, not blame each other.'

Once Pat had made the first-team grade, there were other things to contend with – such as David Speedie. 'We hated each other,' Pat grins. 'Absolutely despised each other. We were very opposite characters. He was really volatile, and I was very different – really quite laid back. But I didn't like his methods of trying to be in control of me and my play. And I knew why he was doing it, because he wanted the ball as often as possible – he wanted the ball more than Kerry! It went on for a long time, but what made it particularly difficult was that my understanding with David was probably better than the understanding I had with any other player in my life.

'I knew where he was all the time. And I knew where he was going to go. He was always frustrated because sometimes I didn't play the ball where I knew he was going to go because I'd seen something else. He knew I'd seen it and that's why he got upset with me. A couple of things changed it. After a few years we actually became very good mates. We kind of openly discussed it. We had a big blazing argument with Ernie Walley in John Hollins's time. I think we could have done without Ernie being there, to be honest – he didn't add any depth to the conversation! And then we both hated each other and got called up for the Scotland squad. So they thought, "Two Chelsea players – put them in together for four days!" Well, we sat down and we talked. And we got to know where each other was coming from. And finally clicked.

'He was more a one-track mind. He had tunnel vision as to what he wanted. Whereas I had, I hope, a wider kind of view of everything, from life to the way people should treat each other. He was just a football player.'

The other big problem was Pat's. 'In those days, right at the start, I had a bad attitude towards footballers. I had little respect for them. My peer group was very different from theirs. I just didn't have anything in common with them and I didn't like some of the ways in which they behaved. But hopefully, I've matured a wee bit. A couple of years on I began to realise that I did respect them for what they did, and what they coped with.

'I suppose I was a character, or I am a character, never had to have any dealings with them. I was just me all the time. I don't care whether I'm in a football club or nightclub; I'll be me. When people go into a group, they maybe alter a little bit, there's a bit of accommodation. I made absolutely no attempt. Never argued back. Just smiled. If you're confident in who you are and what you are, you don't argue with someone to justify yourself. I didn't feel I had to justify myself; I still don't. Certain people in the Chelsea team changed my attitude and have shaped it since then. (It's strange: I'm saying all this and I'm now the chairman of the players union! – all this has completely turned upside-down.) I have respect for very unusual people really; respect because of knowing what they're doing, and the wider effect. Tony McAndrew left Chelsea, and Chelsea died for a while. The team spirit fell apart.'

Now who would have thought that? 'Exactly. As far as I was concerned he was the most important person at the club. I was always interested in group dynamic stuff and all that. I was like an outsider inside there. I was kind of looking at it as a study for me as well, the first couple of years. And he'd get slaughtered, because the fans were hammering him. Now and again I'd tell people, "He's great Tony, because he does this, does that . . ." But he was always the scapegoat. I liked him as a player but I can understand why people didn't. He held others in check who needed to be held. He was strong enough; you hear this phrase to "do the right thing". And he was the kind of, not father-figure, but "liked-uncle" figure for the players at the club.

'And I found it interesting that the fans all loved the one or two who were maybe bad influences, and they hated this one guy who was probably more important to the club than anyone else. And I began to respect how he coped with that sort of stick knowing, himself, as he must have known, that he was important, that he was holding the group together, shaping it in many ways.

'And then other people affected me, like Rougvie. When Doug came down, I think that was the turning-point: I became pro-footballers after knowing Doug Rougvie. I liked the man – nice big daft Scotsman. Lovely fella. I remember I tried to tackle him once in training. It was like trying to tackle a lorry. But it was hard; it made me very upset. He loved his football at Aberdeen, where he was a cult figure and Scottish Footballer of the Year. They knew there he wasn't going to do anything except tear into the boys he's playing against and work hard. And he came down to Chelsea, and if the fans had just formed the right opinion, there's a good chance he would've turned into a cult hero like Joey Jones or Micky Droy.'

But Doug Rougvie was sold to us as the finest footballer the European Champions had. He had pace, but didn't always make the best decisions. Pat played in perhaps the most exciting match in recent memory, the comeback from 3–0 down against Sheffield Wednesday in the Cup at Hillsborough in 1984. It was supersub Paul Canoville's glory night, as he scored twice and we stormed back to lead 4–3 with minutes remaining. Then the big Scotsman was caught out of position, made a, well, flawed challenge in the box, and conceded the penalty. You could see the disappointment on his face. But, again, Blues fans don't forget things like that. It erased the loving memory of playing snowballs with him after we dispensed with Shrewsbury 1–0 in the Cup.

'So the fans turned on him. I felt no pressure, never did. But I remember this one day – Dougie's getting slaughtered by the fans, really the most vicious you could imagine: "Fuck off back, you Scottish bastard" and all that. And his wife is there in the stand, crying her eyes out, because he'd left Aberdeen, and home, and Scotland, and lovely warm people and come down to that. To me Chelsea fans were family, brilliant – but to him . . .

'And he handled himself so well, and he dealt with the pressure so well – most of the time. I loved that dignity; the strength of character that coped. He coped with it because of his family, and because it was his job and money. I remember writing an article about how you come home after a bad day at work and 40,000 people slaughtering you for your mistake, and then some smart-ass on the telly goes on to the rest of the country about what a shit you are. And you think, oh, sod that, I'll read the paper and . . . smart-ass journalists again. And then you go and talk to your wife, but she's crying her eyes out, she's so upset. You go and try and give the children a hug, but they're embarrassed because the kids at school are slaughtering them and it's down to you. And it just goes on and on . . . I'm not saying that happened to Doug. But that can happen. And from then I just thought he deserved respect for what he put up with.'

Pat believes there's more to being a footballer than mere talent. 'At about 15 I got good results in my exams, but it didn't stop some of the lads calling me cabbage: "You're just a vegetable, you are, just playing football, you're thick." But I wasn't thick and they knew I wasn't; it was just that if you're a good footballer you must be thick.

'And there was this teacher who was great. He goes, "I've run these football teams for years. See the best player in my team every year: it's always just about the sharpest guy in the class." It kind of stayed in the back of my mind and then I realised when I got into football, the vast majority are so sharp, and streetwise. Try and spend two or three weeks in a football club and see if you survive. It's absolutely white hot; the stick flying around. Plus you have to deal with all the pressure. How many jobs do you hear about where there's a guy coming into work every day, "Hiya, how you doing? I want your job." And you go to work on a Saturday afternoon and the guy playing against you wants to stop you doing your job.'

Pat's toughest opponents from his Chelsea days were the sharks, the cold assassins. 'People think I should like skilful players,' he says, 'and I do like players like Gullit, that kind of style. But I like Stuart Pearce's total honesty, and I love the fact that you get battered now and again. I remember one time down Stamford Bridge I had a right kicking. Turned round and spun and he's gone whoosh, straight through me. I was lying there rolling about – I've got a big video of it – and he leans down as if to pick me up. And I remember having to turn round and look away. Didn't want it. Because he would give you that; he was cold. I loved that.

'In all the times we played against each other, we never spoke, never shook hands at the end of the game, and we just had a silent kind of respect for each other. I knew that he was going to give me nothing to play with. No weakness in the eyes, or in the personality. Nothing. And I always showed as little pain as possible if I got a bang. I got up, got the ball. No smile, no nothing, no eye contact. Blank. Straight back in there.

'I love that side of football. I love the various psychological tactics people try. I remember when Vinnie Jones came after me. I had the ball and was going towards him. He was saying, "Go on: take me, take me, take me."

'"All right." Straight past him. And as I went past, I took a wee look back and he was laughing. So you knew it was an act, not like Pearce. Never show any weakness – I stole that from Jimmy Johnstone. Read his book when I was younger. Watched him as a kid, playing against Atletico Madrid. Got booted absolutely everywhere, thumped and hammered. Then he'd get the ball and he'd head straight for the player that did it: "I'm not frightened of you. I'm not going to worry about you. You'd better worry that if I get round you and you bring me down, you're going to get booked."

'I think that's dead interesting, all those relationships. At Chelsea I tried to make sense of what was going on, and for two or three years I was a complete fan of the writer Albert Camus, a well-known football fanatic who wrote about it brilliantly. I was seeing so much of it in his work, and he understood the traumas that people go through.' Such intellectual pursuits marked the young Scotsman out as different. Once, on the Chelsea coach, he was reading something by Bohemian writer Chekhov. 'At last,' said one of his team-mates, 'you're reading something I recognise – he's the bloke off *Star Trek*, isn't he?'

Pat would speak his mind whatever and, including the time when he slammed Chelsea racists barracking Paul Canoville, the effect was profound. Even the neo-fascists respected his views, occasionally inviting him, politely, to speak at their meetings. 'I suppose that's just me,' he shrugs. 'I'm the worst of things: I tell the truth all the time, and I find it easy. Instead of hiding things, I just go and say what I think. Certainly, that racist thing that started early at Chelsea – when I stood up against that I wasn't making a big stance; I wasn't being a martyr. I'd seen something wrong and I thought I'd say it.

'Maybe some of the players were wary of getting into that. I remember there was one argument that turned into a blazing row between me and, well, the rest of the team. The lads were all pissed, and they thought they'd have a discussion with me about apartheid. I never usually lost my cool, but I went absolutely mental. I look back at it now, and I reckon I was missing the point. They weren't political animals (they were animals in other ways!). They thought that any reason to take the piss out of me was good and I was a wee bit serious-minded . . . and a bit drunk. Which was *very* unusual, to be drunk with the boys. But I look back at the guys with a lot of fondness. People like Patesy. Brilliant humour, really deadpan. There was never any nastiness behind it with Patesy. He was the one who found me hilarious, I think. He just found me a riot with the long words and things that I'd done.

'One classic was this party one night. It was a fancy-dress party and I was a cute wee boy at the time and I dressed up as a schoolgirl. I was lovely! It was a mad party. I'd had a few drinks, and I said to one or two of my mates, "Hey, the Chelsea lads are all having a party. I've got the address here. We'll go along."

'"Aye, great."

'So we went along and knocked on the door: perfectly normal party, everybody with suits on, and I walked in as a schoolgirl! Patesy's story is, "I looked up and I said, 'Cor, she'd have it . . . Oh no, it's Patsy.'" From that point on they just knew I was strange.'

His girlfriend (now his wife) still in Scotland, Pat shared a flat with

NME music writer Adrian Thrills – known in Chelsea circles as Adrian 'Don't-we-all'. Pat was the only team member who lived in London itself. 'Well, I must try and make it sound rougher than it was,' he smiles. 'Glasgow, you had "Easterhouse young team ya bass OK" sprayed on the walls. So I started my gang: the Kensington young team OK. But we were nae mad enough, because there was this other, madder gang called the Young Conservative Club.'

One aspect of Scottish life Pat was pleased to leave behind was the sectarianism. A week before Clyde signed him, he was approached by a fellow he knew to be a Rangers scout. Rangers didn't sign Catholics at the time. (John Spencer was their first.) 'He says, "Brilliant, wee man! Well played there, you scored three!" And I says, "My name's Patrick Kevin Francis Michael."

'"Great, wee man . . . " He did a U-turn, turned round, walked away to a centre-half and said, "Brilliant, big man! Well played . . . " That was David McPherson, who signed for Rangers within weeks. It didn't anger me at all. It was wrong, but he laughed – he knew the joke as well.'

Armed with his passion for Joy Division and the arts, Pat took in the cultural riches of cosmopolitan London. John Neal used to joke that he'd only secured Pat's signature on a new contract once a clause permitting time off for top gigs and the Edinburgh Festival was included. A typical gathering at his place involved an actor, two ballet dancers, Willie the roadsweeper (a confidant of Sir Peter Hall), a dustman, and Simon from indie band the Cocteau Twins. 'It was a weird set in a way. Wildly interesting and unusual.'

For the first season, Pat travelled to training and matches in London by public transport. 'The tubes and buses were too good,' he explains. But a valuable learning experience changed all that. Adrian Thrills used to take Pat to Tottenham games when Chelsea were a division below and not playing, but he failed to point out to Pat the fervent loathing between the two London clubs. 'I'd stand there enjoying the game, watching Hoddle and Hazard. And then afterwards catch the tube home with the Spurs fans. And the next year, obviously, we got promotion, and when we played Tottenham there was all this hatred. So after the game the lads were going in the team bus back across London, and I said, "Och, it'll be quicker going by tube." And it's a long walk down to Seven Sisters tube and amongst all these Tottenham fans, thinking, you were all right with me last time!

'So I'm on the tube, and I had my bag there and my boots in it. And this guy comes up. I could see it coming. He says, "You're Nevin, arncha?"

'I said, "Don't know what you're talking abaht."

'"Nevin, Chelsea!"

'"Nah."

'"Who d'you support then?"

'I went, "Spurs."

'"Oh yeah, who's your favourite player then?"

'What a thick twat! As if I wouldnae know a player. "Micky Hazard." And I'm thinking I'm just about to see a big knife. I thought, I'm in deep shit here. And the train *stops* in the tunnel. And I'm thinking to myself, "If I get out of this I'm buying a car tomorrow."

'Then the tube starts again. And he comes over to me. And the tube comes to a halt, and he's kind of half blocking the door. And I pointed up and went, "What the fuck's that then, man?" and thumped him, battered against the carriage wall – Glasgow upbringing you see – and I sprinted out on to the platform, him after me. And there's two policemen standing there and he got back on the tube. And the next day I went out and got an old banger. Within three months I'd passed my test and bought a wee green MG.'

The first Chelsea footballer Pat bonded with was John Millar, a fellow 'discovery' of Dave Skinner, Chelsea's Glasgow scout (who also tipped us off about Billy Dodds and Craig Burley). He was the only Chelsea connection at Pat's get-togethers. 'John was a lovely-looking boy – all the actresses fancied him. The problem was all the actors did too. I think the friendship arose because I needed someone to train with in the afternoons as well. I'd get bored with the cones after an hour or so. It just so happened John was a left-back, and so was Graeme Le Saux, later. So I dragged him along, and said, "D'you want to do some extra work?"'

John was with Pat on the fateful mid-season trip to Baghdad in March 1986 when Chelsea – sponsored by Gulf Air at the time, you will recall – played the Iraqi national side. 'It was a nightmare,' says Pat. 'Quite a strain, to be honest. I would write Hunter S. Thompson-esque letters to people. John and I were followed in Baghdad because we went for a walk around the bazaar and got lost. I'd missed the point again: you go on these trips for camaraderie; I thought I was a tourist. I just read my books.'

Millar was a talented player, but one nightmare game in the Hollins era against Nottingham Forest ended his career. Ernie Walley said he wanted the young back to mark their quicksilver winger Franz Carr. 'Right,' said John, 'he's got the beating of me for pace, so I'll stand off him.'

'No,' insisted Ernie. 'I want you to mark him tight, right up his arse.' The young Scot didn't stand a chance, and was absolutely roasted. He was sold to Hearts just as Graeme 'Bergerac' Le Saux started.

'Graeme and I are very good mates,' says Pat. 'I had a lot of time for Graeme, really worked hard for him, spent a lot of time on him. We'd go to the theatre and do various things. And he saw that I could talk about the arts, talk about the theatre, talk about anything I liked. And it got good reactions. And he and I would go back out in the afternoon and work for hours on various things.

'The thing I'm most proud of is that Graeme was a left-back and I'd run at him and take him on, and he'd learn how to deal with it when someone ran at him. I never had to teach him a lot, because he was a good, knowledgeable defender, and he was natural. And for the next half an hour we'd turn it round, and he would run at me. And maybe he thought, that's a stupid idea, but I said, "You're here to learn everything. Don't learn one position, learn more positions; you never know what's going to happen. And anyway, I need to learn how to defend." And we'd work really, really hard. I'm not saying I made him into an England player, but certainly his game went in a different direction after that.'

Pat doesn't enjoy reminiscing about old matches. Even his exceptional display at Liverpool in 1987, when we drew 1–1 and had a blatant penalty appeal turned down after he was clobbered in the box, doesn't interest him. 'It's a game of football, it's there to be enjoyed, and it's gone the next day,' he shrugs. 'I remember unusual things. One of the special things that sticks in my mind was at the end of my first season, and I was walking out of Stamford Bridge as usual. After games everyone would be jumping into cars and I'd walk out and off up the Fulham Road, get on the bus, or walk up to the tube station. Sometimes, there were a couple of restaurants on the Fulham Road and I'd pop in there. My dad would be with me sometimes, others I'd be on my own.

'Now and then someone would fall in step and chat to you: "It was good today, wasn't it?" And then they'd drop back, which was great. And one day this old man must have quickened his step to catch up with me. And he chatted away to me: "You're the Nevin boy. I've never been to see Chelsea for five or six years no, but I heard a bit about you so I came down to see you." I went, "Oh, right." This guy got out of his bloody house and came down here and paid money to see me! This is effort! "You had a good game; you made it worth while. Can you remember . . . " and he said something I'd done. "It's been a few years since I've seen that. And you seem to enjoy what you're doing as well. I enjoyed it this afternoon."

'I said, "Great." And I was just about to carry on talking and he went, "Bye. Thanks," and walked away. And I thought to myself, "That's exactly what you want out of football." You don't want anything more. Any journalist can write hyperbole about you, but him saying the few words that he said there meant more than anything. The bottom line, the reason you're doing it, is to entertain people. He may have had a lovely house, or he might have been in a wee house and not that happy, and I may have helped take him out of things for a while. You can't quantify that. Something like that happened and you just got a glimpse.'

Pat's philosophical approach often masked a less serious side of his personality. 'The Sun came and they liked to pigeon-hole me as this curiosity. And I was talking to this bloke and he started on, "Oh, so you like the arts then? So d'you like painting?" I thought, oh, very good. I'll get this bugger back. So he says, "Music as well?"

'"Yes."

'"What bands?"

'So I said, "I really like this girl called Joy Davidson . . ." Back page of The Sun: "Pat Nevin likes Joy Davidson". So he came back to me and he was furious, and said, "Think you're clever, do you?" And I said, "Well, you were treating me like I was stupid, and I just treated you stupidly back." And he says, "Gis your number then."

'"All right . . ." But I was prepared for him, and I gave him the number of "Big, Black and Busty" from Earl's Court tube station. I was having wee bits of fun.

'I also found the media image of me hilarious. I found my own situation funny. It was a scream. People expected me to be talking about the meaning of life all the time. I mean, once they knew me they'd find I actually had a filthy sense of humour, and loved the absurd things in life. Anything that was wild and daft just cracked me. Quite often giggling fits were a problem I had at Chelsea.

'One in particular was after missing that penalty against Man City, this famous one in the Cup that people still talk about. We were 4–0 up and I'd probably had one of my best games. I ballsed-up the penalty, and I turned round thinking, "Don't laugh!" And if you ever see a video of it, you'll see me walking round with my head down, and then you just see the shoulders going like that, and I laughed my head off, and I'm thinking, "If the manager sees me laughing – deep shit. What'll the fans think? That I don't give a shit!" There were only five minutes to go but I was in stitches. "Try to make it look as if it upset you." Patsey was going to try and console me, but he'd seen me laughing and cracked up as well.

'Big Joe McLaughlin came up with a classic once. Batesy used to poke his head round the door before games, say, "Good luck", or tell a joke. He came in one day with a visual gag and made this gesture [Pat rubs his fingers together] and said, "What's this?" And Joe says, "My signing-on fee." Batesy just turned round on his heels and walked out. And we all burst out laughing.

'I have a lot of respect for Batesy. There are a lot of negative things and some people, through certain bad times, slaughter him. But I love Chelsea and still do, and he saved that club. And when someone's done a certain thing, don't forget it if it's a big thing. Chelsea wouldn't be around today were it not for Ken.'

Pat thrived at Chelsea for three seasons, becoming part of the family. 'It kind of sums up how I felt about Chelsea that I remember a game against Liverpool when David Speedie scored the opening goal, and I missed the game through injury, so I did what I thought was the natural thing: I went and stood in the Shed. Not one person said hello. Stood there the whole game and not a word was said. Dozens of people were around me looking and shaking their heads: "No, it'll not be him." I loved it; it was brilliant. And it was fantastic to go and watch a game in the Shed. It was almost a metaphysical thing with me and Stamford Bridge. I was at home with every inch of that ground. I never felt that at any other place.'

Tragically, John Neal's ill-health eventually forced him to relinquish the reins. The new regime was less sympathetic towards Pat's delicate skills. 'He had a great season when we got promoted and the first season back in the top flight,' says Gwyn Williams. 'If it hadn't been for that Heysel tragedy, we would have been in Europe that year, and who knows how far we would have gone. But at the end of that season there was a change and John Hollins took charge. It was a little bit difficult, to say the least, so we had a few problems. The influx of new players unsettled things, and what was looking to be the start of a big, big castle being built was all of a sudden blown away in a matter of months.

'Pat was a player of flair, and I think John was looking for something a little different, but he never got us playing together. The departure of Mickey Thomas and the appearance of Jerry Murphy on the scene completely baffled most punters, I would imagine. But there you are; managers see things differently, and that's how things are done. The makings of that team were quite good, but it was broken up drastically, wasn't it? The defence never really settled down, and to be fair to John Hollins, Eddie Niedzwiecki was a big loss to him.'

Ernie Walley's arrival along with Holly must have appealed to Pat's sense of the absurd. He could be unorthodox. At one training session, he split the squad into two teams and had them play against each other – without a ball. 'Ernie I liked because I like honest people, but we were just totally opposite in our attitudes towards how to play football. So it was quite bad, really, when Ernie came in, because he suggested I should never take more than two touches. I was going through a period when Chelsea didn't want me to do what I liked doing, and that eventually led to me leaving. That was quite difficult to handle and I really wanted to say to the fans, "I hear people saying I'm not having as good a season this time round, but I'm doing what I'm told to do, and if I do what I want to do I'm told I'm going to be subbed."'

When Bobby Campbell took over in 1988 Pat's status rapidly deteriorated. 'I could have sat down and said, "Look, if they'd treated me right they would've got more out of me and I could have happily stayed for ten years,"' says Pat. 'But I felt I would be cheating the fans by slagging the club. I cared, and do now, so much about the Chelsea supporters. There were plenty of ex-Chelsea players and current players going to the papers, moaning about the club that they loved, and I didn't want to be one of them.'

'There were rumblings,' says Gwyn, 'and Pat came to the end of his contract, and rightfully said, "I've had enough of this", and decided to go to Everton. I think we got a more than fair price.'

'It was a terrible end to the season,' says Pat, referring to the dreadful play-off defeat at the hands of Boro which meant relegation. 'And it was upsetting for me because I felt Chelsea fans would finally say I was a rat leaving a sinking ship. If only they knew what had been made clear to me by Bobby Campbell. It was obvious, shall we say, that my presence wasn't crucial to the manager's plans.'

The wee man needn't have worried. We knew where his heart lay. We knew there was nowhere he felt right, more at home, than Stamford Bridge. That's why, when we saw him in our end at Goodison a few months after he'd left Everton, we finally spoke to him in the stand. 'Right in the middle of these 10,000 Chelsea fans,' he laughs. 'Trying to watch the game. And then all of a sudden, the whole end starts singing, "One Pat Nevin, there's only one Pat Nevin." All pointing at me. And I'm saying, "Oh, lads, give it a break." I imagined the Everton fans saying, "You wee bastard, you. Is that it? You left us three months ago and you go back and support Chelsea against us!"'

But, of course.

9

The Rat

Around spring 1984, Gwyn Williams received a curious phone call: 'Oi, Taff – I've got a free transfer from Southampton and I want to come down your gaff.'

'Those were his exact words,' smiles Gwyn, Chelsea's long-surviving Welshman, wryly. 'And I said to him, "Look, we're top of the South-East Counties League" – as we were in those days with Keith Jones, Keith Dublin, Phil Priest and all those lads – "with a really good team. I can't give you a game; you wouldn't get in our team."

'"What d'ya mean I can't get into your team! I'm telling you I'm better than anything you've got!"'

The pip-squeak Cockney voice and the typically combative manner belonged to none other than Dennis Wise – aka the Tasmanian Devil of Shepherd's Bush and an old acquaintance of our then youth coach.

'I tried to get him to sign as a schoolboy for Chelsea, but he had this allegiance to Bob Higgins and Southampton Football Club at Montem Sports Hall round the corner from where he lived in West London. So he signed for Southampton. They were talking about him being a big superstar midfield player, and he got a long way in the England trials and did really well, but was disappointed. Then two years after that, when he was at the Under-17 stage, he phoned me up. Obviously he got frustrated on the Chelsea front, and ended up at Wimbledon with Dave Bassett. Of course, a few years later, we ended up paying £1.6 million for him.'

In August 1996 BBC commentator John Motson answered *The Observer*'s questionnaire. 'Q: Who is the least intellectual player you have ever interviewed? A: Dennis Wise. Q: Who would you most like to spend a Saturday night out drinking with? A: Dennis Wise.'

There's something lovably downmarket about the diminutive west Londoner, a naughty, sometimes reckless, scamp. He is one of the few characters in today's game, and it has been a struggle for him to establish his credentials as a footballer since he is – sometimes as a result of his own misdemeanours – characterised as something of a street urchin. He is, after all, The Rat. Part of the problem is his chirpy, unapologetic working-class manner and the snobbish attitude towards that. Dennis was a precocious footballer as a child, which was just as well, because his academic career doesn't bear examination. 'I was at school with Les Ferdinand, funnily enough,' he remembers, 'and I think he was the only one that bunked off more than me.' One day playing hookey, Dennis was scrumping apples and caught in the act. In the resulting panic, he fell off the wall and banged his head. We shouldn't place too much emphasis on that episode and its effect on his attitude to life, however. Look at photos of him then and three things strike you. Firstly, the eyes: intent, determined. And secondly his size, which has increased only slightly. Finally the cheeky grin with its piano keyboard of tiny teeth, which has changed not a jot.

Dennis played for Montem Boys, amongst other near-local clubs, and once scored nine goals in a 33–0 Under-9s game. He had a drawer full of medals before he was ten in his parents' house, the bosom of which he vacated just a few years ago. They're a close family, the Wises, a feature of the local Bush community with their stall in the local market. (Hence the otherwise bewildering propensity for some Queen's Park Rangers fans to taunt him with cries of 'Fruit 'n' veg, fruit 'n' veg . . .' Ironically, Dennis was a QPR fan as a kid.)

Dennis arrived in the summer of 1990, during a strange period in Chelsea's history. Stylistically there was little worth cheering about in our football, particularly for those who'd witnessed the fluent teams of the '60s, early '70s and mid-'80s, but we could be effective. Promoted under Bobby 'The Meat' Campbell, the club had won the second of its Full Members trophies. There was pace and flair in Dorigo and Clarke – though this fine servant was being asked to temper his natural, attacking instincts – and muscle in Erland Johnsen and Kenny Monkou. Yet the midfield lacked quality. Dennis arrived, along with another cultured middle man – Andy Townsend.

'I came to the club because I felt that the club would enjoy some glory,' he says. 'We've been very unfortunate. Since I've been here, we've been in four semi-finals and one final, and it's my seventh season. So we ain't done bad, but we just need a little bit extra. You know, we just seem to muck it up at the wrong time and we miss out.'

'Basically, for the £1.6 million we paid for him, he's a snip,' says Gwyn. 'His quality's still there – same with Andy Townsend. The two were bought in Bobby Campbell's time; unfortunately we needed a bit more to go with that quality. That's what happens; it's like blocking a hole in a dam. You've only got five fingers, and there's ten holes. We made a good profit out of Andy, and we're still going to make a big profit out of Dennis, because he's going to be here for another three or four years and he's a great kid.'

In his first season we notched five consecutive victories at one stage – including the traditional triumph at Old Trafford – and rose to a heady sixth in the First Division. We also progressed to the penultimate stage of the League Cup. But there was a brittleness and ugliness about our play, which could slip from sublime to ridiculous in the blink of a misplaced pass, and a lot was expected of supporters watching the kind of play that was alien to Stamford Bridge. As Dennis realised, there was no disguising the need for improvement – across the board – at the club. In April 1991 at the City Ground, Forest casually knocked seven past us without reply. Chelsea fans played a blinder compared to the players, and were responsible for the first recording of the Monty Python song 'Always Look on the Bright Side of Life' in its natural football-terrace habitat.

Dennis couldn't voice his reservations publicly at the time of course – that's not what new boys do: 'Within a year or two I think this side could mature into one capable of challenging for and winning the title,' is what he told the fans.

But the League Cup semi-final against Sheffield Wednesday that year was typical. We'd turned Spurs over 3–0 at White Hart Lane after a listless 0–0 at home – Wisey was superb and scored a penalty. But the Second Division side seemed to present a different obstacle: indifference. The crowd was a poor one and, for a semi-final, strangely subdued.

'It was an odd game,' agrees Dennis. 'There was no one there and that was the disappointing thing about it. We expected it to be a full house roaring and getting behind us but it wasn't. We lost 2–0, gave two sloppy goals away, and it was all over. Now we have got full houses when it comes to important games. The punters are roaring and that's what we need. Since Ruud's come, especially, and the players we bought this year, people will want to come.'

The major repair work performed by Glenn wasn't foreseeable back in 1991. Instead The Meat was put in the freezer and Ian Porterfield, his former coach, took over. Dennis himself was finally settling in after a period when he failed to wow Stamford Bridge. 'I think I won the fans over when I stuck my two fingers up at them!' jokes Wisey. 'Nah, but it does take time, because I was the most expensive player at the time. There's also the Wimbledon thing –

people didn't like Wimbledon players. But as you can see with the likes of Warren Barton, Phelo, Scalesy, all ex-Wimbledon players, a lot of them that's moved on have shown they're good players. I think people realise that and they respect Wimbledon in a way now, so it's a little bit different.'

At Plough Lane Wisey had been used as a winger – steal a yard with a trick and get a cross in. At Chelsea he had to reacquaint himself with the more central role he always favoured. It took time. 'So the crowd's views on me changed I think when I got an injury. We'd been doing well and I got a problem in my foot and I was out for about eight weeks. We'd been playing really well up to that point, though people weren't really mentioning me. And I don't think we won a game while I was out. Being absent from the team – it's quite funny, you know; you can become a better player when you're injured, because if the team doesn't do well everyone thinks, "Oh, he's missing, so we're missing him." It doesn't necessarily work like that; it doesn't mean anything that some players aren't playing. But people think that way. And then I came back, and we started to do okay again.'

Dennis's absence coincided with the growing sense that Ian Porterfield's days were numbered as we failed to win a league game in the two months the midfielder was out. A promising start to the season dissolved in gloom. Wisey felt sorry for Porters. 'He was a lovely fella,' says Dennis. 'The lads said when he came here that he was a better number two – you know, under someone – because everyone loved him and he was a nice man. The fact was he perhaps couldn't deal with all the pressure. I think it was a lot to deal with and I think he preferred to go out and train with the lads and be part of the lads, you know, which he couldn't when he was the actual manager. He needed someone there who was going to say, "Right, now, knuckle down chaps." It was hard for him.'

Don Howe, brought in to coach the first team, was good at his job, but it was the other duties of management that troubled Porters.

Dennis was adaptable, though. He was the latest in a long line of Chelsea characters too, and probably the first since the gesticulating Dave Webb. 'It's nice to be liked by the crowd – it's a great feeling. Wherever I've played I don't think I've been hated – I hope I never will be. People come to be entertained, basically, and to enjoy it. You play football but you want them to be a part of it as well. You want all the punters not just to come, say, "Oh, we've watched the game" and go home.

'If there's a little kid who's there and I see him I'll pull him on to the field or do something. It's just the way I've always been.' There was the moment when Dennis played head tennis with someone in the west stand benches while a player received treatment. 'It doesn't bother me,' says Dennis. 'Some geezer, instead of throwing me the ball, headed it back to me and said, "Come on, head it back!" Why not? It's just making it a bit more enjoyable for the punters while someone's being treated. There's no harm in that. The supporters enjoy it, and the kid, well, it may never happen to him again. You think, "That's great, that." I sometimes think that's what it's about: you've got to let them enjoy it and show a bit of passion and show a bit of appreciation to them for their loyalty to you and the club.'

So Dennis it is who whips up the crowd surreptitiously when he arrives to take a corner. Dennis it is who singles out someone from his team – usually Hitchy, to remind him of a bet – or the crowd to join him in celebrating a goal. His winner up at Villa Park in 1995 was particularly baffling to commentators: he slapped his head as he ran grinning past the grandstand. As he explained later, a 'slaphead' Villa fan had been giving him some verbal abuse during the warm-up, and it was the least he could do to acknowledge the fellow's baldness in public. That's why Chelsea fans alone love Dennis Wise. Like David Webb, he's one step from the terraces, doing his best every week. 'It's just that some players are like that and some players ain't like it,' he reasons. 'You don't see it much now: there's Ian Wright at Arsenal and that's about it, you know? I think certain clubs have one of them, and most clubs have none of those players who the supporters can respond to, and they like and that. You give your all and you want to win. I think that's what they mostly appreciate, and that's all I want to do.'

With the veteran prankster Kerry Dixon, Dennis also enjoyed some less public laughs. There was the time when he and 'The Wig' threw all of the contents of young central defender Jason Cundy's room out of the window – clothes, cases, bed and all. And, allegedly, an occasion when The Rat's droppings found their way into someone else's bag . . . Dennis is incorrigible.

Meanwhile, Porters's first investments had seemed astute. Dominating centrist Paul Elliott was bought from Celtic and settled in superbly. Prolific goalscorer Clive Allen added punch up front. And an old friend of Wisey's from Wimbledon arrived to give bite to the midfield – Vinnie Jones. That jesting trio became the pivot – barometer, even – of team morale. 'They're my friends, simple as that,' says Dennis. 'I've known them for a long time. I knew Andy when he was at Southampton; I knew Jonah when he was at Wimbledon, and we got on very well. It's nice to bring players like that to the club and know them already. It takes time to get used to some players, but not them.'

The old Crazy Gang influence was never more potently expressed than at Anfield in 1992. We hadn't won there in the league for 56 years. But with Jamaica and Erland bolstering the defence, we approached the game with a certain cockiness. 'That was a nice game,' smiles Dennis. 'We played extremely well that day. We used our midfield three differently; it was a tactical move on Ian Porterfield's part. They had three in midfield as well: Jan Molby, Ronnie Whelan and Ray Houghton. The manager wanted us to cut out their supply lines from deep, so I was playing in the hole and having to help Clive Allen when I could, but I also pushed on Molby and stopped him from getting the ball. Vinnie marked Houghton and Andy Townsend was on Mark Walters or Marsh, the sub. Everyone used to play 4-4-2 against them and get murdered in midfield. Porters said, "Right, we're going to put three on three and see what they do then."

'So we worked man to man on them, and we let them come to us and counter-attacked them and we caused them a lot of problems. We had Graeme Le Saux wide left and Bobby Stuart wide right, and it was great because they had so much pace and I could pick them out with balls. That day the whole midfield played exceptionally well. Vinnie scored a goal with a great strike. It was the first time we'd beaten Liverpool at Anfield for years, and we played them off the park.'

The local newspapers, though, saw it differently. The old Crazy Gang guttersnipes Wise and Jones, according to the Merseyside press corps – including Tommy 'Voice of Moderation' Smith – had 'mugged' the aristos of Liverpool, or somehow desecrated the high temple of football. The reason for the outrage was an irreverent incident that went some way to unsettling the home side (who were anyway still conscious that we had beaten them 4–2 at the Bridge the previous season).

'It was a laugh, actually,' recalls Dennis. 'They've got this sign up above the tunnel as you go out that says "This Is Anfield". So Vinnie got a felt tipped pen, wrote a big note saying "WE'RE BOTHERED", and stuck it on the sign. It was up there when we came out of the tunnel and the Liverpool players must have thought, "Oh no, not these two again!"' (Vinnie and Dennis had, of course, been instrumental in Wimbledon's 1988 Cup final win over the Anfield mob.) 'But they're like that, Scousers,' chuckles Dennis. 'They won't turn round and admit the better team won on the day.'

Dennis was masterful throughout, snapping at heels, creating chances and driving his team-mates on to greater effort. He missed a penalty and even found time to score the winner in what remains one of his finest Chelsea games. Blues fans there will never forget him for that – and the relief that we'd finally done it after 56 years trying. 'It was nice to score as well,' he smiles. 'I got the Man of the Match award, which they say they don't give to opposition players.' It is rumoured that Dennis was the first non-Liverpool player to earn the accolade.

Yet after that hiatus the season fell into disarray. There seemed to be no resilience or direction to the team for the most part. The quarter-final display against Sunderland in the FA Cup was a classic example. Once again a lack-lustre home performance which should have been won by Clive Allen's goal saw us lose the home advantage. The replay is locked in Dr Caligari's (disturbingly full) box of Chelsea horror shows. On a freezing night, an inferior side fighting off relegation was allowed to hold on to a lead until Dennis, almost single-handedly carrying the fight to the north-easterners, equalised. With extra time beckoning, we fancied our chances finally to make quality count. Instead, almost immediately, we conceded a poor winner to a free header from a corner. A mixture of ill-conceived tactics and on-field apathy realised a desperately poor result. 'Sunderland got to the final,' groans Dennis. 'We felt that would have been a great chance to win the Cup but we missed out on it through sloppiness, basically.'

You sensed, after that, that we would never get to Wembley again – there was a mental block. A drastic solution was needed. 'I think what it boiled down to was that you had a lot of people who'd been there a long time,' reasons Dennis. 'You needed fresh faces to liven it up. What happens is it becomes stale. You need to have a change; some players need to go.'

But the lack of goals was a problem, and even the record-breaking signing of Robert Fleck – another panic buy of someone who'd scored goals against us – couldn't obscure the fact that we needed something Ian Porterfield's quixotic management couldn't provide. 'We've needed someone who could get 20 or 25 goals ever since I came here. We've had people who can get 14 or 15 – I finished top scorer for us with 15 in 1991–92. I was playing in midfield at the time as well – although I think three of the goals were penalties. We've always needed someone there. It shouldn't be midfield players or someone behind the front one or two being the top scorer. Like John Spencer last year or Hughesie. We've always had one striker who can get 13, 14 goals, and midfielders who can get their eight to ten goals, but we've never had an Ian Wright, Alan Shearer, Les Ferdinand or someone like that. Well, we've never had one of them for a long, long time. But that's what we've got now, in Gianluca Vialli.'

To get from there to here, though, took the arrival of an important figure in Dennis's football career: Glenn Hoddle. 'I don't know,' Wisey muses. 'I think that Chelsea needed a big lift, and when Glenn Hoddle came, he gave it that lift. He did certain things to improve the football and the set-up off the pitch as well, to make it more professional.'

Dennis was looked upon as one of those who would thrive under Hod's stewardship and he proved to be one of the few who could adapt without too many problems (though occasional argument) to Glenn's tactical approach. 'Oh yeah, I knew I'd be all right with Glenn's style of play,' says Dennis. 'I know what to do. I've got the reputation as an aggressive midfield player who never gives up. But I've got a bit more about me than that. Still, they can say what they like; it doesn't really bother me.'

Gwyn Williams always had faith too. 'He can play wide,' says Gwyn, 'he's got an engine to get up and down, he can tackle, he can score goals, he's good at set plays. And he's a hustler, but he's got a good temperament. He knows what he can do, he knows that when it's down to the nitty-gritty, one against one, he can handle it, and he can wind them up as well as they can wind him up.' More importantly, perhaps, was his winner's mentality. 'You have to have that,' says Gwyn. 'When you're a 400-metre runner against the best in the world, you don't think, "I'm going to finish sixth here." You look around the field, trying to psyche them out, and it's the same on the pitch. There are one against ones all over the pitch and Wisey's excellent like that.'

Discipline, though, could be a problem. Dennis collected too many petulant bookings and earned himself a reputation as a hot-head amongst referees who were only too happy to show him the yellow or the red card at the slightest opportunity. 'He's got that cheeky little image,' says Gwyn, 'but he's never ever going to change. He's not malicious or anything like that; he just likes a laugh and gives as good as he gets.'

There were famous occasions when Glenn didn't always agree with that view. When Dennis was sent off at West Ham (Chelsea were losing 1–0 at the time) for a two-footed tackle on 'The Gremlin', David Burrows, in 1993, the manager subtly but powerfully chastised his player for his conduct. We lost the game in part through that irresponsible act. The threat to hand the skipper's armband to a more responsible soul couldn't have been clearer.

In any case, the first year brought an FA Cup final which Dennis still hates to talk about. Losing 4–0 to a team we had beaten twice in the league – Man United – was a dreadful end to a season that promised much. 'For me, one of the games at Chelsea that I've enjoyed the most was against Luton in the semi-finals at Wembley,' says Dennis. 'Just the atmosphere, and the punters, and the way we played. I thought we played really well that day and what it meant to get to the final for all the punters. The celebrations after – it was like a final . . . '

In Glenn's second year Dennis began the best he ever has for the club. Then there was the dismissal at St James's Park for allegedly mouthing obscenities at the linesman. On this occasion Glenn supported his captain, publicly querying the official's ability to hear what Dennis was saying in the raucous arena – especially considering he was in the middle of the park at the time. But the most damaging disciplinary problem for Dennis happened later that season, when a taxi driver took him to court (having first taken him to the tabloids) over an incident outside Terry Venables's Scribes West club. His eyes like saucers, moist and haunted like a mad cow's, Dennis walked away from a court conviction in February 1995 with a forthcoming appeal and three-month sentence hanging over him.

It shook him up badly and made him take life more seriously, but fundamentally it didn't change his attitude towards football, which is his life. 'It didn't change me as a player,' says Dennis. 'It didn't change me much at all, to be honest; it just made me think about life a bit more and appreciate things a bit more.'

Glenn responded the instant the news broke about the incident, relieving Dennis of the captaincy and handing it to Mr Clean, Gavin Peacock. Dennis wasn't overjoyed by Glenn's actions. 'He had his way of handling things,' is all he will say. 'That's how he felt that he had to handle it, and that was his decision.'

Jamaica, meanwhile, believes that Glenn's decisiveness actually helped Dennis in the long run: 'Glenn dealt with it the right way I felt, taking the captaincy off Dennis, but doing it at source, nipping it in the bud. He made Dennis earn the right to the captaincy. And I'll tell you what, let's be fair, Glenn Hoddle revived Dennis's life, on and off the pitch. He gave Dennis a sense of responsibility. He said, "Dennis, you are my captain, you can't conduct yourself like that, you can't go round doing the things you've done. I need you on the pitch. You can't go round mouthing it off." And you look at Dennis's disciplinary record thereafter. Glenn's managerial skills are brilliant, and that comes from respect.'

'The good thing about it is my disciplinary record's got a bit better,' agrees Dennis. 'And it needed to, because I was in front of the FA at one stage. But we've got Mark Hughes now, so that's handy – it takes a bit of pressure off me!' Dennis now makes a point of trying to get to know the officials. 'I think at first the referee's not sure what you're like. I think now they've met me and they've spoken to me, they think, "Oh, he's okay, he's not bad, he's not as difficult as he's made out to be."'

One of the worst aspects of the taxi business was that immediately prior to it, Dennis had been playing probably the best football of his career. For much of 1993–94, he was our most consistent player. He was showing maturity in Glenn's teams wherever he was deployed. The three-touch mantra chanted by his manager and coach had converted Dennis's sometimes meandering movement into direct penetration. His passing was outstanding, over whatever distance, and he ran games with assurance and single-mindedness. He was intensely focused. His free role permitted movement from flank to flank and made him incredibly difficult to pick up. He was able to score two magnificent goals from distance, one against Zizkov and the other at Man City.

Suddenly Terry Venables could include him in his England teams without the ritual sneers. He became the first English footballer to sign a contract into the twenty-first century. The European Cup-Winners' Cup campaign of 1994–95 was just the right platform for Dennis and he starred in what games he was fit to play in. 'I enjoyed Zizkov at home,' he says, 'because that was the first Chelsea game in Europe for a long, long time, and I thought we played extremely well. They came back into it, and we showed a lot of bottle because we could have been out quite easily in the first round. Plus I scored one of my best goals for Chelsea.

'I also enjoyed Austria Vienna away because we went and did a job, and Spenny's goal was second to none – I've never seen anything like it. Then in the semi-final I was very disappointed. I wish Glenn Hoddle had taken me to Zaragoza, because I didn't go – can't remember the reason why – and I remember sitting at home, thinking, "Come on, lads, just hold on for 20 minutes, and we'll be okay". Because if we were to lose 1–0 it wasn't a problem. And then – bang – 20 minutes: 2–0 down. And I thought, "Oh-oh, we're in trouble", and I was thinking, "Just hold on to 2–0." And then it went to 3–0. And you think, "Please, just hold on to 3–0."

Despite a 3–1 rally against Zaragoza at the Bridge, we fell at the final hurdle again. 'We showed a lot of bottle at home,' says Dennis, 'but it was never really on. I think they always knew they had it under control. We were under too much pressure after the 3–0 away performance. They came out in the second half and got the goal straightaway. But that's the way it goes.'

The aftermath of the courtroom saga coincided with a period of frustration for Dennis on the pitch in Glenn's final season. There was the nagging thigh injury, of course, and the mental legacy of the trial to contend with. Early on, like others, he sometimes seemed to be hard-pressed in the 3-5-2 system with Ruud as sweeper. But once the teething problems were over he was back to his old self. Even when called upon by Glenn to fill the holding midfield slot left vacant after Eddie Newton – playing such excellent football too, poor fellow – broke his leg.

'Last year I did okay there, to be honest,' says Dennis. 'I played in the holding role and I enjoyed it. But it stops you from creating goals and scoring goals, and that's how I've always played football. I feel that I can create things, and by playing me as a holding player, I still get long passes and put people in but I like to try and hurt teams in their own third – and you can't do it as much. But it's a team game, and if the manager wants you to play there you play there, and I played there for a reason, because Eddie Newton was injured.'

The 1995–96 season wasn't one of Wisey's best, it has to be said, but there were reasons for that. He still managed to seize games by the scruff of the neck, as in the rampaging 3–1 victory over Southampton at The Dell, when he scored twice and bossed things from start to finish. Then there was the triumph at Selhurst Park over the Dons – a distinctly unusual success for the modern Chelsea side. Dennis showed incredible mental strength in that game, even though he missed a penalty: 'What a crap penalty that was,' he says. 'The only thing I'm pleased about is every time I miss one we win the game.'

Glenn Hoddle, mindful of Wimbledon's aerial strength, decided to have Dennis take short corners, and it was just such a move, with John Spencer coming to collect then picking out Doobs, that led to our second and decisive goal. But Glenn was most impressed by Wisey's strength of character after the spot-kick setback. 'Dennis had a good record from the spot,' says Glenn. 'And I talked it through with him at the break and said, "I fancy you if there's a second penalty," and he goes, "Yeah, I'm up for that." Which says a lot about his personality, because a lot of people wouldn't have fancied it after the miss.' Ruud Gullit was increasingly taken with The Rat's work on the pitch too. 'He plays differently now,' says Rudi. 'He used to run with the ball more; now he plays one-twos and short touches, and he played very well last season.'

Ruud, John Spencer and Dennis had become quite close during the season, despite their cultural differences. Wisey found a way to bypass the Dutchman's ice cool. 'Me and Spenny knocked him about a bit,' says Dennis. 'He's a great fella, and a lovely man as well off the field. I think when he first came everyone was a bit in awe of him, and you always wanted to give him the ball. Now he makes everyone express themselves. He became one of the lads.'

Ruud's arrival confirmed Dennis's conviction that the time for failure is past. Ask him about the excellent 1–0 victories over Man United in the 1993–94 season and he responds with typical frustration: 'They were good times, but doubles over teams and things like that, they mean nothing, really. We need to win something. We want a cup, we want to turn round and say, what about the FA Cup-winning side, what about the day we won the Coca-Cola? What about when we won that European trophy? – not what about when we did the double over Man United in normal league games. I think those times have got to go, you know. Doing doubles over people mean nothing unless you follow it up.'

He despairs sometimes of our self-destruct mechanism, evident in Chelsea teams since 1972 and the League Cup final against Stoke. 'We always seem to give away silly goals at silly times: Sunderland away, the FA Cup in January 1992 when it was wet at Crystal Palace – a back pass that stuck in the puddles. Two goals given away against Man United when we were 1–0 up in the FA Cup semi-finals last season. That was a sickener. We were absolutely cruising, and we put ourselves under pressure. We were unlucky, and that's the way it goes, but I'm fed up with it. I think all the lads are fed up with it now. And there comes a time when you think, "Come on, now's our chance, let's take it," and you really have a go at it. Well, we have had a go at it in the past, but I think we've got the quality now, you know?'

Dennis is re-energised by the changes at Chelsea in April 1996. 'I think it was a great decision by Batesy to bring in Glenn Hoddle,' he enthuses, 'followed by another good decision by giving the job to Ruud. I think it's great. Everyone knocks Batesy but he's done everything for the club and the club can only get better now. We have made a lot of progress in the last three years. The club is taken more seriously. We've got the right players in now. I think Ruud knows it and I think we know it and there's a lot of competition, but that's what we need – competition for places – and we've got it. There's been competition before, but I don't think it's been high and I don't think the quality of the squad overall has been that high. You need strength in depth in every department. We've got it now.

Everyone needs to be on their toes, which is great. And if you get injured or suspended then people will come in and take your place, and you will come in after a while or whatever. And that's the way it goes.'

There were before, believes Dennis, some faults in our tactical approach at times: 'I think we attacked too much, to be honest; we always looked to go forward and that's what Ruud will be concentrating on – keeping the ball and making them run instead of us. That's what he wants us to do. They play it on the Continent so well; they keep the ball and make you run and they don't look half as tired as the English sides, because whilst they're roaring about trying to bury people and trying to win balls, they're just nipping it round you and making you run. Ruud wants to keep the ball, and I think if we keep the ball the other people can't do us any damage. It's simple, what he says, and it makes sense. You keep the ball and the other team doesn't score. It's as simple as that. Plus we have the ball more than them, and we have more chance of scoring ourselves. But we need to fill the ground. When the ground's full and the punters are roaring, that's when we're at our best. When we play someone like Man City on a Wednesday evening and you've got about 14,000 and it's dead, that's when we're not at our best, for some reason. So if we're doing well, there's no excuse for the fans not to come on a cold Wednesday in February.'

To those close to the heart of the club, Dennis's good work extends way beyond the business on the pitch – a lot of it given less publicity than the less savoury incidents. 'He's a great lad, Dennis,' says Gwyn Williams. 'I've got a lot of respect for him. Wholehearted, great worrier, and he more than anyone else would have known the kind of problems he faced this time last year when we had the taxi driver business. He is excellent as a PR frontman – he's magnificent with kids who are sick or disabled. And he's got so much time for everybody.'

So Dennis belies his public reputation behind the scenes at Chelsea in many ways. With old sparring partner Mr Gullit firmly established in the manager's chair, there are now presumably no more rude names in the dressing-room banter: it's 'gaffer' or 'boss', not 'big nose'. 'It's funny, I do call him Yeti sometimes but all that stuff about there being a problem between us was just some silly paper story. There are certain things in people you can't change. Ruud is all for pasta and health foods and that's fine, but I still like my biscuits now and then. But that's just it: Ruud is Ruud and I'm me. No problem. We treat each other the same. I'm happy with it. It's just harder for him, I think, cause he's a player. He's been part of us last year, and he still is part of us. Sometimes he has to step back, I think, because he's the manager . . . well, he calls himself the coach – the coach is easier, isn't it? The good thing about it is that I can go up to him and ask him things and speak to him, where it wasn't so easy with Glenn Hoddle. Glenn Hoddle had his ways, between him and Peter, but now I can speak to Graham Rix and I can speak to Ruud and Gwyn, you know, which is good.'

That wasn't the only change that Wisey has seen in his six years at Chelsea – all for the better. 'It's a lot different,' he says. 'The facilities, the ground, the people – the standards are higher now. The spirit's better, everyone's enjoying it, but enjoying it in a nice way, a serious way. Everyone's relaxed about it and I think they're looking forward to what's coming, which is nice. We are all looking forward to playing under Rudi with a lot of confidence. Ruud's come in and had us working very hard – much harder than before. He expects certain things and you have to come up to his standards, because he's the boss and he's done it himself. I'm enjoying it. It can only lift you when players like Gianluca Vialli, Roberto di Matteo and Frank Leboeuf are brought to the club.'

Ruud's three summer '96 and '97 signings represented a different calibre of player to some that have arrived since 1991. 'They have come here to win things,' says Wisey. 'They know what they want and they know what they want to do. If we can all gel together, I'm sure we will win something. I wouldn't like to predict anything, though – every time I've said something, we've ended up 11th!' The former Lazio midfielder Roberto was taken with Dennis straightaway: 'Dennis loves to have a joke now and then but he is deadly serious on the pitch and a wonderful player to lead the team,' he says. 'I've already formed a very good understanding with him. He works so hard and has very good skill in making space for other players. He is the greatest influence on the team and I am very happy to be playing with him.'

The stage was set for Dennis to enter the most successful period of his career, personally and professionally. More than anything he wanted to authenticate his arrival at the top with silverware. By the time we reached the 1997 final, we'd been singing 'When Wise goes up to lift the FA Cup . . .' for some six years, fruitlessly.

Dennis had genuinely become one of the Chelsea greats, though, by becoming a lynchpin of the side. When he played, we did too. Whether he was asked to play at the front of a diamond midfield, the holding role in a 3-5-2 (which he adapted magnificently to in Eddie Newton's absence), or wide left or right to accommodate the likes of Robbie or Eddie, he was fully concentrated, responsible.

During Luca Vialli's testiest first period at Chelsea, when his public fall-out with Rudi was at its peak, Dennis put on a vest with something written on it – he had a feeling he would score and might be able to expose it to the press, as was the trend of the time. Sure enough, he slotted one in and hared over to Luca, who was warming the bench as usual. 'CHEER UP, LUCA, WE LOVE YOU xx,' it read. It did more for mending team spirit than any players' meeting could. Typical Wisey – except the spelling was immaculate (he had his scriptwriter Steve Clark to thank for that).

This later model, the Wise mk III perhaps, was the most impressive yet. The feistiness was still there, but the nastiness had left him. (The clamouring for his England recall fell on Hoddle's deaf ears, of course – he remembers the skipper's outspokenness during some of the old dog days.)

Dennis had become the consummate club man, too, organising social events, plucking lucky kids out of the crowd as he did after the FA Cup semi-final at Highbury when he helped overcome Wimbledon so superbly.

In the final, harrying, distributing and buoying up a side that had no other real leader of men, he was magnificent. Though he's almost universally disliked outside of Chelsea circles, it was his delight that inspired Wembley to its biggest party in years at the final whistle.

A year later at the same venue, it was his gesture to ask on behalf of the players that player-manager Luca accept the Coca-Cola Cup. In captaining the side that day and in Stockholm two months later, Dennis became our greatest skipper since Ron Harris, if not Roy Bentley.

At 31, to be recognised as Chelsea's greatest ever captain must now be his aim, even though he'd never admit it. He may even go into management. Unthinkable two years ago.

Back in the summer of 1996, one day the little midfielder was running repeats round the pitch with Ade Mafe, looking for all the world like a kid being punished for scrumping when he should have been doing sums. 'That's what you get when you call the gaffer Big Nose,' chuckled Dennis as he ran by, loveable as ever. The more things changed around Chelsea then, it seemed, the more he stayed the same. Now, like the rest of the club, he's Wised up.

10

Jamaica

Like Clint in the spaghetti Westerns, a tall, slim stranger strode into town when the townsfolk faced a doubtful future. But he didn't stay long, and when he'd gone, the people missed him, so they chanted his name at every home game and wrote to him in droves.

Few footballers, if any, have made as profound an impact in such a short space of time as Paul Elliott managed over 54 games in 14 months starting in August 1991. His rapport with the fans was instant; his heart, within a squad of too many players patently lacking that vital organ, was immediately apparent. And there was something about the troubled rock star dying young in the way we clung to the hope that he would return to lead us again, when injury stole him from our plans.

It was all rather different from his first Stamford Bridge appearance as a willing, willowy teenager ten years earlier. He was with Charlton at the time, and a minority of Chelsea fans were dragging the club into the gutter with their verbal attacks on black players. 'Wooaah!' Paul recoils at the memory. 'If they'd seen how things were, not even Lloyds of London would have insured me to go to Chelsea in those days.' Luckily for us, the likes of Paul saw the broader picture – this was not a Chelsea problem, but a social problem.

When he signed pro at 16 in 1980, manager Mike Bailey had warned Paul, 'Son, you're gonna get it, not because you're black, but because you're a good player as well, and people will want to put you off your game, and they know there's certain nerves they can touch.' Paul never exposed those nerves and was all the stronger for it. His career was a fine one tragically curtailed. An England Youth, Under-21 and 'B' international, he progressed from the Robins, his local club, through Luton and Aston Villa and then abroad with Pisa in Italy, to Celtic, before ending his career, tragically prematurely, at Stamford Bridge.

Paul was 27 years old when he left Celtic and signed for Chelsea in the summer of 1991. Many people, excluding those who followed

150

the increasingly dull game north of the border, knew little about him since he'd left for Italy in 1983. And there were ominous portents. The last Scottish Footballer of the Year we'd signed was Doug Rougvie. But God, we needed Superman at the back. And we soon believed we'd found him. 'I'm not sure I was a hero,' he frowns. 'I loved my time at Chelsea, and I still did as Coors's match-day host. I also took great satisfaction, particularly in my first year, because I won Player of the Year and obviously I had an instant rapport with the fans there.

'I was a confident guy. I'd done well in Italy, enjoyed my football, the continuity was there in Scotland, but I desperately wanted to play for England and I knew I had to go south to do it. I'd been at Celtic for two great years and saw the racial problems that I'd inherited diminishing. The same people who were throwing the bananas and sending the unsavoury letters and whatever, they were begging me not to leave. People used to say to me, "Where are you from, what school did you go to?" At the end of the day I'd say, "I'm black and I'm British and I don't give a damn." My second year I won Celtic Player of the Year, Scottish Player of the Year and Scottish Football Writers' Player of the Year. And that way you can influence people's attitudes. But I felt like I'd gone there and done my job on and off the pitch, and it was time to move on.' Just like a superhero: *My work here is done. And the England football team needs me . . .*'

'I knew I was good enough,' says Paul. 'In my first year in Italy I was voted in the top three foreign defenders.'

We know why Chelsea wanted *him* – as a replacement for the too-young Jason Cundy and to shepherd our frail back line. But why did the England 'B' skipper choose *Chels*? Ian Porterfield, who'd just returned to the Bridge as boss, having taken over in the summer, must have played up the fact that we were the only team to beat Champions Arsenal (2–1, you'll recall) and glossed over the fact that we had leaked seven to Nottingham Forest and finished the 1990–91 campaign with the worst defensive record in the division except for Derby County (whom we cleverly scored eight against).

'When David Pleat bought me at Luton one of his comments was that he'd signed the player who could be the bung to block the hole in the sink, and it was a very similar situation at Chelsea: great going forward, but defensively didn't have anything there, so maybe I could relate to that a little bit. Basically, Ian said, "Paul, this club, if it goes well, forget Tottenham, forget Arsenal, this club will be the best." And it's sad – six years later we're still singing the same tune, aren't we?'

Paul wasn't the only newcomer. Vinnie Jones, curiously, arrived from Sheffield United ('Chelsea are a sleeping giant, etc.'), full-back Tom Boyd from Motherwell ('We'll be pushing the front-runners, etc.') and striker Joe Allon from Hartlepool ('Why aye! Chelsea! etc.'). Paul cost almost as much – £1.4 million – as the other three put together, and that was just about right.

His introduction to the existing squad and the other new boys came on the pre-season jaunt to Ireland. 'We were in Dublin,' he recalls, 'and we'd gone out and had a couple of drinks, and Boydy was never one to hold the drink. All the Liverpool lads walked into the bar, Boydy flat out on the floor, and I remember Andy Townsend saying, "That's our great new 800 grand signing down there."' Tommy was also responsible for bringing south Paul's nickname, acquired at Celtic: Jamaica. And when former Celts team-mate Tony Cascarino arrived soon after, Jamaica it was. He was always talking about the island of his forebears, listening to reggae, and dreaming of his next visit.

As fans, our first introduction to him was distinctly 'irie'. 'I scored two goals in the first four games. I scored on my debut, same as Joe Allon, in the 2–2 at home to Wimbledon, and then scored, again with Joe Allon, and again in a 2–2, against Notts County at the Bridge.' Jamaica's debut goal was, auspiciously, a smart header from a corner; Geordie Allon's was more unusual: it came, as he joyously put it later in that sing-song accent, 'Off me cock!'

Goals from a defender who showed himself to be assertive, incisive and – crucially, since the departure of Graham Roberts – a leader, was an added bonus. His timing of tackles was immaculate, pace explosive, passing – after a shaky start – sound. He was everywhere. And we'd been used to players who were wont to treat the ball like a leper. Even in those early stages, against the likes of Spurs – squashed 3–1 with goals from The Beak (Andy Townsend), The Wig (Kerry Dixon) and The Moustache (Kevin Wilson) – Sheffield United and Aston Villa, he drove us to victory through sheer force of personality. He looked the part, all right.

'I think the goals took the pressure off. It was a big fee – I was the second most expensive player Chelsea had ever bought, and there was a great level of expectation. And I was consistent that season. I know my games when I've done well. I think about when we beat Everton away in the FA Cup. Another one that stuck in my mind was Sheffield United in the Cup at home. I felt like a mountain that day, I don't know why. Vinnie stupidly got booked after whatever happened and we were just under continual pressure in the second half, but held out to go through. I was playing against Brian Deane that day, and there was a continual avalanche of balls coming into the box.

'I enjoyed the game early on against Notts County when I scored. I enjoyed myself in the games when we played Nottingham Forest at home and I hit the bar and headed on Vinnie's long throw for Kerry to score, and Tottenham away – Wisey was blinding and Beak scored a good one. I also enjoyed Tottenham at home because I was playing against Paul Stewart, and I did this little shimmy and he tried to clump me.

'I remember when we played Hull in the Cup when I was playing alongside Cundy. That sticks in my mind and we won that one too. I remember West Ham away when it was very hot. That was one of my early games there, and Stuart Slater was playing. We drew 1–1. I also remember playing Arsenal in October and we got beaten 2–1. I was playing with Kenny at the back. Tommy Boyd had a difficult time down the right-hand side – Kevin Campbell was superb. You know, I loved that game. I've always loved playing at Highbury. It's very tight and compact. I remember playing against Wrighty on his home debut then. And then on New Year's Day we played against Man City and I was playing against Niall Quinn; that was some battle that one. Boom, boom, boom.

'I felt such a sense of belonging at Chelsea at such an early stage. That's what surprised me – to make such an impact in such a short space of time. But that season, the essence of my game was consistency. People could rely on me.' The fans relied on him. Player of the Year Kenny Monkou was a big, fast, effective centre-back who could shoot from the halfway line – with his head. And he may have dished it out on the quiet to opposition strikers, but his presence on the field was cool, pacific. People could relate to Jamaica's clenched-fist coaxing, his leading of the line. He may even have set the Chelsea record for winning over The Shed and being honoured in song: *'Elli-ott, Elli-ott, Elli-ott . . .'* 'I wasn't aware to begin with because you're so focused on your job. But then I loved it.'

At the time of the 'boom, boom, boom' game against City, we were in no danger of relegation (how aspirations had faded) and could cruise into a semi-final place by dispatching Sunderland. 'Then it all went belly-up, didn't it?' says Paul. 'I played in the Sunderland game . . .' For once he has little to offer on that desperate replay. You will recall that we decided not to call on Clive Allen, and then conceded a pathetic second goal seconds after Wisey had equalised. It was too late for a response.

On the plus side, we won at Anfield in the league for the first time in 56 years, Vinnie Jones and Dennis Wise, the old Crazy Gang duo, out-psyching the 'This Is Anfield' mob. (Mind you, they did have Souness in charge at the time.) 'Yeah, the signs were there,' says

Jamaica. 'It was a transitional stage for the club, I felt. There were some good youth-team players coming through, and they've come through well since. I always liked Graeme Le Saux. He was a thinker, a more rounded person. But I always saw that the boy needed guidance and careful management, because he's brighter than the average lad, and a single-minded player, to his credit. He was a little bit unpopular with some of the lads, but he wasn't unpopular with me because I knew where the boy was coming from. He was a lateral thinker. He'd see things from a different angle and because others didn't have that level of intellect, they'd have the arsehole with him. But he was a super player, with great potential.'

Since the departure of Pat Nevin, antique-loving Kenny Monkou was Bergerac's pal. And while Jamaica and the Surinam-born Dutchman were friends off the pitch, there was clearly no chemistry between them on it. 'Yeah, I liked Kenny very much as a person; he was a nice lad, a genuine lad,' muses Paul. 'But professionally, people always felt he was going to make a ricket somewhere, which was sad. He could be a colossus for 89½ minutes and all of a sudden . . . Physically he was awesome, had pace, everything. I think that one of Kenny's problems was that little bit of extra time he had on the ball in Europe. In the equivalent situation in the UK you'd get punished if you made an error. We both had height, we could both head the ball, we both had athleticism. Generally we could both use our pace and tackle, just sometimes it felt that I worked better with Cundy as the younger man, and I could guide him more, and have a bit more influence on his game. I think you need one main man.

'I played how I played. I don't know how much of a problem it was to Kenny. I just think the continuity wasn't there, whereas I could read Jason Cundy's game better. He was young, he was impetuous. I could tell him boom, boom, boom . . . gee him up. Kenny was very unpredictable. There were times, for example, when I was going to attack the ball, and I saw Kenny out of my peripheral vision going for the same ball when really he shouldn't have been; he should have been tucking in behind me. Whereas I'd say to Jason, "If I go tight, you tuck around me, and if you go tight, don't worry about me, I'll be behind you." His rawness made my job very simple. Unfortunately Jason should've stayed with Chelsea for another two years. He was at least five years away from maturity.'

Tommy Boyd was a man who couldn't bridge the gap between the Scottish and the English game. 'Very good athlete, could get forward well,' says Paul. 'But he wasn't used to coming up against players who were going to test him every week. He had good recovery, and he was quite strong, but people were getting the ball and running at him continuously, as opposed to Boydy bombing on. It's a different ball game here, and that's the gap that he couldn't bridge.'

Goals – or at least, one more goal than the opposition – were proving hard to come by too, as the season closed with six defeats in ten matches. 'Kerry Dixon was probably just past his peak,' says Paul. 'Kevin Wilson was always going to be a poacher but not one who could sustain it over a period of time. Mick Harford was a short-term signing. Gordon Durie, well, Juke Box was Juke Box. His heart wasn't in the club, so really you had problems there. In midfield Townsend, excellent in the first year, second year . . .' Paul saw too many treading water, lacking the hunger of himself and Wisey: 'There was an acceptance level, a taking for granted. Some of them played within themselves as well, done enough just to get by. If you have three or four like that you're not going to win anything; you just about survive. A rapid reconstruction was needed, make no mistake.' But reconstruction of a different kind, poignantly, was on the agenda for Paul Elliott.

There were new faces in attack: Harford, John Spencer from Rangers, Robert Fleck (sharp intake of breath), £2.1 million from Norwich. Mal Donaghy arrived; Spackers was back. 'I started the second season sluggishly. My timing wasn't quite right – I was going for things and I kept missing, and then all of a sudden we played Aston Villa in midweek, we won away and my game just came together. That was the fifth or sixth game of the season, and I thought, "We're flying now." That Villa game brought everything together. We won 3–1, battered them, and I felt like a mountain. Dalian Atkinson was up front, and I did well against him. Great performance all round: Wisey scored, Flecky scored, Eddie Newton scored. I thought, here we go . . . bang!'

The bang refers to the incendiary incident at Anfield the following week. 'I remember reading in the paper, believe it or not, prior to the Liverpool game, something like "Elliott number one man for England". And I thought, "Wow, this is how I'll end the season," and that felt good, you know.' It was 5 September 1992. A 50:50 ball between the surging Jamaica and then Liverpool striker Dean Saunders, where the latter appeared to go 'over the top', left our centre-back writhing in agony. It was surely one of the worst challenges of the season. But the famously sporting Kop jeered as Jamaica stayed down – and the referee, crucially, gave a free-kick *against* him.

'To be honest, it happened in a split second, and I don't know what was in Saunders's mind, but I knew there was a reckless disregard for my safety. Not that it was deliberately done; you can't say that, you don't know what's inside a man's head. But I've never felt so much pain in my life,' recalls Paul. 'The scars are here to bear witness. That's Saunders's boot marks from when he made contact with my knee.' He reveals a leg that looks like it's been through a serious car crash. 'There was an eight-inch abrasion and swelling and I had to have emergency surgery on the lateral complex to give the leg a level of stability.'

The more serious injury, the ruptured right anterior cruciate ligament, wasn't repaired then. Paul had 'done' his left cruciate in Italy and knew it was best to build it up for six to eight weeks and see how things were. 'The surgeon said that if they'd done the cruciate ligament straightaway I would have had so much trouble straightening the leg, because it was such a violent contact. Had I had both operations my leg would be like a chicken's, I would have spent so much longer in plaster.'

Paul's long-time consultant David Dandy explained the situation to his patient: 'Paul, I've seen your broken leg at 18. I've seen your left cruciate ligament injury from Italy. Ninety-nine per cent of players don't get back from those two injuries. This is a third one. I know your capacity, I know your character. It's career-threatening – make no mistake. But if anybody could do it, it would be you.'

'That was all the incentive I needed,' says Paul. 'Believe me, I did my nut. The same way I used to go out and play and give my lot; I attacked my rehabilitation with the same vigour.'

So Paul applied his customary diligence to the task of building up muscle and fibre around the damaged ligament. But come December Paul met his specialist, David Dandy of Cambridge, and the knee was still unstable. The cruciate needed surgery. It was the day of Cantona's Manchester United debut at the Bridge, and the Frenchman scored. How Jamaica would have relished that battle of wits. But Paul was already having to think beyond such joys. 'By that point the priority was my health, my mobility and my quality of life; coming back as a footballer was secondary.'

Paul was regularly introduced to the crowd at the Bridge. The deafening chanting of his name (home and away, as he still travelled with the first team) was one of the most uplifting aspects of that dreadful time, and showed Chelsea fans, and the club as a whole, at its best. Ken Bates was robustly supportive. It was almost family. 'Phenomenal . . . supporters wrote from all around the country, saying we've not seen tackles as bad on a Sunday pitch or whatever. That's why when I read the conjecture about Saunders going abroad, I was saying, "Man doesn't have to run unless he has to hide."'

For his own part, Saunders, the player who'd already called

Chelsea a small, Mickey Mouse club after his father was refused entry to the tunnel area, was barracked whenever he faced the Blues. 'I appreciated that the fans had lost Paul Elliott the footballer,' Jamaica says, 'but Paul Elliott the man couldn't conduct himself in such a fashion, you know. I underestimated the affection of the fans, I must admit that. I mean, I only played 54 games for Chelsea, and I felt like I'd been there 12 years. Even now I still feel like a Chelsea player just by the warmth from the punters.'

1992 rolled into 1993. The fans were beginning to despair. But when physio Bob Ward suggested Jamaica do ten laps at Harlington, he would do 15; 25 repetitions? No, Jamaica would do 40, so determined was he. 'All that Italian discipline for me, eating the right things, doing the right things, that's when it was so applicable,' says Paul. 'Over there people have such a desire to be a professional footballer that they're overwhelmed if they reach that level. It's more profound. They call it a sacrifice. I heard so many players say, "Paul, sacrifice. Because we can work for ten years and not have to work again for the rest of our lives. What's ten years of staying in hotels, behaving yourself, saying the right things, conducting yourself in the right manner?"'

If anything, Paul's stature grew most during this period as fans witnessed the dignity and determination with which he fought his personal crises. One of Glenn Hoddle's first acts as new Chelsea manager in the summer of 1993 was to make Paul club captain. 'Great honour,' says Paul. 'He said he felt that I had an aura, I had respect from third parties, and he felt that I wanted to lead from the front. He felt there were characteristics that were important to Chelsea at that time. And I was proud. Despite my own problems, I wasn't so indulgent to forget about other people, and I think he respected that. I thrive on responsibility.'

Despite Jamaica's discipline and determination, there was no substantial physical improvement. He was devastated not to get back, but not surprised. It was April 1994, 19 months after the Liverpool game. 'Bob Ward put out a slalom, nine or ten cones, to go round. The knee just went away from me. I couldn't do it. I thought it was going to buckle underneath me. Bad blow, bad blow . . .'

Still, there were distractions on the pitch while Jamaica was still registered as a player. The FA Cup run ended in bitter disappointment, but the post-match reception was a brilliant, rousing, emotional affair with superb speeches form Glenn and Batesy. But the reception there for Paul was heart-warming when he announced his retirement from playing. 'It said it all,' he recalls. 'We were at the Strand and we were so sad. And I spoke, and I was touched by the incredible reception I got . . . it brought me to tears, because I didn't realise. The problem with me is I probably underestimated my importance to other people, and didn't realise the level of influence I could have, whether it was children, adults, people of the National Front element who come to me and say to me, "Paul, I want to shake your hand." Your Frankie Sinclairs, Bobby Stuarts; they'd want to come and speak to me and I'd give them time. Sometimes it takes certain things to bring out aspects of your character and adversity brought that out of me.'

At least Paul's burgeoning career as a TV summariser was allowing him to apply his immense skill in communicating to football. His locution was noted by fellow south Londoner Colin Pates on one of his returns to the Bridge. Patesy took his old chum to task in typical fashion: 'Oi, Jamaica, what's all these long words you keep using on the box, then?' he teased. 'What's wrong wiv a bit o' Sarf London, eh? I heard you the other day say, "The pitch isn't conducive to good football." Not conducive? Why didn't you just say it was a "crap pitch". Where's yer sarf London gone?'

The South London is still in Paul, don't worry about that. And he needed the perseverance he learned on the streets there again when the ground-breaking litigation against Saunders for damages began in 1994. 'I knew the risks,' he says. 'I knew I could lose as well, seeing as I was before a judge who probably doesn't know the offside rule. When you cross the white line, there are certain things that you do and don't consent to. If I were to have got injured within the laws of Association Football it wouldn't have even gone to court. The referee, Richard Keys, says, "I never make mistakes." Yet after my game he got disqualified from the lists.'

The likes of Don Howe, John Hollins, Brian Glanville and Patrick Barclay supported Paul's case, as well as Ronnie Whelan, Saunders's team-mate on the day. But Vinnie Jones changed his evidence, and Andy Townsend, Chelsea skipper at Anfield but now with Saunders at Aston Villa, crucially failed to back up Jamaica's claim.

'Andy Townsend dithered and dithered. He was a man who, I felt, was easily led. I liked Andy as a person, but I always knew there was a hidden agenda with him, and with Vinnie Jones. It didn't surprise me with Vinnie. I'd known of him for a long time and he's always the one that gives it the "brothers" bit when it suits him. I saw him sometime after and he couldn't look me in the face. I always saw that in them. They go with the flow: if it's black it's black, if it's green it's green. I never let that bug me, how some people did. I've learnt in life that what goes around, comes around. They reap as they sow, and indirectly Vinnie Jones has had his comeuppance, and he knows how. I never sent out any bad thoughts towards them or even towards Dean Saunders, because I know if you do that it's going to rebound against you.'

When the case was lost there was a substantial legal bill to add to Jamaica's woes. 'The biggest blow in my life was not losing the money,' he says. 'I've got acumen. I can always earn money. But losing my career was devastating. I felt I was the best central defender in Britain and it was all going to happen. I was on the brink of England recognition. When you lose it that way you can't just walk away. I don't regret anything I've done. Had I not gone to court it would have always been eating inside me and I wouldn't have the calmness I now have about life. That would affect my relationship with my children, with my family, my day-to-day life. I would be walking around with a chip on my shoulder.

'I'm very peaceful now. I have my faith, I have a lovely family, great children. I would have loved to have played for another five years, no problem. I had a desire and a love for football. The greatest love I had was playing and training. I loved that. I loved the big games but because of my experience in life, it's like I treated every game like it was my last, treated every training session as my last. I always wanted to win, whatever I've done. Some people talk about it lightly as if it's a game of snakes and ladders. With my background, we came in the '60s and we had it tough. I earned the right to be a professional footballer, but I was privileged. People talk about pressure before big games, and that's rubbish. I used to say, "If you want it to be a pressure game, it's a pressure game, but if you go out and be professional, treating every game the same way, then all those big games aren't a problem."

'One of my greatest attributes is my psychological strength. I just thought, "I want to win." Win, lose or draw I give my best. Thursday, Friday, I'd always relax. I never trained too hard on a Friday, but did enough. A lot of it's mental, but at the end of the day, if it's important, well, just go and do it, son. Self-belief is a great thing in football. Confidence is 90 per cent of the game. Ability not so much. There are players with not a lot of ability who have made a lot of money out of the game. I've always been my own man. I never had hangers-on or people to feed my ego, even when I had a crap game, telling me how well I've played; I didn't need that. I'm a private man, an individual and I think those qualities are possibly the reason why I've made a reasonable success since I stopped playing. I don't need third-party baggage around me. I've got a very realistic view of life. Football is about having the ability to do it. When I was coming through, you had to be twice as good to break through.'

Times have changed since Paul entered the game, even since he had Napoli's Maradona in his pocket playing for Pisa and had his eye lashed by Ruud Gullit's dreadlocks against AC Milan. Life is calmer now. New challenges to face. He's no longer Coors's match-day host which had, by association, made him a fine PR man for the club. But he has a contract with BSkyB, and one with Channel Four and their *Football Italia* – he speaks the language fluently and flies out regularly. Then there's his 'charriddy' work – boys' clubs and stuff – and the important contributions to the Commission for Racial Equality's initiatives to drive bigotry off the terraces. He's completing a sport and law degree (his mum always wanted Paul to be a lawyer), coaches children at a school of excellence, and covered for Graham Rix with the Chelsea kids at the tail-end of the 1995–96 season. He's still 'Chels' despite those diverse interests.

'The problem with a lot of players today,' he reasons, 'is they only see it today and don't realise there's a massive life tomorrow. There's a great complacency there. When they stop being a footballer they have to become individuals and human beings. That's the area that so many players can't cope with. What am I going to do? At 32, 33, I've got another 30, 40 years to enjoy my life. Football breeds the camaraderie, which is good, but you have to take life seriously as well – they never do. There are 400 players on the dole and another 70, 80, coming out of the game every year through injury. You need diversification. At the end of the day you're only training for two and a quarter hours a day on average, you're playing for 180 minutes maximum a week – that doesn't work out to three working days at most, and it's used too much as an excuse sometimes, I feel.'

Paul Elliott never played in any semi-finals, finals or European games, relegation or championship deciders. But he arrived at a time when Chelsea needed a hero and he became one. His, and our, main frustration was that he wasn't able to survive the bread-and-water football of the Porterfield regime and enjoy the banquet of the Hoddle era. 'It's a huge disappointment, not playing under Glenn. He would undoubtedly have improved my game. He would have given me more vision. Put it this way: I felt he could have done more for me than what he's done for Duberry. And you see, he's made Duberry a good player. Duberry had a young raw potential, whereas I was more of a finished article. So I felt my rate of improvement would have been quicker.'

Paul's pre-season testimonial against Porto in 1995 – an indulgence offered by the club after four years' service rather than the customary ten – was the second chance Paul had to reassess an old adversary from his Italian days: Ruud Gullit. 'The Tuesday before I sat in the stand at Gillingham,' said Paul, 'I could see the way Gullit was playing at the back and I had this little thought: "God, what would I have given to have been able to play in front of him in the same team?" I'd have him as sweeper behind me, and I could be the man-marker. Yeah, that would have been amazing.'

It must be awful to think that he could never be part of Chelsea's renaissance. 'Yes, initially it was tough. I loved the game. A lot of professional players don't enjoy training; some just enjoy when they play. But let me tell you something: there's no better job in this world than playing professional football in this country. It was wonderful while it lasted, and I'd have liked to have had some more but I always say to myself, even in the midst of adversity, I was still one of the privileged few.'

11

Judge Dread

There is a joke that goes some way to summing up Chelsea fans' feelings towards the three most prominent personalities on our playing staff of the last three years. It goes like this:

Glenn Hoddle, Ruud Gullit and Dennis Wise are driving to training when their car breaks down. There is a wide river between them and the training ground, and the closest bridge is some miles away. After a moment's thought, Glenn has an idea: why don't they try running across the river to save time? And so they give it a try.

Glenn goes first and skips across, managing not to sink beneath the surface. Rudi goes next and swiftly joins his manager on the far bank. And so to Dennis, who confidently sets off, lands on the water – and promptly sinks. So the diminutive midfielder has to swim the rest of the way in his designer togs.

'Erm, Ruud,' says Glenn softly. 'D'you think we should have told him about the stepping stones just under the surface?'

'Huh?' replies Ruud. 'What stones?'

Oh, the nonchalant godliness, the diffident 'What-is-all-the-fuss-about – it's only walking on water, it's not the second coming'. Ah, but to us it is. The shock of such a deity deigning to come to Stamford Bridge! It wasn't as if we had much of a track record in great overseas signings. All right, we'd audaciously tried to hire George Best in 1975. And, yes, we'd humiliated ourselves by publicising a bid for Johann Cruyff after he'd starred for New York Cosmos in a testimonial against us in 1978. But you really had to go back to Nils Middleboe in the '20s to find a similarly world-class foreigner in a Chelsea shirt. World Footballer of the Year, European Champion, AC Milan star, buddy of Baresi, coming to Chelsea!

That is if we could trust the stories. Was he really signing? Would he arrive in July and leave in August? There was only so long we would be able to shield the tumultuous state of the ground from his gaze . . . We all wanted to see him in the UK. Meet him. Touch him. Thank him. Three days before he was due to arrive, I did just that.

I was sitting on the Habitat sofa in the Chelsea reception area waiting for the summons to interview Colin Hutchinson. The lift doors opened, and out walked a tall, dreadlocked man in a suit. Well, it wasn't Gregory Isaacs. At this stage, if memory serves, a celestial choir began to sing and shards of light sprang from behind his head. I stood up, ignored the papers which fell from my lap to litter the floor and locked his hand in a vice-like handshake. I managed about three words, all three of them 'Welcome . . . '

Once Colin Hutchinson had used his national service assault training to break my grinning grip, Ruud was gone. He was coming to Chelsea. But I must say he looked a little pensive . . . 'When I saw for the first time the pitch and the stadium,' he says now, 'I was thinking to myself, "What am I doing here?"' Some season-ticket holders in the west stand – 'Poland', as it's known; last refuge of the Panda Pop – have been thinking that for years as they queue for their Waggon Wheels or wait to use the roofless toilet in the last refuge of Iron Curtain facilities. During the previous season, a game at the Bridge was postponed because bits of the ground were blowing around. Fit for a king?

'It was such a mess,' says Rudi. 'Everyone was working on the pitch, the stands were not all there, there was such a mess with excavators and things all over the place. I thought it was really – ahhh! It was more the disorder that was there, you know, than what was underneath it. They were working on the whole area; everyone was working. But then when I met the staff and the fans I knew it was a club that desperately wanted some success. That is something you tasted everywhere you went. People kept saying they could not believe it; "Why?" they said. Everyone was a voyeur. Everyone wanted to see me and know why I had come to Chelsea. But I just thought that it was for me the best solution for the rest of my career.'

He rejected lucrative swansongs in Japan and Monaco. 'I had different kinds of offers and it was just one of the offers; I didn't even think about Chelsea itself. I didn't have any preconceptions. I didn't know what Chelsea was. I couldn't imagine how Chelsea was, you know, I just put the offer with the others. I didn't choose a big team. In my career I always chose a team which didn't have a lot of luck.' And there was the white socks: 'I have always won things with teams wearing white socks,' he said at the time.

A genuine football genius had arrived at Stamford Bridge. Credit to Hod, Hutch and Ken for that. And for that one day, when Ruud Gullit signed for us, everyone in the world knew about Chelsea Football Club. We made the nine o'clock news for perhaps the first time ever where a punch wasn't thrown – on the pitch or at board level. I can't remember feeling so proud of my team. The rain forest was a little smaller after frequent visits to the newsagents that week. David Platt, a team-mate of Gullit's at Sampdoria, effused: 'I know Ruud was impressed when he met Glenn Hoddle. He played against him in the past and likes his ideas about the game. Two years ago, it was impossible to think of the likes of Klinsmann and Gullit going to England. Klinsmann paved the way and I think Ruud will do even better for Chelsea.'

Ruud agreed with the Hoddle approach. 'We always liked him on our side of the North Sea! He was known as a very good player and we would have based a team around such talent. And you could see that he had experience of playing in Europe. He knew what he wanted from the players and how he wanted the team to look. Also the players believed in him.'

When Colin Hutchinson and Glenn Hoddle initially flew out on their secret missions to engage Ruud and Gazza, two things were striking. First was that the talented Geordie employed a series of tough advisers whereas Ruud looked after himself. And secondly Gazza, though pleasant, would only discuss money – whereas Ruud talked football with the Chelsea contingent for three hours. Shortly after that, Glenn departed on holiday to Florida. Ruud had promised to call Colin with a decision, and he answered in the affirmative. A delighted Colin, clearly forgetting Miami's past Mafia connections, left a cryptic message at the Chelsea manager's hotel: 'The man from Italy says yes.' After that news, for Glenn the new season couldn't come soon enough.

'You could see he had some ability, but with all that long hair and everything I was worried he might be a bit undisciplined,' remembered Terry Neil, explaining how he turned down a young Ruud Gullit for £35,000. Chelsea had valued him rather greater (though in waiting a dozen years to sign him they got him buckshee). Ian McNeill, John Neal's managerial assistant, was scouting for Chelsea abroad, looking at a couple of Danish players playing against the Netherlands. He wasn't impressed – Denmark lost 6–0. But the tall, confident young Dutch sweeper was a different matter. He still has the note and the rough valuation: £300,000. How much would Pat Nevin, Speedo and Kerry have liked Rudi to ping those 50-yarders back then?

The atmosphere for his first competitive game in a Chelsea shirt against Everton on 19 August 1995 was almost feverishly charged. Merchandisers had a field day. T-shirts were everywhere: 'The Ruud Boys', 'Judge Dread: Chelsea's Ruud Boy: Judge, Jury and Executioner'. And those silly Milli Vanilli wigs with the beads. In the centre circle as the teams ran out for the first home game, the Independent Supporters' Association unfurled a Dutch flag with the old Chelsea crest on, amended to give the lion dreadlocks and a Ruud expression.

It was building up for a huge anti-climax. And 0–0 against Everton, perhaps, was just that. But in the second minute, when Ruud's raking pass out of defence alighted perfectly for Mark Stein, it was evident another star in Chelsea's pantheon of greats was born. 'Sometimes out there it was like watching an 18-year-old among 12-year-olds,' said Glenn Hoddle afterwards. Throughout the match Ruud waited, pointed, prompted, shrugged – and shook his locks occasionally in despair. Don't make him do that, chaps, we thought, don't show us up.

We still looked like a team searching for a pattern, although the Ruud boy was magnificent. We were goalless after three games. It all came right in mid-September when Southampton arrived at the Bridge for the ritual Le Tissier versus Gullit event. The Channel Islander – perpetually linked with CFC by everything from press to estate agent reports ('He's buying a house near the M3 so he can get to Chelsea's training ground, you know') – was utterly eclipsed, even outclassed by Ruud when the Dutchman was sprawled on the floor. Frank Sinclair grabbed the first on 74 minutes. Fifteen minutes later, the whole stadium erupted. Scott Minto advanced down the left and tickled it in to Mark Hughes, who headed down for Ruud to hammer in his first goal, a heavenly, unstoppable volley. It merely added to the occasion that Sparky, so often our tormentor with Man United, added a third – also his first – with an even more spectacular volley a minute later. It was the 90th anniversary of the club's founding and we were looking like a team fit to grace the famous turf at last.

Paul Elliott was at Pisa when the big Dutchman was in his pomp at Milan in 1987. Jamaica was instantly impressed, even if Ruud's dreadlocks lashed into his eye and temporarily blinded him after a challenge. He now watches from the stand rather than defence, and could see clearly enough the impact the charismatic foreigner was having at his club. 'To be honest,' Jamaica marvels, 'I've been around in football a long time – and I saw first-hand the influence he had at AC Milan and it was phenomenal – but I've never seen one player in English football or around the world have an influence at a place the way Ruud has at Chelsea. I worked at the training ground when I was looking after the kids at the end of the 1996 season, and even with the pros who have achieved a lot, he still held a great aura and had a great influence on them.'

His impact on supporters who thought they'd seen it all was quite simply astonishing. He made it into some fans' all-time Chelsea XIs (including mine) after a handful of games. There was an adrenalin rush and an expectant roar every time he got the ball or surged forward into space. We hadn't known anything like it, certainly since the days of Pat Nevin or Ossie and Charlie Cooke. But this was different. The admiration for Gullit was personal, not tribal; it transcended race and team allegiance.

'I think Ruud is more than that because he has the aura as a man and exudes that as a player,' says Paul again. 'Look at all the foreign players who've come to this country – and Cantona's been mega – but because of Ruud's aura off the pitch he's a colossus. As a player I remember papers were saying he's on his last legs, taking a pay-day, what's he going to be like in the winter . . . What these idiots don't realise is that the winter in Milan is colder than it is here. They haven't got a clue. It was never going to bother Ruud. Sometimes I think there's a little bit of a chip because our own players aren't developed like that, and that's why they're sometimes too critical, too demanding, on the overseas players.'

There was some annoyance in certain quarters of the Chelsea squad at the attention Ruud was getting. It's true that praise was unevenly heaped on the Chelsea side of 1995–96, but it was typical, of some of the players that instead of responding positively, they simmered with resentment. At least Scott Minto brought some humour to it. Asked what his magic moment of recent weeks was, he nominated the day when Ruud 'only got a seven out of ten for his performance'.

The most sickening sight, though, was the fawning of the British press. It's interesting to see the no-nonsense, barking style of the knowledgeable Italian journalists at press events. In contrast, most of the English seem beguiled by any foreign footballer who can speak their language better than they can, as Jürgen Klinsmann found a season earlier. 'Sometimes they think that there's always something unusual coming out of your mouth,' says Ruud. 'You know: "Oh yeah, oh, I never thought of that." Only some of them. But then I think that's because of what you've achieved and it is normal. If you have a professor who has done a lot of in-depth research into the heart, then you ask him questions about it because he knows more about it. Of course, I don't always have the answer because I think that football is something more global than that. But I have some answers.'

Harry Harris and others followed Ruud around like sycophantic courtiers, but their love went unrequited. Ruud rarely did one-on-

one interviews. When he did he would quickly switch the conversation from football to real life. (How Eddie McCreadie would have loved to have perfected that technique!) The funniest occasion was after an evening game. Rudi strolled into the press room at Stamford Bridge where a few hardy tabloid hacks remained hammering out their copy on laptops. They immediately threw an adoring cordon around him for some wisdom on British football.

He trotted out the now familiar phrases about English football being 'stuck in third gear' and that it was too early to judge how good he and his colleagues could be. Then he veered off the chart. Did anyone see the documentary about a man who shook uncontrollably with Parkinson's disease and had an operation to cure it? Blank faces. Ruud took five minutes to explain the fabric of this moving small-screen epic. The press men half-smiled: the lights were on, but the occupants had metaphorically nipped round the pub for a drink. He'd lost them – as he often did when talking technically about football. It was a fine way to set out your stall with them – not impolite, just intellectually impressive.

Oddly enough, sometimes he couldn't be further from that image when out of the public gaze. There's a less mature side to him. 'Football appeals to me as a child,' he says. 'We all have different personalities inside us, and I prefer the child in me so I enjoy football.' So he shares dirty jokes with the worst of them, and spars verbally against the smallest team-mates with the biggest personalities, Dennis Wise and John Spencer. To the press he was the Dutch Master; to Wisey and Spenny he was 'Big Nose'. They seemed unusual soul mates. 'It just happens,' says Ruud. 'It's just a friendship, it's not that we are going out a lot together, though sometimes we see each other for a meal after games or playing golf, but not all the time.'

Variety makes a better mix, Ruud believes. 'I think that everyone has an outlook on life in a different way. It depends on what you talk to them about,' he says. 'The joking and the playing around, that's not the whole story. They are also good for team-building, for building team spirit. That's also important. You know sometimes it can be boring always having the same types of character. You need some types who are totally different from the others that gives you a good team spirit, a good blend.' Ruud accepted there was a certain amount of responsibility on him to set an example at Chelsea, 'but everywhere I've played it's like that. It's no more at Chelsea, just the same. I know wherever I play I have the same responsibility.'

In the meantime, Ruud's impact, up until his injury in the autumn, was every bit as powerful as Klinsmann's a season earlier, if not more profound. Yet the system, and his best place within it, didn't click until that enforced sabbatical. Up to that point, Ruud would leave his sweeper position to kick up rumpus in more advanced positions, and his languorous retreats often left us misshapen at the back. David Lee, his deputy, was less inclined to rove, but more importantly, after several months wrangling, Dan Petrescu, the wing-back from Sheffield Wednesday, arrived. Suddenly the 3-5-2 made sense. We started to turn it on, even without Dutch inspiration. 'Of course, the system needed Dan Petrescu,' says Ruud. 'It was better then. We played some good football. I think Newcastle was good, in the League at home and away in the Cup. Those were very good performances. First you have to understand the system. Everyone came to realise what the system can do for you. You can only do it by having results, and when we had these results, I think that we got a lot more optimistic about the system.'

The point where people had started to take notice was the home defeat of runaway leaders Newcastle United in December. Without Ruud, we won 1–0 from Dan's intelligent volley. On the return of our inspiration, now deployed in midfield, a Radio 5 Live commentator was moved to describe the team as one that could, on its day, annihilate anyone. Since the FA Cup first-round draw had paired us with Newcastle – in the tie of the round – such a display was the only type that would suffice. As it was we surrendered the hard-earned 1–0 advantage through sloppy goalkeeping and faced the trek up to the north-east – not our happiest hunting ground – for the replay. 'I think the Newcastle atmosphere for each game was very nice,' says Ruud, 'and it's good, they were made quiet, so that's what you play for.'

But the mood at St James's Park was carnivorous at first, so few Chelsea adherents were allowed into the ground. Those Blues fans who had made it were treated to a fantastic display by the Ruud boy, whose guile and timing were stunning. Spraying balls with pinpoint accuracy, he set up chance after chance. We ran the Geordies ragged. Even so, a deflected free-kick and a penalty, seemingly given by the ref to re-ingratiate himself with the locals after Wise's successful spot-kick, gave the home side a 2–1 advantage.

With minutes remaining a Petrescu cross to the far post saw Doobs beat Watson to the ball and it dropped perfectly for Ruud to stab it past Srnicek. The photo of Doobs and Ruud running in celebration is burned into the memory. And, of course, thanks to Eddie Newton's cool completion, we progressed after the penalty shoot-out. 'That goal was very nice, and it was a vital one as you know,' says Ruud. 'It was good for team spirit because we had to go six hours back on the bus, so everyone was happy. That's different if you play well.' He rates it as his best performance in a Chelsea shirt. And this was January, when the 'dodgy knee' was supposed to play him up.

That was a crucial victory for the new Chelsea. People have taken us seriously ever since. And there were highlights still to come, as Rudi fitted into midfield and began to worry defences more with his pace and intelligence. 'I think that Middlesbrough was a very good performance too,' says Ruud. 'I think the whole technical side was good.' We tore the Teessiders apart 5–0. Then there was Southampton away. Ruud's rampaging run from his own half was met with a Sparky flick. His clip over Dave Beasant was magical. 'I think that Dennis played very well there,' Ruud defers. 'Dennis came back from a very difficult moment, he was injured, he didn't play the week before and everybody was thinking would he be captain again and so on. And so I think that it was more his game, not my game.'

The boggy Selhurst Park quarter-final replay against Wimbledon saw another fine performance from Ruud. It was a Gullit-esque reaction to Vinnie Jones's sneering comments about Ruud's attitude following an earlier Premiership encounter: 'You don't respond . . . in my heart I always think about myself, not others. I never criticise other players about what they do and don't do. It is my philosophy. First you have to look at yourself before you think of the others. So if people point their fingers at me that is not a problem for me.'

The same self-confidence stood him in good stead in his early life. 'As a child my father told me that I would have to work harder than others for what I would achieve with my talent. For me, that was the stimulation: I took it positively. If you feel attacked by the way you are, then you have a problem. I felt proud of what I was, of my colour, of everything.' He appears utterly fearless, on or off the pitch. 'Sometimes I think we gave teams too much respect, like Wimbledon in the first FA Cup match. We are better playing our own game.'

Ruud's quality did the talking at Wimbledon in the Premiership – a game in which Glenn Hoddle harked back to the winter of 1963 under Tommy Docherty, by fielding a team tailored to the conditions and the opposition. Rudi left the Jones boy for dead on several occasions. Ruud is incredibly confident and very self-aware. He was used as a decoy at the free-kick for our goal at Selhurst Park that day. After Vinnie's pathetic public assessment of him 'squealing more than a pot-bellied pig', all eyes would be on him seeking revenge, and he was smart enough to recognise the potential for misleading people in that direction. And again in the Cup replay, Ruud punished the Dons every bit as much as Craig, Dennis and Dan did. He hit the post and tore through their defence down the flanks where the pitch was least debilitated. He also made one of the goals – if not the crucial header that Doobs powered in.

And so to Villa Park and Man United – again. Ruud played it down; no 'Klinsmann's dreaming of twin towers' stuff here. 'It's nothing, just a semi-final,' he shrugged. 'Nothing counts until the final.' Not everyone agreed. The banners decking Villa Park said 'In Hod we trust' and 'Chelsea's Ruud Boys', 'Rudi Can't Fail'. As the teams came out onto the rutted, sand-covered pitch, the balloons and streamers supplied by the Independent Supporters' Association (those that hadn't already succumbed to the fans' premature excitement, anyway) flew into the air to a deafening roar. As David 'Rodders' Lee trotted up to our end he smiled broadly; it seemed all he could do to stop himself from cheering with joy.

We won the first battle, of course, outsinging the red hordes to such an extent that a rosacea-cheeked Alex Ferguson emerged before kick-off to try to whip up his subdued troops. And we won the early skirmishes on the field too. Ruud himself topped a superb first-half display of tempo change and patient teamwork by harking back to the Milan days with a storming header past Schmeichel to set up victory. And if it hadn't been for the injuries to Steve Clarke and Terry Phelan we may have held on. As it is, Cole and Beckham – the latter latching on to a poor back-pass from the otherwise exemplary Craig Burley – steered United to Wembley.

'The team did everything to win,' said Rudi. 'And the supporters were tremendous for us. Unfortunately it didn't go well, but Wembley can wait – there are bigger goals to achieve. Just one match at Wembley was not so important to me as seeing this Chelsea team develop and take shape in the way we want. I'm looking to achieve much more with Chelsea and I'm happy with the way we are going. There can be too much attention on one match and it can affect your overall aim. That was the case against Manchester United and we lost because of two injuries and the fact that we created two goals for them that they didn't create themselves. It was a pity, but we will be better for the experience. Maybe we will be a little more cynical in the future when we are in the lead.'

The lessons of life under Rinus Michels and Arrigo Sacchi weren't wasted on Ruud. The Dutchman was the first to comfort the Burley boy after his unfortunate misdemeanour. 'Craig was understandably upset with himself,' he says, phlegmatically. 'After that goal I went to him straightaway and told him not to worry. I think everyone knows we didn't lose just because he made that one bad pass. I said at the time that when we win, we win together and so when we lose it is together also. It might have been me who made such a mistake in another game.'

The shockwaves of that defeat scuppered any chance of playing in Europe the following season, something Ruud clearly had an appetite for. And the nature of it was telling – it was one of 17 occasions on which victory was within our grasp but relinquished. 'I think it was lack of concentration,' says Ruud emphatically. 'Concentrating for 90 minutes is always hard – it's the hardest thing in football, perhaps. And, really, you either have it or you don't. It is difficult to improve it once you have played some time. After the semi-final, it was as if we had nothing to play for. Teams wanted it more than us and they beat us. Then we got annoyed with ourselves, and the gaffer showed he was not happy with how we were playing, and our game came together again against Leeds. But by this time it was too late.'

The 4–1 defeat of Leeds was the final fling in another season of highs and lows. But the greatest buzz rose from the deepest disappointment. Once it became obvious that Glenn was set on quitting Stamford Bridge for Lancaster Gate, there was only one consolation that could possibly make amends. On the final day of the season, Chelsea fans were unequivocal as to what that prize was. Even before he emerged from the tunnel against Blackburn – enigmatically last – there was no point in the board considering anyone else as Glenn's successor. The nearest credible alternative – Peter Shreeves apart – was summarily dismissed as if he had never won a Championship or a European trophy in his life. 'You can stick George Graham up your arse!' rang round every part of the Bridge. Sealing the issue, Ken Bates made as if to conduct the choir. And in case he doubted who was wanted instead, 'We want Rudi! We want Rudi!' was chanted on and off for 40 minutes.

The 'lap of appreciation' turned into an impromptu coronation. Ruud was visibly moved by it all, looking almost humble. 'Without doubt the reception the fans gave me was very important,' Ruud smiles. 'Before, when the rumours started, of course as a football player already you start thinking about it – that's obvious. So when they wanted me that bad I was, oh! . . . It was a big surprise to me. You know it was a strange experience and of course when I was thinking about doing the job the reaction of the fans made it a lot easier for me to make the decision. And also I knew I had a lot to do back for them.'

Ruud took the additional duties seriously. 'Player-manager is totally different,' he says. 'You have to take some distance from being a player. Sometimes you have to make some decisions that are very difficult. It's not a position everyone can play.' Glenn never asked his advice, but that one season stood him in good stead: 'The good thing is that I didn't come in really unaware. All my ideas on the team, what I had in mind for it, was always there.'

Ruud's appointment was rubber-stamped almost immediately, and we had our first-ever overseas – and black – manager. 'Make no mistake.' Paul Elliott insists, 'it was a great day for Chelsea Football Club when Ruud Gullit was appointed manager. That was a significant breakthrough – with a capital "S". We'll probably appreciate it even more ten or fifteen years down the line.'

Ruud had shown enough commitment to the development of the club and its players in his first season to make the board's decision a simple one. He was to some extent identified with the progress of the youngsters. And he'd always been a team member – 'If I wanted to play on my own as an individual, I would be a tennis player' – and it showed. 'I think they did well in the season: Michael Duberry, Jody Morris, Mark Nicholls,' he says. 'Duberry has been a surprise, but for now this is where it starts for Doobs. To get there is easy; to stay there is the hard part. It all depends on himself. Now he has to show us that he is what he was. He's not there yet. No. This is where the hard work begins because he has set a standard and must also show he can still do better. It is the most important thing.'

There was the celebrated occasion captured live on Sky Sports when Ruud strolled off at half-time, arm around unaccustomed wing-back Andy Myers. The microphone picked up 'Tyson' complaining, 'I don't understand.' As they strode past the camera, Rudi responded, 'Come with me – I will show you.'

'I don't remember that,' says Ruud. 'But I think it's nice if you see that people can do more than you or they think they can. You just hand on to them something and then they realise and they go a step further. I have done the same thing with important players. Eddie Newton has played very, very well, consistently right up to his injury – as I said, he was the silent force in the team. John Spencer played very well, he plays in a different way now, uses his head more. I had a word with him. I said I didn't want him to spend so much energy running and tackling, I just wanted him to concentrate on scoring goals. And you can see it worked.'

Ruud was generous in sharing his vast experience with fellow players and he would play mind games with them: 'Who is your toughest opponent?' he would tease. 'Yourself!' He's big on individual responsibility within the team: 'We all have assignments. You all must do the job assigned and then you can express yourself.'

Recalling the Milan side of Baresi, Maldini, Rijkaard or Donadoni, he says, 'If you play at a high level, you're used to those high-level players; everybody has his skill and admires others for theirs, but it was part of the job, and for the team after all. If you didn't do what is expected, then we got angry. It belonged to the team.'

That goes for off the pitch as well. Ruud was amused but appalled by the biscuits-and-sausages diet of some English players, and he was aware that they liked a drink. He believed the best way to stop them over-indulging was to leave the responsibility for moderation down to them. 'If players play well and want a beer or glass of wine,' he says, 'then they can have it. But you must know your own limits. You must know you are also with the team.'

He adapts the principle to all situations. During a reserve-team game at Chelsea in his first season, Rudi was talking to a young professional struggling to break into the side. 'You're too good for this, aren't you?' he encouraged, quietly. 'You deserve first-team football, don't you?' The youngster nodded. 'And you know who can do something about it?' A shake of the head. 'Only you.'

In fact football is one of the few things about which he is invariably serious. When the Colombian goalkeeper Higuita's scorpion kick wowed 'em at Wembley, Rudi related how Dutch national coach Rinus Michels – the 'Sphinx' – would have responded to such flamboyance: 'He would drop him from the team for two or three games for playing a dangerous game in defence. Once one of his club players did a back-heel in his own area. So Michels played him in the reserves for a few games to teach him a lesson.' He would also explain how Milan prepared for world domination (and the 1989 European Cup final where they obliterated Steaua Bucharest – Dan Petrescu included – 4–0), how Arrigo Sacchi drilled the system into his team until they dreamt about it at night. His presence raised the sights of the players and the club. He's been there, done that. He's a winner at the highest level. He's worth listening to; it might rub off.

Ruud had his simple thoughts for the day: 'You never talk about a player on another team,' he would warn. 'Don't think about them. Just think about your own game.' Another was 'If we keep the ball, they can't hurt us.' Or 'We win as a team, so we lose as one.' Then there's his favourite old Dutch proverb, thrown back at those who blame defeat on circumstances beyond their control. 'If only,' they'll say. 'Yes,' he will smile, 'but if my grandmother had a penis, then she would be my grandfather. What happened, happened. You can't change that.'

Ruud was, if anything, more of a no-nonsense 'gaffer' than the studious Glenn. He immediately released the nutritionist (whose 'nuts 'n' muesli' regime, despite what the papers say, was never rigorously enforced) and reflexologist, 'Tootsie'; banned the players from using their beloved mobile phones on match days or on the team coach; broke up the 'black table', 'white table', 'kids table', 'staff table' that existed in the training-ground dining-hall; and brought in a professional fitness coach, former Olympic sprinter Ade Mafe – there were times, it must be said, when Chelsea had looked like a team that was trained to the fitness level of a 37-year-old player-manager.

'It is very important to be as fit as you possibly can be,' says Ruud. 'When you get to that extra level you feel more confident in your ability and everything is possible. I was certainly comfortable at Chelsea with the methods Glenn used. But the people he had are no longer here and I will be trying just to use my own methods at the club. I am not saying there are big changes but what I will put in place comes from the experience I have had from many top coaches and specialists during my career.'

His reign ushered in a mood of cool professionalism buzzing with conviction. Ruud set the terms. He was aloof when he wanted to be – from the outset. When it seemed certain the fans' hero would be offered the management chalice, Graham Rix, then still youth-team coach, saw Ruud walking off the pitch on his own and seized his chance. 'I went up to him after training, when Glenn looked like leaving,' says Graham, 'and I said to him, "Look, Ruud, if you get the job, I'm ready." He said, "I know," and just carried on walking.' Such is the lofty coolness of Ruud, the way he sets his own agenda. 'He knows exactly what he wants,' says Colin Hutchinson admiringly, 'and he's very definite about how he can achieve it.'

In Graham Rix he found a fine foil, though Ruud perhaps underengaged his café crème-smoking assistant in tactical conversation during his tenure. It was an aspect of his management that was typically left unexplained. Like the team selections, pinned on the dressing-room wall an hour before kick-off, as much to the curiosity of Ricco as those picked, or the sudden experimentation with callow youths. 'Of course,' Ruud insists, 'the manager must also be a good psychologist because he has to deal with a lot of players with different kind of characters. And you have to know how to handle them and it's not that easy. It is important to get the blend of players and also their personalities. Then you can get the best out of them.'

In summer '96 Ricco described a smooth realignment under the new manager. 'Our philosophy won't change,' he said. 'But we have to win more games and that means being more solid, which is what

Rudi is after. Look at the most successful teams and they had a spine – that's what Rudi's talking about with the lads he's brought in this season. He's looked abroad for experts like Leboeuf, who's been a libero throughout his career and can read every situation. But there's more to it than that. 'We've always asked questions of the players here, ever since Glenn arrived, but are trying to carry the process further all the time.'

Our first enticing glimpse of Ruud as manager came during his stint as a summariser for the BBC during Euro 96. Having successfully predicted the positional changes Italian boss Arrigo Sacchi would make at half-time during one game, he chastised the Czechs for their hidebound lack of ambition in another. 'My philosophy is to create things for yourself and to win. It's very easy to destroy things. I prefer to create.' But how does that square with his other maxim: 'We have to be more cynical [clinical?] – one chance, one goal'?

Maybe it's all in each player knowing their individual responsibility within the team system. 'His team-talks last about five seconds,' said Wisey, soon into Ruud's reign. 'He just says, "Look, this is what I want you to do . . . and I would also like some goals." He wants us to express ourselves, but he also wants us to win. Before his first season as manager he said, "I only want to win the first match, and then after that the second match, and the third match . . ."' Unlike his predecessor, though, Ruud could be open to discussion of tactics. He listened to what people like Dennis or Ricco had to say, then ignored them and made up his own mind. Now, Dennis's views on the midfield and his role within it are considered.

But there's much more to Rudi than that. 'Football is not my whole life,' shrugs Ruud. 'Of course, I enjoy playing it. But I don't like talking about it all the time.' Not surprising, coming from a footballer whose all-time favourite film is *The Miracle Worker*, an old biopic of deaf, dumb and blind girl Helen Keller and her incredible mentor. His heroes include Nelson Mandela and Bob Marley. He has other things to think about.

Now, outside the goldfish bowl of Italian football life, he can indulge other passions in a more private lifestyle. 'I play some golf with Dennis and others – Dennis says I am the only black man who can beat him! – I go out with my kids, I go to the city just shopping, and I go to concerts, things like that. And here I can go to restaurants. Those things would normally be trouble for a well-known footballer in Italy. I don't like hero worship. That's why I went to London – just to be swallowed by the big city.'

Little wonder that when Ruud was enticing the great Gianluca

Vialli to choose Chelsea over other clubs, he knew that London was a big selling point. 'What do you want out of life – football and non-football?' he inveigled, confident that his own magnetism was something he didn't need to press home. 'Here, when people see you out they say "Hi" to you and then they leave you alone. They have a lot of respect for your way of life which is important. It's part of the big city mentality. Big cities are all the same.'

Just as easily as discussing tactical switches at the training ground, Ruud could engage in debate about racial issues with Dennis or Eddie Newton, then chat for ages about mobile phone technology or computer games. He was personable, sometimes haughty. He would sometimes leave the chairman chewing air because of some sudden pressing engagement elsewhere. There was always a spark when he was in a room. And how he enjoyed himself at Chelsea. 'If I can pass on this feeling to the rest of the team,' he said, 'then we can make it fun together. But, of course, we all have our assignments.'

How times changed between 1990 and 1996. 'All of a sudden,' commented Paul Elliott at the time, 'the players that we've got now, your Viallis, your di Matteos, your Leboeufs, your Gullits . . . Arsenal and Tottenham couldn't get the players that Chelsea signed. Five years ago the other clubs would have been a priority. So the trend is definitely changing, and it just gets better and better.'

Homegrown youth also meant a lot to Rudi. Blooding youngsters was his smart pre-emptive strike against the xenophobes of the British press, sharpening their knives at the Bosman hordes' invasion of Britain. His first team selection featured internationals from eight different countries. Equally noteworthy, there were three promising youngsters from our youth scheme, aged 17, 19 and 20. Jody Morris, the youngest, and at one time the best graduate since Ray Wilkins, came on in the second half.

As a result, Ruud was able to play the exotic imports off against the sprouting of young English oaks. It was a hallmark of his management. Paul Hughes, Mark Nicholls, Nick Crittenden, Joe Sheerin, Stevie Hampshire and Neil Clement debuted under him. There could have been more.

Rudi rarely watched the kids play, nor the reserves. But he saw enough quality in one 15-year-old schoolboy in five minutes to want to blood him immediately when first-team injuries were piling up. He had to be persuaded forcefully that this wasn't a good idea. Rudi, a young debutant himself, liked the idea of throwing in the odd youngster to see how they fared.

Twenty-one-year-old Michael Duberry cemented his first-team

position under Rudi as the ex-YTS vaults were raided. Eddie Newton was habitually praised by his manager for his growing influence in the holding midfield role. 'He is our silent force,' Ruud announced proudly. (It was misquoted in one paper as 'silent horse'. Now that would have been an oblique adage, even by Ruud's standards.) Perhaps most surprisingly, Mark Nicholls and Paul Hughes blossomed enough to warrant positive exposure in the papers. Rudi had the magic touch.

Mark Hughes ('Hyoogsie' as Ruud pronounced it, having known Welsh coach Barry Hughes in his Dutch playing career), Dennis Wise, the returnee Graeme Le Saux and Steve Clarke were all singled out, as senior players, to help knit the team's morale. In the Italian way, always Ruud's strongest influence, he communicated with the team through them, principally Dennis.

But something else happened during his time. He raised our game – the supporters' – immeasurably. We learned how to be winners again. Chelsea were considered genuine title challengers for the first time in years by that loose fraternity, the football community. Even by Ruud's biggest admirer, Alex Ferguson. And it wasn't simply the fluid, attacking flair on the pitch.

Ruud's presence was talismanic, no matter how inattentive his management style appeared. His personality placed us on the world football map. Van Basten and Rijkaard popped in to see the lads train. Dani Behr leched after him on TV. Des Lynam and Alan Hansen fawned over him.

He enjoyed London, so rang up his friends and invited them to play 'sexy' football with him for the great city's most fashionable club. And they came, because of him. It took a plane journey sitting next to his compatriot for the superb keeper Ed De Goey to be convinced SW6 was where it was at. The brilliant Uruguayan Gus Poyet was hand-picked by Gullit. Norwegian striking sensation Tore Andre Flo too. Celestine Babayaro, the solid, exciting full-back, heard that Ruud wanted him and couldn't sign fast enough. Even the mighty Gianfranco Zola, one of the greatest footballers of his generation, was lured by Ruud. Zola, the one Tottenham and Arsenal couldn't get. The one *Hoddle* couldn't get. And the loveable Sardinian delivered just when we needed him to. As Ruud took a back seat, he destroyed teams with mesmerising runs and staggering strikes: Man United, Liverpool, Wimbledon. There was no player in the world, it seemed, who wouldn't fancy playing for Rudi's Chelsea.

Under Ruud, other supporters didn't simply respect us, they actually *liked* us. He was the piece we'd missed for so long, and suddenly the whole mystifying puzzle of 26 years' under-achievement was falling into place.

He often said he wanted us to be more 'cynical' (again, he probably meant clinical), yet he presented a more congenial face than the club had had for 25 years.

How dignified was he – in contrast to some we could mention – in mourning Matthew Harding's tragic death? It is difficult to conceive of another person, let alone player-manager, who could have combined respect, optimism and professionalism during that period as Ruud did. Even if the hand-holding at the start of that memorable Tottenham game wasn't his idea, it was Ruud's presence that made it imaginable. We became a club more confident and at ease with itself.

How good did he look coming out at Wembley in May 1997, at the end of his first season in charge? To Chelsea fans, the contrast between Robson's tight-lipped shuffle and Rudi's languid swagger put us one-up over Boro before a ball was kicked. That it took one of Rudi's brilliant acquisitions – the mighty Robbie Di Matteo – and one homegrown 'brother' in Eddie Newton to win our first major trophy for a quarter of a century was so fitting it might have been Hollywood scripted. He became the first overseas manager to win a major English trophy. (Luca, oddly enough, was the second.) Des Lynam was moved to suggest that he couldn't remember such scenes of joy as at the end of that final. At the centre of the extended 'Blue Day' celebrations, handing his chairman the cup, was Ruud. He'd turned down the offer of Bates's lucky leprechaun as he collected the trophy because he thought it was a joke.

Just ten months later, in a Chelsea hotel, the same chairman handed his manager a letter explaining that his services were no longer required. This time, there was definitely no joke intended.

Whatever it was that led to Ruud's dismissal – conspiracy, communication breakdown, cock-up – the club was the poorer for the loss of its figurehead. At the time Chelsea were second in the Premiership (albeit temporarily) and in the last four of the Coca-Cola Cup. Nevertheless, there had been doubts over Ruud's recent 'performance'. His judgement had been called into question in the buying, unseen, of squad reinforcements from a mysterious French contact. He appeared over-occupied with extra-mural commitments like his Dutch coaching badge or over-priced clothing label.

He seemed to have lost his spark of genius in team selections too, and was off form on the pitch. Worse still was his judgement in taking the money for a pizza advertising campaign! 'Corners?!' He'd turned one.

'You don't win the Premiership by beating the other top teams,' he said, 'but by beating those below you.' Up to February 1998, when Ruud was sacked, we had not beaten a top-six side, and had tumbled to inferior sides in Coventry, Bolton, Southampton and Everton.

In mid-January, following the infuriating 3–1 defeat by a weak home side at Goodison, Ruud looked genuinely ruffled for the first time. He seemed to be feeling it. Whenever we lost, he always had a happy knack of accentuating the positive in post-match briefings, exposing the rich vein of optimism that was one of the gifts he brought to the club. Not this time. Nor at Arsenal, following the dismal spell of defeats that were the sad culmination of his management.

People protested that he didn't explain his actions. That didn't mean he wasn't accountable. He was, and is, a genius. Geniuses should never be required to explain. Quite often they can't.

None of these issues was a hanging offence. All to be expected of a manager in his second full year in charge. There was enough in the six-goal demolitions of Barnsley and Tottenham and the emphatic eclipsing of Derby and Sheffield Wednesday to suggest that some things were progressing. Ruud wasn't given a chance to make any more mistakes.

And so Luca was anointed. Luca, whom Rudi was said to have 'mistreated' by keeping him on the bench and saying hurtful things. Luca, who had maybe become a better Premiership player for Rudi's handling of him. Luca, who was another world-famous name. So, from Hoddle to Gullit to Vialli – the king is dead, long live the emperor. A seamless transition, or another avoidable gamble that sets us back in our quest for the Championship? Time will tell, if we choose to listen.

Luca's first nervous job was to overturn a fortuitous 2–1 deficit to Arsenal in the Coca-Cola semi-final second leg. Picking himself – of course – he led the Blues to a famous 3–1 victory on an extraordinarily rousing night. A number of celebrants afterwards found time to toast Rudi's health in The Jolly Maltster, a boozer near the ground. 'I feel sorry for him,' someone mused. 'He got us to the semis.' There was a pause. 'But would we have won with him in charge tonight?'

'No,' we chorused, unanimously.

Chelsea fans secretly knew we didn't own Ruud Gullit. He was always passing through, gloriously. He belonged to the world, as we were frequently reminded. But wasn't it brilliant to have him for those sweet 30 months? Wasn't it great to be associated with a man who will go on to make history elsewhere and always carry a little piece of Chelsea with him?

Weeks after his departure we were back at Wembley, back on top of Boro (a 2–0 repeat) and back in the silverware. After that there was the little matter of another glorious finale to our Cup-Winners' Cup campaign, masterminded for the most part by the dreadlocked Dutchman. We never got to wish him farewell and show our appreciation for his too-short stay, for bringing back the swagger to SW6.

So here goes. Thanks for everything, Rudi. Goodbye, genius.

12

God

There came unto that sea called Chels a prophet beloved of the people
of Tott-en-ham of the north and not greatly cared unto by those
Chels-ites who forgave not the many smotings he had delivered even
unto them in battle at the lane of the hart of white and the bridge of
Stam-ford. And his name was Glen-Hod. And in the first year of our
Lord of playing and management at Chel-sea, yea Glen-Hod did
perform an miracle. And the Chels-ites saw that the powers of Glen-
Hod were mighty, for he delivered unto them the Cup Final of FA, an
celebration denied of them almost an generation. They cast their eyes
upon the towers twin of that place called Wem-ber-lee. And they saw
that it was good. And two summers passeth and Glen-Hod look-ed
upon his people and saw that they were still sore afraid for the want
of silver-ware in their cabinets, yea even were they afeard of the fate
known as the mediocrity of the middle table. And so from over the sea
where wheat is pummelled into the myriad shapes of the Pas-ta,
came at his beckon an new and famed champion, of the locks of
dread, whose name was Gull-it. And the people of Chels looked upon
this new Gull-it. And they saw that he was bloody good . . .

'Morale wasn't bad, but the direction was wrong and I think people
had got unnerved with the whole situation. I actually put a team
together for the first game at Blackburn and I hadn't seen them
play, and I just went on what everybody said to me.' Dave Webb
performed a vital job for Chelsea. When he took over from Ian
Porterfield in 1993 it smacked of the time The Doc assumed control
from Ted Drake 30 years earlier – the club had lost the plot and was
in a spiral of decline.

Webby secured our Premier status and was asked by Ken Bates
to perform an independent audit of the club. If he'd been appointed
permanently at the end of the season, he'd have placed his faith in
the products of Chelsea's youth scheme. 'To me,' says Webby, 'Eddie
Newton was the one it should have started around. People can say

about Graeme Le Saux. I don't know why he was unpopular with the players. I'd just got there, and they came up with a fee, and I said okay. Lovely boy. There was nothing wrong with him, I just genuinely didn't see the position that you could play him in. Didn't see him as a natural left-back and didn't see him as a natural winger. I couldn't see myself playing with wing-backs.

'You can be a hero at Chelsea in whatever position you play in; it's been proven over the years with people like Eddie McCreadie. And if I did have an inclination, that was the way I was going. I wanted people to be individuals in their own right, and there weren't enough of them in the club. As time got nearer to me leaving, I knew that in my heart of hearts I was going through the motions, and it was very awkward, very hard to go in and keep your head up. I always remember someone said to me after, that on the last day at Sheffield the crowd weren't too appreciative of me at the end – not that they were meant to be. And that supposedly indicated to Ken that he didn't feel I was the person because of that.'

Meanwhile, Glenn Hoddle had been waiting for a sign from a higher plain than even Ken Bates. He was looking for divine inspiration. Few in the game would plan their careers in such a way. But then few players were as great as Glenn. (Once he'd left Tottenham, of course.) He's not your traditional common-or-garden Christian, just as he was never your straight-up-and-down footballer. And so, two days after shepherding Swindon safely through the play-off final in 1993, Spurs legend Glenn succeeded Chelsea FA Cup icon Dave Webb as Chelsea's player-manager. It was a brave appointment by Ken, and a quite brilliant one. The first player the new boss had to value was himself – Swindon were bitterly disappointed and wanted compensation for losing Hoddle the player as well. Seven hundred and fifty thousand pounds might have been one of the bargains of the decade, had we seen more of his influential presence on the field.

He was more than aware that there was a challenge ahead of him. The fact that Chelsea was a club horribly becalmed and lacking any footballing direction appealed to him; he could bring in a new crew and take it any place he wanted. (Tottenham were too modern and successful for his plans.) He believed he'd have the ship on course in six months. 'I am very much aware that the fans crave success,' he said, setting about eradicating another problem – the association with White Hart Lane he was acutely conscious of.

Another two days and the Hoddle revolution began. The youth set-up had been upgraded by Gwyn Williams, but it was radically renovated by Hod's first appointment, his old England spar and

Arsenal rival Graham Rix arriving from Dundee as youth-team coach. 'He said I'd have to stop playing,' says Graham, 'but that it would be good experience.' Ricco trusted him; after all, if you share a secret passion for concerts by the Eagles, it kind of binds you together in ignominy. 'We decided straightaway to play 3-5-2 throughout the club. It allows the style to go through the whole club. So a kid in the Under-14s knows that if he works hard and makes it, he'll know exactly what to do when he's playing in Terry Phelan's position, or Dennis Wise's position. A lot of kids come to Chelsea because they like the way Glenn had the first team playing. They say, "That'll do me!"

'Jimmy Nicholl came up to me when we played Millwall once and mullered them 3-0. He says to me at half-time, "God, your lads ain't half knocking it about." I take that for granted, so I just agreed with him. He says, "And they play like that at Under-16s as well?" I says, "We play like that at Under-11s." He was astounded.

'At most clubs it stops at the youth team. They just want players rather than a system they can work to. We want our youngsters to know what's expected of them. Somebody, maybe not me or Ruud Gullit, is going to benefit hugely from this in six, seven years' time. Seven or eight youth-team boys will not only make the numbers up in the first team, but will be exceptional players. Which is what you want, isn't it?'

Glenn's admiration for the Ajax method of nurturing talent revealed itself in the new structure he immediately established at Chelsea under Graham, though in private it was the German model of mental strength, stamina and skill that he most often cited. 'At Ajax they have a formula,' says Graham Rix. 'They call it TIPS – technique, intelligence, personality, speed. For me, though, it's PITS. Personality comes first because if you can't perform under pressure, you've no chance.'

Personality was something that was lacking at Chelsea – our colourful chairman apart – as Webby had diagnosed. From being the nearly-men in the mid-'80s, we'd become the nowhere-nearly-men of the '90s. Hod had always been a top-drawer player. The last of the glamour boys of the '70s; a player with glitter in the blood coursing through his veins. With the arrival of Glenn, the new Ken Bates tactic was clearly stated: sign big names to get the media interested, and bring the glamour and the crowds flooding back. The opening game of the 1993–94 season brought a crowd of 29,189, which roughly translated into 41 per cent more optimism in Glenn's much-heralded passing game than the midfield by-pass tactics under Ian Porterfield. We lost 2–1 to Blackburn, but in the patient passing the

Hoddle hallmark was clear. 'My simple belief is that if you don't master the ball, the ball will master you,' he often said. He was right.

'To be honest,' Glenn says now, 'I didn't really enjoy the football in the first two years, apart from the cup runs, but the final year was completely different.' That was when the pieces fell into place. They were very much up in the air when he arrived.

The Hod era had begun as well as it could for everyone at Chelsea. We slaughtered Spurs 4–0 to win the pre-season Makita Trophy. Okay, so it wasn't the Champions Cup, but as Blues fans we've become used to accepting any tinware going. And 'God' was able triumphantly to ally himself with his new club for the first time. Sad, but it was special. 'I know it meant a lot to the supporters to beat Spurs,' Glenn said, and conceded that the slaying of his old club would help people accept him as a true Blue rather than a faded lilywhite. And in Glenn's first season there were other such magic moments. We were the first team to beat eventual double-winners Man United, and the only side to do the double over them. In fact, it was Glenn's most important early signing, Gavin Peacock, who did the damage in both cases.

The Glenn effect was pronounced. We beat Liverpool as well, from a Shipperley strike and a goalkeeping error of Grobbelaarian proportions. Yet some of the finest hours in Glenn's three-year reign came in the darkest moments, when his tactical nous and conviction were stretched to the limit by a depleted squad: look no further than the FA Cup campaign in '93–'94, or Europe a year later. Glenn was to ensure his place in the Chelsea history books by becoming only the fourth manager to take us to a Cup final.

Despite the trumpeting of a new era at Chelsea, there was an early jolt that threatened to dislodge his halo. The team was performing with irritating inconsistency; 'the old Chelsea problem since the '70s', as Glenn called it. Professionalism is the art of producing a good performance when you least feel like it. That was not CFC. Many of the players seemed incapable of adapting to the system, and without Glenn in the sweeper's role and full strength in other departments the 3-5-2 was temporarily consigned to the recycling bin.

Then in December 1994 the club slipped into the relegation zone. The Southampton game was the nadir. We lost 3–1. The performance, the situation, the shame . . . they were a heavy burden on him, and had a profound effect on Glenn. Alan Hansen publicly urged Glenn to change his tactics. In a tense, noisy dressing-room after the game, Dennis Wise agreed: 'It's no good us trying all this pretty stuff without the right people . . . we've got to get stuck in, close them down and stuff.' Glenn's steadying influence, Peter Shreeves, mediated. 'What I think Dennis is saying is that perhaps we need to compete more when not in possession,' he offered.

Relegation was not part of Glenn's agenda and it shook him. The sound of the trap-door opening was an embarrassment, but it had a more profound effect. 'I learned some important lessons in those days,' he said. He came to recognise that graft was needed alongside the grace. The consolation of the game at the Dell was Mark Stein's first goal since his signing two months earlier. His second in as many days marked a turning-point: we beat Newcastle 1–0 and never really looked back. Stein's Premiership record, set then, of nine goals in seven consecutive games, still stands. Slowly we sailed into less troubled waters.

It's possible he felt disappointed by the slow progress of some players. Whatever, he didn't look upon them as 'my boys' until after the preposterous 4–3 game against Spurs later that season. By then, there were other distractions as we progressed in our most successful FA Cup campaign for 24 years. In truth it was almost over before it started. Glenn admitted he had dreamt that we would face his brother Carl's team, struggling Barnet, in our first Cup game. What his vision hadn't confirmed was how poorly we would play. It was 0–0, but Barnet had a chance to steal victory. The replay was won, annoyingly, handsomely.

Oxford almost upset our progress too. After we had equalised their opener and gone ahead, goalscorer and Hod favourite Gavin Peacock inexplicably handled in the penalty area. The spot-kick wasn't converted, however, and we pursued our dream. Sheffield Wednesday, predictably, blocked the road to Wembley. The now traditional nervy home draw in the Cup looked set to presage an iniquitous exit at Hillsborough, but the replay proved one of the most triumphant nights in Glenn's reign.

It remains one of his favourite team performances. 'It was an excellent performance,' he says. 'Our hunger and spirit were fantastic. We closed them down, never gave them time to settle and created great chances on the break.' One incredible move, where six passes tore through Wednesday's lines, ended with Spencer's early opener. Wednesday equalised to earn extra-time, but there was only one team in it. Powerful running off the ball, fluid passing movements and immense concentration, with Eddie Newton, Craig Burley and Gavin Peacock again outstanding, made us easy 3–1 winners.

Wolves were professionally disposed of 1–0 in the quarter-final live on BBC TV, and the dream semi-final – a Luton team featuring former Bridge hero Kerry 'Mary' Dixon – came at Wembley. It was a magical, tension-free occasion. FA Cup hero Gavin Peacock maintained his goal-every-round habit with the two that sank the First Division side.

Under Glenn, the team was scaling heights inconceivable a year earlier, and if the stylish play came in fits and starts, the overall direction of the team was clear. And after a period of adjustment, during which Glenn and Peter would hammer away at the principles of understanding, faith and patience, insisting that we were playing progressive football, the fans came to believe in the Hoddle method. After we'd reached a major final for the first time in 24 years, we were all converts. And if it hadn't been for a future Chelsea player – Mark Hughes – the outcome of that dreadful day might have been so different. Sparky grabbed a spectacular late equaliser against Oldham for Manchester United in the other semi. Before the replay there was a quandary: who did we want to win? Oldham's muscular approach had seen us off twice that season; Man United had similar problems with us. Would lightning strike thrice in either case?

Whatever, Man United it was. And David Elleray was the referee, as if anyone could forget. Gavin Peacock hit the woodwork as we subdued the Mancs in the first half as we had in the league games. That was perhaps the decisive moment. Like so many, I guess, I turned to the fellow next to me and, in one of those prophetic comments you hope will reduce the likelihood of fulfilment, said, 'I hope we don't live to regret that miss.' Of course, we did. I've watched the video clip a hundred times, and Gav's shot still never goes in. And Frank Sinclair still gets penalised for a perfectly fair shoulder charge for that second killer penalty. Four bloody nil. All that, for this.

As the team filed off the pitch disconsolately, Graham Rix patted them in one by one: 'You've tasted it, you want some more' was his mantra. At the post-match party, Glenn made a gracious speech that took the sting out of the defeat and praised the efforts of his players to the highest. And – more salve for the wounded pride – since Man United had won the 'double' we were back in Europe for the first time since 1972–73.

Glenn has always wanted to pit himself against the best at home and abroad. Our excellent European campaign gave him the opportunity to shine. While other British clubs faltered – Rangers, Man United, Blackburn, Aston Villa – only Chelsea and the robust Arsenal flew the flag. Hod and Shreevesie's tactics were tailor-made for the competition: 'We went away first and foremost with the intention not to concede a goal, to play tight,' says Glenn. 'And with that roar you get from British crowds we felt we could always unsettle the Continental teams at home and have a go at them in spells.'

Viktoria Zizkov in the first round proved the model. A thumping, see-saw match at the Bridge ended 4–2. The 0–0 second leg in Jablonec – assisted by the brilliant penalty save by Dmitri Kharine – was played out perfectly. As the campaign continued, Glenn's approach appeared in sharp relief to that of other managers involved in European competition, from Dalglish and Atkinson to Ferguson and Walter Smith, who naïvely opted for a full-on attacking approach and were punished for it.

Glenn's proudest moment came in Austria, patiently defending a 0–0 home result in an intense game against Austria Memphis in February 1995. An injury-ravaged team including Andy Myers and John Spencer in midfield battled fervently against the home side, pressing and harrying from the front, and looking for a breakaway opportunity. It was now a familiar style to Chelsea players and they responded quite brilliantly. So that when an Austrian corner broke down and a ball rebounded off Erland Johnsen to the unmarked John Spencer, everyone knew it was vital the chance was exploited. The crop-haired Scotsman, fresh from reading *Bravo Two-Zero*, had told team-mates he was 'on a mission to go behind enemy lines', and his lightning 80-yard raid, aided by Eddie Newton's equally brilliant 90-yard decoy run, finished with a clinical strike past the Austrian national keeper, was one of the finest moments in Chelsea's illustrious history. 'Europe helped us a lot with the fans' understanding of what we were doing,' says Glenn. 'Tactics in Europe have to be different home and away, and that experience helped the supporters take on board what we were trying to do. The good thing was that in my final season they could see it with their own eyes.'

The exertions of that eventual 1–1 draw in Austria cost the services of three more players, as Dmitri Kharine, Gareth Hall and Dennis Wise were all injured. We drew 2–2 with Coventry the next weekend. (Curiously, we never beat Coventry under Glenn, but the Midlanders were beaten 2–0 in the early stages of Ruud's rule.) The obvious shallowness of the squad was the cue for the machinations that would eventually lead to Glenn's departure from the club. Glenn even issued a veiled hint that he would consider quitting if Chelsea's ambition failed to match his own. All this with the pathetic, egotistical wrangling between chairman Ken Bates and his aspiring successor, the emollient financier Matthew Harding, rumbling in the background. Again, Chelsea looked set to grab disaster from the jaws of triumph.

In Europe, things began to unravel. A 1–0 defeat in Bruges was overturned at the Bridge in a game that even had Alan 'Captain Scarlet' Hansen raving in excitement at the quality of our football. But at Real Zaragoza, with the influential Wise and others missing and in front of a ravenous Spanish crowd, two dreadful defensive blunders and a third goal for the home team destroyed our chances. We won 3–1 at home, though the Bridge crowd never believed like they had against Bruges. It was no shame to lose in a semi-final to the eventual winners, but Glenn knew the Chelsea team was too limited. 'It was a fabulous achievement from everyone at the club to have got so far. Of course it would have been terrific to have gone one stage further, and we weren't that far away from doing it.' He played for half an hour, and was to hang up his boots, along with Graham Rix, in an emotional match at the end of April 1995. 'I've done four years of player-managing,' he said at the time, 'and no one can appreciate how tiring it is.'

Already there was amongst fans the feeling that Chelsea was keeping his mind busy until the England tenure of another Chels old boy, Terry Venables, was loosened by lawsuits, and the FA rang Stamford Bridge. With two former clubs, Monaco and Tottenham, lurking ominously in the wings and his own contract not up for discussion, Glenn went on the record with a piece of gamesmanship that looked calculated even then. 'I'm worried about the long-term future,' he said on the back of that Coventry draw and the lion-hearted performance in Vienna. 'We need a bit of help. I'm not prepared to continue playing survival football. Two league draws doesn't satisfy me and we can't camouflage it any further.'

It was tempting to think that the camouflage was more likely festooning Glenn's personal ambitions. It was no secret to those who knew him that he coveted the England seat, even though he deeply respected Terry Venables's performances in keeping it warm for him. Such public declarations were equivalent to sending your CV to every top club in Europe, yes. But it is equally likely that Glenn was trying to engage the fans and force the board's hand into its pocket. (And, let's be fair, at the end of the season Ruud Gullit arrived.) It was a familiar tactic to Hod-watchers. He is a player of the psychological game. Bob Paisley was another. The Liverpool manager was keenly aware of the brain game, and would frequently feed the press with a story to put the opposition's preparations off-kilter, or disarm a particular opponent. He was 'chucking them a bit footballer could be so irresponsible as to get involved in a violent struggle with a member of the public. He was also very self-aware and always took matters like that very personally. So the captain's armband was instantly handed to nice, safe Gavin Peacock. And relations between Dennis and the gaffer never seemed fully to recover.

In such circumstances, Glenn would act alone. If he had a failing, it was perhaps that he didn't consult widely enough. He could be a remote figure at the training ground and the Bridge, making decisions in isolation. It was perhaps a conceit of ultra-confidence that could be betrayed at press conferences, where the nervy mannerisms – that vulgar flash of fat tongue, pick-and-swipe of the nostrils, exaggerated grimace and departing frown – revealed a man who was less at ease with the media than people thought. Glenn was always intensely private, and his personal aura was not always enough to win over his players. His spiritual side was often brought to bear on vital decisions. It had long been rumoured that some sort of 'sign' convinced Glenn his future lay with Chelsea long before he came to the Bridge, while publicly he cited the potential for improvement he noticed when invited to recuperate with us after serious injury ended his influential spell under Wenger at Monaco in 1991. As a rich man, it was certainly not pound signs he saw.

Ostensibly, when the conjecture surrounding his acceptance of the England role rumbled past us like a Texas goods train, the pros and cons mentioned were again all valid, practical concerns. But there is always another dimension with Glenn. Someone – perhaps inadvertently – pressed the button in Tottenham's press prefab at the height of the 'will he, won't he' charade. Hardened hacks read between Glenn's every line for 15 minutes, looking for a chink of light. But his portcullis was down. Until, that is, a voice from the back queried, 'Glenn, are you waiting for a sign?' It stopped Hod in his tracks. So flustered was he that he couldn't believe his ears and asked for the question to be repeated. Then he muttered that he was not prepared to discuss private matters like that. None of the press corps picked up on it. But there was obviously something in it. And whatever the eventual revelation was, it surely wasn't embodied in Graham Kelly.

In the uncertainty, fans began to take stock of the Hoddle reign. Much has been made of Glenn's transfer dealings – the money laid out and the return in silver. There were obviously acquisitions that proved questionable: unfortunate David Rocastle and Andy Dow, a Rix recommendation. But others since discarded repaid their fee.

Gavin Peacock was worth the outlay for his two decisive strikes alone that brought us six points against Man United (and for hitting the bar and giving us something positive to talk about after the FA Cup final). Mark Stein's Premier League record-breaking sequence of strikes kept us in the Premiership in the New Year of 1994, was flying until crocked by Irwin at Old Trafford, and has never been the same again. Paul Furlong scored some important goals too: the first against Bruges (after fine work by Steino) and the winners against Southampton and QPR in the Cup and League. That leaves the unlucky Jakob Kjeldbjerg, whose potential was never realised because of injury, and Scott Minto, who has suffered his share of knocks, but has yet to justify the 'future England full-back' billing.

Intrinsically, though, Glenn inherited an inadequate squad and a youth system that had been renovated under Porters (don't forget that contribution) but was yet to bear real fruit. On the plus side, in his second and third years he resolved the problem of a squad that often appeared to be playing in deep-sea divers' boots (and with the same ponderousness of thought) by bringing in new boys fleet of foot and mind. In 1994, when we lost 4–2 at Newcastle and Fox scored, reacting quickest to a Kharine penalty save, Peter Shreeves noted, sagely, that it wasn't the winger's pace that got him there: 'Physical speed is nothing; mental speed is all.' In other words, the fastest car doesn't always win the Grand Prix. But the management also realised that a team of family hatchbacks wouldn't win you anything. Buying Mark Hughes, audaciously, from Man United was the first signing of genuine class Glenn had made, but Sparky's assets didn't include lightning pace.

Yet in late 1995, the money was found to purchase Paul Furlong, Dan Petrescu and Terry Phelan. Now Furs, speed merchant, fine shooter and lovely fellow that he is, didn't have the greatest football brain. Phelo's pace makes up for any shortcomings in the intellectual department and was vital. But in the 'X-Files' man, a player we'd chased for the best part of a year, Glenn thought he'd found the key to the system he'd wanted since 1993. 'I want to play football,' said Dan, setting out his intentions in no uncertain terms. 'I want to play with Ruud Gullit and Chelsea.' Like most Chelsea fans I couldn't remember the last time anyone worth buying had said something like that.

Glenn had struck gold: Dan is intelligent, consistent, pacy, ruthless and a winner. His remarkable initial sequence, beginning with the clinical finish against Newcastle at home and closing with his astonishing strike in the quarter-final at Wimbledon, completed of toffee', giving them something to chew on. Glenn was not averse to serving up the confectionery. He would disguise or exaggerate key injuries, as all managers should, and he would talk up his players' ability, as most managers do.

But he would also attempt to influence the opposition. Perhaps the most transparent and celebrated occasion was in the 1995–96 season when we faced Wimbledon. Aware that the famously xenophobic Vinnie Jones would want to throw his weight around in a midfield also occupied by Rudi, Glenn handed round the toffee at the pre-match press conference, explaining that he had often considered buying the Wimbledon (and former Chels) midfielder, and insisting that his skills and passing ability were ridiculously underrated. It worked for the most part – a subdued Vincent did indeed try knocking the ball round more than usual, and was pilloried by his manager for it. Glenn basked in a minor psychological victory. Glenn enjoyed that side of the game. His studious manager at Monaco, Arsène Wenger, Bruce Rioch's replacement as Arsenal coach, was a master of motivation and mind games.

Glenn had learned not to make snap decisions except when absolutely necessary. His selection of Dennis Wise as captain on the departure of Andy Townsend was, in the light of Dennis's maturity as a player since, an inspired choice. 'There is a common fallacy about captains ranting and raving and putting their fists in the air,' says Glenn now. 'The best captain I ever had was Stevie Perryman at Tottenham. He was a sensible talker and a very unselfish player towards those who were more gifted than himself.' But Dennis was the most gifted outfield player in the team Glenn inherited and the clear leader. He isn't the sort to take his team by the scruff of the neck, but he'll keep chatting all the time, issue the bollockings where appropriate, and has a firm tactical grasp – something he's never credited with.

On the odd occasion when Dennis proved himself unworthy of the honour, Glenn acted immediately. When the skipper rashly got himself sent off at West Ham early in his tenancy, Glenn reminded him of the responsibilities inherent in the job, and issued a veiled warning that he would be stripped of the captaincy. (The dismissal coincided with our drastic dip in morale and form approaching Christmas 1993.) 'It's important that the skipper is a fellow who can handle himself on and off the pitch,' is all Glenn will say. But the taxi incident in early 1995, where Dennis was accused and cleared of attacking a cabbie outside Terry Venables's Kensington club, absolutely infuriated him. He was taken aback that a professional the elusive system. Suddenly it all came into focus as if in one of those 'magic eye' pictures. A collective sigh of understanding rose like pipe smoke from Chelsea's players and fans at Elland Road when he made his debut. It didn't matter that we lost. Dan's surges into enemy lines made sense of the wing-back slot where Clarkey, who had lost some of that same buccaneering spirit over the years after Bobby Campbell took a hammer to him, and for all his qualities could not. Every player who took on the role found it inordinately demanding, constantly running up and down the flanks. 'Dan,' says Glenn tellingly, 'has been playing that role all his life in Romania and Italy.' Phelo's running made even more sense of the system.

Equally important was the emergence of three homegrown players: David Lee, Andy Myers and Michael Duberry. 'Rodders' and 'Tyson' we knew had potential. It was just a matter of remaining injury-free in Andy's case, and for Rodders to apply himself more. Both responded superbly to the system in the autumn of 1995. Doobs progressed from ugly duckling in his awkward debut at the end of the 1993–94 season to elegant swan at the centre of defence almost by accident. Glenn had allowed Bournemouth to take him on loan and he'd done exceptionally well – there was talk of a six-figure move to the south coast. But the injury crisis in Glenn's final season meant a shock recall and Doobs was an absolute revelation to the fans and the media. He would go on to win Capital Gold's Young Player of the Year award, having silenced strikers as voracious as Ferdinand, Cantona and Wright.

It was the first sign that the Hod youth system was bearing fruit. 'On my first day,' Graham Rix recalled recently, 'I was asking a squad of boys I had not chosen or even seen to change everything they had learnt. I said there should be no more knocking the ball behind full-backs and chasing it, that they should give each other passing options rather than lash the ball upfield.' Doobs, schooled as a conventional centre-half in a flat back four, was shifted to the right side of a three-man defence. 'I told him he'd enjoy it,' says Graham. 'I told him, "We'll have three defenders and a goalkeeper against their two strikers and the rest should clear off down the pitch while our goalkeeper throws it to his defenders. That leaves four men against two, playing in half a pitch. Theoretically, you're never going to lose the ball."'

In 1995–96, given his chance, the penny dropped. 'Duberry,' cooed one writer, 'was tackling like an Englishman while passing like a Dutchman.' So the elusive 'three-at-the-back' – a term we hadn't heard at Chelsea since the days of The Doc and marvellous Marvin Hinton – returned in style. It was the cornerstone of Glenn's strategy and he'd finally cracked it a third of the way into his final season. Naturally he was relieved. 'We'd been trying to play that system from the start, but what with injuries and situations, we couldn't get a run on it,' he says. 'It was a pleasure to see it reaping benefits at last. Technique will always be number one in my eyes but, on the tactical front, the boys have had to learn very quickly. We kept the commitment of the traditional English game along with its mental toughness, but blended that with a little bit of the Continental style and patience.'

It led people to dub Chelsea 'Ajax-on-Thames'. 'Some teams use three solid centre-halves at the back for a defensive reason,' says Glenn. 'We did it for an offensive reason. Since the '70s and '80s, teams here played 4-4-2 against each other, cancelling each other out. Football, tactically, became sterile. Your centre-half couldn't pass the ball from the back when he was up against two strikers. The three at the back gives you that extra man to get you off the hook. You can knock the ball into the middle rather than welly it up the field. The last couple of years, what you've got in the Premiership is what Europe has had: different tactical formations. Suddenly people are saying: "We'll play someone in the hole, have a diamond shape in midfield, play three at the back, push full-backs in." And a lot of that is down to the new managers. A lot of us were players who played abroad or internationally: myself, Bryan Robson, Kevin Keegan. We've got that experience of playing against different systems, and have seen it work well or not so well. And each of us has put some of that knowledge into systems for our own teams.'

Glenn wasn't surprised that the system was working at last. 'People who came into the first team knew what their jobs were,' he says. 'It's never easy to step up but Michael Duberry and David Lee had a head start because they knew the system. Jody Morris too when he came into the picture. The reason why I had had to change to a back four for the first two seasons was because of the injuries I had to key players. It was only really in the last season that it functioned how I knew it could function – because it had worked at Swindon.'

The 3-5-2 sometimes evolved into 3-6-1, a radical formation for an English side, that encouraged the most sophisticated passing and flowing movement we had seen for decades. Glenn was also discovering assets players didn't know they possessed. In the 3-5-1-1 formation, John Spencer played behind Sparky, and initially his lack of enthusiasm for the quasi-midfield role was well known. 'I was stupid,' reflects John. 'I even said it to Glenn Hoddle before we played at Old Trafford in his last season. He had said to me that I would score and make goals from the inside-forward position if I were to believe in myself. And he was right – I was top scorer and had the most assists.'

We passed our way to a 3–1 at West Ham, a 5–0 against Middlesbrough and a 4–1 over Leeds; we had the better of a draw at Old Trafford and won at Newcastle to become the first team to win at citadel St James's in the Cup. 'We are playing good football, excellent at times,' Glenn said after the Boro match, 'but that's going to stand for nothing unless we go on to win things. While I'm enjoying watching the boys play, and enjoying the job more than at any time here, we've still got to go out and win something. That's what the supporters will demand in the end.

'Graham Rix, our youth-team manager, said to me only yesterday that the letters have come flying in after the game against Middlesbrough. That's nice.' He and Shreevesie were also grateful that at last all the investment in ball skills at Harlington was paying off in competitive games. 'We always put in 20 minutes of touch work,' he says, 'working two or three at a time. Some people wondered if the players would ever use that particular skill in a proper game, but that's missing the point. We wanted them to be touching the ball and getting confident caressing it, controlling it. We had two shooting walls put up at Harlington for the players to kick up against. The kids worked on it all the time, and that improves touch.'

There was always something exciting happening at the club during Hoddle's time there. The crowning glory was his audacious achievement in bringing the mighty Ruud Gullit, former world player of the year and football genius, to London SW6. Without Glenn there would have been neither the vision nor the incentive to lure Ruud to this new challenge. And after all he'd achieved, he still called Glenn 'the gaffer'. Even though, like the manager himself, he proved a short-term occupant of the sweeper's position, Ruud helped force a radical reappraisal of 'joke' Chelsea. And that was all part of Glenn's often-professed ambition to change the club from top to bottom.

Glenn argued with the board against the downsizing of the pitch to accommodate the new stadium development, and he argued on football grounds. He introduced constraints on the players' diet, kicking out the tradition of each player taking turns to bring in biscuits at training and introducing a nutritionist and a reflexologist. These weren't his most convincing signings. As one staff member put it, 'If a player had had a heavy night he'd go to see

Toots [the reflexologist] for a quiet half-hour lying down.' The nutritionist definitely improved the diet of most players, though sausages and chips were no doubt consumed off the premises.

Before Glenn, the Imperial College training ground at Harlington wasn't even fit for training, let alone eating at. Glenn it was who insisted on a hefty investment to improve the pitiful facilities unworthy of any professional club, let alone a Premiership one. Glenn got the builders in and it is now unrecognisable from old. '"Chip shop", I used to call it,' laughs Paul Elliott. 'I mean, there used to be plastic cups and biscuits all over the place, and the dressing-rooms were crap. At the training ground now, all the dressing-rooms are laid out, the kit is nice and tidy, the boots are done correctly, the balls are pumped up, the food is first class. That didn't always happen before. All those little details that you have to pay attention to, you'd be surprised how much contribution they have on the pitch.'

Glenn also encouraged a family atmosphere where once Chelsea could appear aloof. He opened up a room in the tunnel area for players' families to meet on match days. And he allowed his two secretaries, Jane Wilkins and Judy Walker, to job-share after they started families. 'You'd be surprised,' says Jamaica. 'It's not the big things that make football clubs, it's the attention to small details. Glenn had that quality. He had power, but he used it in the right way, to the benefit of others. For me, as a player he was ten years ahead of his time; as a man he was ten years ahead of his time; and I feel now as a manager he's going to be ten years ahead.'

Yet on the field there was still a brittleness about our play that couldn't be denied. Seventeen times we led and failed to bank the full reward. We were susceptible to lapses in concentration – the final frontier now explored by Graham Rix and Ruud Gullit – and to shots from the edge of the box. Coventry manager Ron Atkinson had it sussed when we arrived during an extended unbeaten run in 1996: 'I was talking to the lads before this game, saying to them about how Chelsea are a sophisticated side, play like a Continental team, clever passes, intelligent runs . . . and a couple of the lads said, "Boss, why don't we just get wired into them?" I said, "You'll do for me."' He was speaking after his side had just beaten us 1–0.

In the semi-final at sandy Villa Park – once more the graveyard of our ambitions – Glenn perhaps showed a purism that may have cost us the place in the final. With Dan Petrescu suspended, when Steve Clarke was injured at 1–0 to us, Hod might have switched to a 4-5-1 to shore things up. When Terry Phelan pulled a hamstring – no matter what the player said – we would have been safer to defend our lead with a packed middle and back rather than dispatch our most effective defender, Doobs, to the exacting right wing-back role and deploy Gavin Peacock on the other flank. It was a principle too far, and a sad note to bow out on. There had been something magically unreal about the whole afternoon. It was almost as if the mere presence of our twin titans – Ruud and Glenn – would bring us some reward. We'll have to wait. We're used to it.

Yet in the end, Glenn can look back on his final season with pride for reintroducing a swagger into the steps of Chelsea fans and instilling pride again in the footballing prowess of our fine old club. We could put a mean head on as well as the passing. In the past there was often too much creativity or too little. At the end there was a good balance. Jamaica has a nice way of summarising the improvements: 'It's like when I first went to Chelsea it was water; now it's Dom Perignon champagne. That's how I look at it in terms of the qualities, the facilities, the attitudes of the players and the style on the pitch.'

'Don't forget,' says Graham Rix, one of the vital components in Glenn's revolution at the Bridge and our new first-team coach, 'the three new lads, Frank, Roberto and Gianluca, have all said they came here because of Ruud. And Rudi only came here because of Glenn. So there is that progression. And let's hope it continues.'

Amen to that.